BIBLE JOHN'S SECRET DAUGHTER

David Leslie has worked for the *News of the World* since 1970. He has covered scores of major stories, including the tragedies of Zeebrugge, Piper Alpha, Lockerbie and Dunblane. He has been based in Glasgow since 1994, concentrating on crime and major investigations. He is also the author of the bestselling *Crimelord: The Licensee*, about the elusive multimillionaire gangster Tam McGraw.

BIBLE JOHN'S SECRET DAUGHTER

Murder, Drugs and a Mother's Secret Heartbreak

DAVID LESLIE

MAINSTREAM
PUBLISHING

EDINBURGH AND LONDON

First published in Great Britain in 2007 by
MAINSTREAM PUBLISHING COMPANY (EDINBURGH) LTD
7 Albany Street
Edinburgh EH1 3UG

ISBN 9781845962289

This book is a work of non-fiction based on the life, experiences
and recollections of those close to Hannah Martin. In some cases, names
of people and places, dates, sequences or the detail of events have been
changed to protect the privacy of others. The author has stated to the
publishers that, except in such respects, not affecting the substantial
accuracy of the work, the contents of this book are true.

A catalogue record for this book is
available from the British Library

Typeset in Sabon

Printed in Great Britain by
William Clowes Ltd, Beccles, Suffolk

ACKNOWLEDGEMENTS

Hannah Martin died in penury. But had her wealth been counted in the number and loyalty of her friends she would have been rich indeed. Many have contributed to the telling of her story, but it is to Hannah's closest friend that I am especially indebted, not just for the generosity of her memories and time but also for her integrity, honesty and determination that this should be a true story. This delightful lady has asked not to be identified publicly, but she knows who she is and I am so grateful to her.

For reasons I explain in the story, Hannah called her own daughter Isobel, a name I retain throughout, even though it is not one by which she is now known. It is easy to see why she has blossomed in the career she chose. Her charm and intelligence have made every one of our many meetings a delight and she opened so many doors for me. To know her is a privilege and she exudes a pride in her mother that humbles the listener.

My thanks also to my photographic colleagues, George Wright and Gary Jamieson; to Graeme Mason for his hospitality and candour; to Innes Smith for wise and kind thoughts; to Deborah Warner, my editor at Mainstream, for patience and positive help; and to Hannah Martin.

CONTENTS

PROLOGUE

It was while researching material for my first book, *Crimelord: The Licensee*, that I first learned of Hannah Martin. She had been the star prosecution witness at the trial of 11 men accused of smuggling cannabis into Scotland under the floors of holiday coaches. It had been the biggest and most successful racket ever, grossing close to £50 million, making very rich some of the most astute and leaving leading European criminal gangs agape at the sheer simplicity yet genius of it. A host of police forces were baffled as to why it had operated for so long without their knowledge.

Time after time, I wondered who Hannah Martin was and why she was so important, but no one seemed able or willing to tell me. For all her significance, very little had been written about this woman, once the mistress of one of the accused men, Graeme Mason. One of the reasons for this was that restrictions had been placed on the reporting of the men's lengthy trial in Edinburgh during the spring and summer of 1998. The other accused were due in the dock once the initial trial was over; therefore, the Crown did not want to risk a defence charge that their own claim to innocence had been prejudiced by sensationalism.

Many of those I interviewed while writing *Crimelord* were

adamant Hannah Martin was a key player in the smugglers' downfall, but finding anyone who knew her or would talk about her proved an elusive and eventually unsuccessful mission. She had simply disappeared; it was almost as though she had never existed.

After the book was launched, I was contacted by its publisher, Mainstream, and told that a reader who wanted to discuss *Crimelord* with me had left a telephone number with a request that I get in touch.

When I called, a woman answered and I introduced myself.

In a pleasant, friendly voice she said she had enjoyed the book. 'Did you try to find Hannah Martin?' she then asked.

I replied I had, then explained, 'She seems to have vanished. Lots of people remember her, but nobody knows where she went or what happened to her after the trial. There were times when I wondered if she really existed.'

'She was certainly very much involved in it,' the woman told me, 'but the drugs and smuggling affair was only one of many parts of her life.'

'Then she must be some remarkable lady,' I answered. By now, I was desperate to learn more. 'You obviously know her.'

'In a way, yes, but I can promise you Hannah Martin's story is an incredible one. Would you like to hear it?'

'Of course, but who are you?'

'I'm Hannah Martin's daughter, something of which I'm very proud. I think we should meet because I would like to tell you about my mother.'

ONE

DANCE CRAZY

Hannah Martin loved to dance, but then so did most in the west of Scotland. In Glasgow especially they were dancing potty and she among the most fervent. If Hannah had had her way, she would have danced seven nights a week, which was possible thanks to the abundance of dance halls the city had to offer. Some even opened at lunchtime. Slow and quick foxtrots, paso dobles, waltzes; each step, each movement was second nature to her. And not only the female pattern: if men were too shy to ask, or if there was a temporary shortage caused by their being late, as they drank courage down their throats or had to work overtime at their jobs, then Hannah would simply dance with a girlfriend, the pair taking it in turn to lead or be led.

Dancing was Hannah's escape from unhappy memories and a wearisome home life with her parents, Jessie and Malcolm. Maybe it was all she needed because while the occasional one of her more adventurous friends looked for a liqueur to end their night's menu of twists, turns, left changes and promenades, a nightcap of sexual dalliance by allowing a fondle or maybe more in a dark place or quiet street before heading homewards, sex didn't seem to especially interest her. Hannah was a good girl, saving the joys her body would offer for Mr Right, if and when he appeared. Like many others, a kiss on the doorstep was as much as she expected to give or receive.

Pals even thought her naive about the subject of sex, but then this was the 1960s, the Swinging '60s, as they would be remembered. In today's uninhibited society, the term 'swinger' has come to mean a man or woman keen to experiment with a variety of partners, but the '60s swung because the music made people want to do just that – swing your partner around the dance hall, or if there was no one to hold nearby just swing yourself. Rock and roll had arrived and, as it established itself, the music encouraged the rise of bands that would ultimately cause the demise of ballroom dancing. The television boom was taking off, bringing with it a change in lifestyle, so instead of bouncing about on their feet some now preferred putting them up to watch others make the effort. The dance hall era, when floors would be packed each night of the week, was on the cusp of decline. The goggle box made groups like the Rolling Stones and Manfred Mann into household names, instantly available at the push of a button, and their concerts money-spinning sell-outs, encouraging hall owners to ponder whether they ought to change direction and fill their arenas with seats. This was the dilemma that would come to venues such as Glasgow's Majestic Ballroom, the Locarno, the Dennistoun Palais, the Plaza, St Andrews Halls, the F and F Palais de Danse, the West End Ballroom and the best-known and much-loved Barrowland Ballroom in the city's east end.

Like the city and its inhabitants, the Barrowland had learned to fight its way through troubled times. It was set in the heart of the Barras, an area in the city centre that had been given its name because it was to there that hawkers and peddlers would push their barrows, packed with any and every conceivable item that would fit into them. Many would first have trundled Steptoe-like along the avenues to the west of the city where the rich and middle classes had their homes, offering to relieve these benefactors of their old clothing, pots and pans that were showing signs of wear, bedding that had become thin and marked, and even scratched or broken furniture. At the Barras, they would seek to out-shout others selling similar wares. Their presence would attract the poor by the thousand, each desperate to pick up a bargain for a few pennies or less. As time passed, more and more barrows squeezed in, and as competition for space intensified fighting between rival traders became commonplace, often leading to the police being called in, though usually disputes could be settled amicably.

Inevitably, the market spread and as it did so policeman's daughter Margaret McIver spotted the potential. Having started with a single barrow selling fruit and vegetables, she and her husband, James, built up their business until they opened a covered market at the Barras. Being able to shop and sell under a roof guaranteed the Barras would flourish even further. Margaret showed her gratitude to those who took space by laying on a free dance each Christmas. Frustrated one year by learning to her horror that someone else had already booked her usual venue, she demonstrated her determination not to be outdone by building her very own dance hall.

Opened in 1934, it was initially rented out to others but soon, realising from the growing headcount of paying customers that laying on dancing was the equivalent to being granted a licence to print money, Margaret formed a resident band, Billy McGregor and the Gaybirds, and sat back as the cash poured in. The Barrowland became a haven for servicemen calling at the Clyde from a plethora of countries during the Second World War and even rated a mention during a traitorous broadcast by Irish-American William Joyce, the German mouthpiece best known as Lord Haw-Haw, who was hanged for treason in 1946.

Margaret died in June 1958 and three months later the hall was ravaged by fire. It was rebuilt and opened again on Christmas

Eve 1960, with a capacity of 1,900, acoustics envied the world over and a sprung floor. Top bands such as those led by Johnny Dankworth, Henry Hall and Joe Loss would grace its stage, while on the floor young men and women from as far afield as Edinburgh, Fife, Ayrshire and South Lanarkshire would hop, bop, jitterbug, polka, waltz and trot the night away.

They came from many backgrounds, those dancers, from homes rich and poor, big and small, clean and dirty, happy and miserable. The doors would normally open around seven, by which time a lengthy queue would have formed, so it was essential to be there well before the doormen ushered the first couples inside. This would mean a rush for the vast majority who were working folk, with jobs that did not let them free until five or six of an evening. The solution, for many, was the public baths.

Scattered all over the city, the baths had largely begun life as wash houses, the 'steamies' to which women would take their dirty clothing and perhaps hire a tub or washboard, then take advantage, while they were doing the family wash, of the chance for a gossip, hence the expression 'talk of the steamie'. If the wash houses did not already have baths for men and women installed, the Glasgow Corporation had these added and so, instead of having to catch a bus home for a wash and brush up, returning not just late but potentially to be told the hall was already full up, the Barrowland fans would make a dash for the nearest public baths, where for just a few pence they could hire towels and emerge scrubbed and fresh faced, their hair still damp, and have time for a fish supper or bridie before joining the line of eager dancers. The biggest of these baths, with 54 private cubicles, was on Harhill Street in Govan, but among the others were those on Douglas Street in Partick, Calder Street in Govanhill and Kay Street in Springburn.

During her first excursions to the Barrowland, Hannah had no such worries about getting to the dance hall on time, even though her journey from Bellshill, seven miles to the south of Glasgow, meant a couple of buses. She was still a schoolgirl at the time, although her level of attendance left much to be desired. Aged thirteen, just entering her teens and encountering young womanhood, she looked old enough to be allowed to pass in and mingle with those two or more times her age. It might have been expected that she would go dancing with her sister Isabella, three years her senior and known to everyone as Isobel (a pattern we too will adopt), but the bonds between them were not strong. In any case, the sisters had little in common. Later, Isobel would no longer be around to join Hannah on her journeys to the Barrowland.

A glitzy, brash spot, widely looked on as the liveliest dance hall in Scotland, the Barrowland was much more than merely a place in which those who were technically capable could show off their skills in public. It was almost a community centre, where the young and those disguising the ravages of time in the hope of being looked upon as young met to admire and be admired, to talk, look for a future, roll away a past.

The doormen, sometimes disparagingly referred to as bouncers, who inspected each new arrival – searching out the drunks and trouble-making deadbeats, even eyeing up a likely candidate with whom to settle an old score later on – were not charged with making moral judgements on the hundreds who passed before their gaze each night. Adulterers, thieves, liars, cheats, shoplifters and, as time would prove, even a murderer or two, would at some stage or another make their way onto the dance floor.

Occasionally, as the buses made their way to Glasgow, Hannah would watch in fascination as a married woman tugged off her wedding ring and hid it in the recesses of her handbag, even using a dab of make-up to hide the telltale pale strip of flesh left on the third finger of her left hand. Others would wait until reaching the ladies' cloakroom to perform this little plot of deceit. Wherever or whenever, it made no difference: the motive was the same. Of course not every married woman making a beeline for the Barrowland, leaving her husband behind or the children in the care of a babysitter, did so with the intention of ditching her moral respectability and vows of faithfulness; however, often a woman, freed from home and housework and sometimes a brutal, uncaring husband, was not going to let the little matter of a gold band spoil her chances of a frolic with a stranger that would end when it was time to dash for the last bus home. There were those who claimed that as the closing hour approached there were often to be found more couples performing in the backstreets around the Gallowgate than stepping the light fantastic in the dance hall itself.

A woman might discover herself spending most of the night in the arms of a good-looking stranger adept at finding his way around the dance floor. If he offered to walk her to her bus or her home at evening's end, well, what could be the harm in that? Or a stop in an unlit shop doorway for a kiss, she allowing his hands a brief discovery of her body, even a sly caress of soft bare flesh at a stocking top? Who was to know? There was no need to explain to those waiting at home what had transpired. Such an innocent diversion could hardly lead to anything, could it? After all, there were lots of others about and her protector would generally seem nice, intelligent, interesting even.

Making oneself available could naturally be fraught with risks. Young men with a weekend in which to blow their week's wages tended to first 'tank up' before making to the Barrowland. Bars and pubs in the area proliferated. And try as hard as they might, landlords found it impossible to prevent the old enmity between Catholics and Protestants, that continues to pervade the west of Scotland, from entering the area. The fact that the dance hall was in the east end, traditionally a Catholic stronghold, meant nothing because Protestant drinking holes abounded there too, and still do.

In addition to the religious differences, Glasgow has long been a dangerous if not deadly meeting place for gangs whose membership is solely territorially based. There was an unwritten law that any member of an opposing gang caught within the boundaries of another would be allowed to continue unmolested if he was accompanied by a woman, in particular a girlfriend or wife. In such a case, the razors would be slipped back into pockets, still shining, at least for the time being. But when members of opposing factions – be it with tribal or religious differences, steaming with booze, filled with an energy that had to be dissipated and indifferent to the consequences – challenged for the affections of a woman, be she young or mature but certainly making her availability evident, then trouble was almost inevitable.

At weekends, the Barrowland would be the scene of special afternoon or matinee dances laid on for those considered too young to join the adult goings-on at night. Known locally as 'unders', these get-togethers would be finished by early evening, but that did not necessarily signal the end of the entertainment, as one unders regular remembers. 'If things seemed a bit on the tame side, we'd wind up a few of the boys by making promises to two or three that they could have a feel outside. That used to start off some real ding-dongs, and we'd walk off leaving them to it.

'At nights, my grandma and I would take a walk down to the Gallowgate and stand outside the Barrowland just to watch the men fighting. There were some really good shows, and all for free: blood everywhere, people being kicked or slashed, and then winners and losers trying to get back inside with their clothes ripped and stained. Loads of people went to watch the fights and occasionally a couple of the women would get stuck in, the men making a circle around them and egging them to rip each other's clothes off.

'It was good fun and very often you'd go back first thing next morning to look for pieces of jewellery that had been torn off or money that had fallen out of the men's pockets. Sometimes the fighters themselves would come looking for bits and pieces they had lost. They'd have swollen noses, ears half hanging off, cut and slashed faces, still half drunk and maybe even have the girl they'd been fighting over with them.'

Then, on average once a month, would come what was looked on as a replay of the ancient battles against the Auld Enemy. In this modern version, the combatants were Hell's Angels and, initially at least in the scraps, Teddy Boys, young men in tight trousers, long coats, greased hair and crêpe-soled shoes known in the business as beetle crushers. The bikers would head north from England – Newcastle, Carlisle, even Manchester – their numbers increasing along the way. Having reached Glasgow, they would make for the Kingsley Café at the junction of London Road and Monteith Place. A one-time waitress remembers that despite their frightening appearance, they were 'courteous and polite', adding, 'Everybody knew they had come to hang around outside the Barrowland intent on fighting. In the café, their language could be a mixture of, to a Glaswegian, the unintelligible and four-letter words. But as soon as one of the girls approached them, or a woman sat nearby, the filthy language would stop, which was more than you could say of the locals. A stranger walking into the café would be able to tell the Scots from the English – the Scots were the ones who carried on effing and blinding, as if swearing was an accepted part of the lingo.

'The Hell's Angels knew they had no chance of getting into the Barrowland, or any other dance hall – men needed a shirt and tie for that, and officially anyone who had been drinking was not supposed to get inside, although the reality was a fair proportion of the dancers were merry from booze – so the bikers hung around until the Teds turned up and then they would be at it, hammer and tongs.

'When knives and razors came out, someone would call the police and one or two would go off to hospital and a few more to the cells. There were some really hard guys among the Hell's Angels, but it was astonishing how they would mostly be meek as lambs in front of women. There would always be the odd exception, and maybe one or two did get carried away as the day wore on, try it on with some girl or other and perhaps not want to take "No" for an answer.'

Vicious though the fighting might sometimes have been, it was generally agreed that this ought to be the limit of the unauthorised violence. The Barrowland was notorious for being the scene of punch-ups; however, these were dances, not wars, and while women did now and then become embroiled, they were the exceptions. Girls like Hannah and women, young and old, expected to be able to enjoy a night out there and arrive home, if not totally unmolested, at least safely.

Like most other parents, had Malcolm and Jessie suspected there was any likelihood that the safety and sanctity of their daughters was being threatened, there would have been an instant ban on them going back to the dance hall. But the Martins did feel secure. Even when, now and then, Hannah missed the last bus home, she need only have made the short walk to nearby Bridgeton, where a relative would give her a bed for the night and send her home after breakfast the following morning.

If other parents occasionally gave their girls a gentle reminder to 'watch yourself', none appear to have been issued in Hannah's direction. Maybe the Martins, like so many other parents, took the view that tragedy happened to others, not the likes of them. It was an outlook that would lead to so much heartache in the years that lay ahead.

The Barrowland saw them all: the good, the bad, the beautiful and the nondescript. But mostly the nondescript. No one, for example, could say that Hannah Martin was other than ordinary.

There was nothing about her screaming out that she had it in her to become extraordinary, but she surely did. That applied, too, to a young man named John Irvine McInnes from Stonehouse, Lanarkshire, a former Scots Guard who had left the army to become a furniture salesman. John had his good and bad points, but an occasional trip to the Barrowland was no crime. Much later it would not seem that way.

There was Helen Puttock, a twenty-nine-year-old mother of two from Scotstoun, who would sometimes take a taxi ride for a night's dancing. How many hundreds of others did the same? Did Helen stand out from the crowd? She would.

And then there was a tall, auburn-haired stranger who called himself John and had an odd habit of sometimes coming out with quotations from the Holy Bible.

TWO

THE STRANGER

Early in 1966, Hannah set off for the Barrowland, assuring her parents there was no need for them to worry if she did not return home that night. She intended to stay with Jessie's relatives on Landressy Street in Bridgeton, a few minutes' walk from the dance hall, and would catch a bus back sometime the next morning. She looked older than her 16 years and could easily have passed for 20, with a ripening body and auburn hair that men found desirable, but out of bounds – although she was not averse to a kiss and cuddle, provided it was on the understanding it went no further. She could not have known it, but this was to be an evening that might have changed so many lives.

Towards the end of the night's fun, a stranger pushed his way through couples milling around the crowded floor and asked for the last dance. Hannah nodded and, minutes afterwards, as the applause for the musicians was dying out, her partner asked if he could see her home. She told him of her destination, half-fearing he would announce that he was heading in the opposite direction, and to her pleasure he indicated Bridgeton was on his route.

Jostling with other couples making their way down the wide staircase and heading through double doors thrown wide open to encourage the swift exit of the night's detritus – as this was how the doormen saw their customers – Hannah and her escort met up outside and turned left, took another left onto Kent Street and a left yet again onto Moncur Street, along the rear of the Barrowland. The streets were dark and murky, leading through blocks of apartments and shops that are now mostly gone. Couples smooched in dark doorways, and Hannah could hear the rustle of clothing and an occasional giggle. They walked slowly through an area known locally as The Dwellings, where they lingered to kiss and cuddle, before entering what was the appropriately named Risk Street. From there, it was a few more minutes' stroll to London Road and then onto Landressy Street.

She felt happy and confident as they set off, humming some of the night's dance-hall tunes, skipping and flirting. They stopped several times to kiss but, after a few minutes, Hannah sensed a coolness developing in the stranger: his kisses were becoming less firm, she was holding onto him rather than he taking the initiative. She had expected to feel his hands make their way under her coat and was surprised, even a little disappointed, at his apparent lack of exploration. He had become quiet, sullen even, and began falling behind her as they walked. At first, there had been others walking in the same direction, presumably heading home too, but gradually they had turned off, vanishing into the shadows, until only Hannah and the stranger remained on the streets.

When he lagged, she urged him to catch up, turning around and exhorting him, 'Come on, keep up, keep up!' She was already ambling slowly rather than strolling, so made no effort to stop. 'Keep up,' she urged again. 'Keep up!'

Then she heard him recite what sounded like a Bible quotation. He was a few yards behind at this stage and she had difficulty hearing. 'What was that?' Hannah asked, half-turning, not really aware of what had been said. She was met with silence and wondered if her companion might be slowing in the hope she would walk so far ahead that he would be able to slip away and leave her to find her own way to Landressy Street.

It was, she felt, a bizarre performance on the part of a man who had asked if he might see her home. Journey's end, her aunt's home, was now only a couple of minutes off and, once reached, any chance of romance would surely cease. Time was short.

Looking back with the aid of hindsight, and all that was to follow in the coming years, it is easy to wonder why Hannah did not take to her heels. But there was no reason to do so. Though she thought she had heard words more suited to a pulpit, there was nothing especially unusual or alarming about a stranger talking rubbish. She was simply a young woman making her way home through residential streets with an escort who was apparently acting the fool.

'Keep up,' she told him once more and was a little relieved to hear his footsteps approaching. A trace of anticipation may even have crossed her lips at the thought of him obeying her instruction. But she did not turn around.

And then lightning shot before her eyes a millisecond after a blow to the back of her head. Her knees buckled. Someone less streetwise than Hannah might have stopped and asked what was happening, and would almost certainly not have been given an answer to their very last question on this earth. Maybe it was instinct, a determination for survival, or possibly just fear, but she kept going, desperately fighting against the urge to collapse, knowing that to look around would cost a vital fraction of a second that could be the difference between living and dying. She felt shocked and faint; she thought she was going to be sick and was oddly curious as to what was going on.

The pain in her head was agonising but, from somewhere, she found the strength to begin shouting for help, a plea that went unanswered. She was strangely unaware of the whereabouts of her attacker, who appeared to have fled at the first shouts.

Soon, she was at the door that promised safety and sanctuary. Her cousins, infuriated by what she had told them, went angrily rushing off in the direction from which she had come, hoping to exact revenge on her attacker, but they returned half an hour later, breathless, admitting they had been unable to find him. What had happened in those dreadful few minutes would always haunt Hannah because her life might easily have ended there and then. Yet it would be many years before she would confide to a close friend the events of that night: 'I couldn't even be sure what the man looked like because it was as if the blow had made a mess of my memory, confused my thinking,' Hannah remembered. 'It was all over so quickly and I wasn't really hurt, just shaken.

'It was no use going to the police because, what could I tell them? In any case, people around Bridgeton had little faith in them. They would hardly go to much trouble over a teenage girl who said she'd been hit by a man she couldn't identify. And so I told my aunt not to tell my parents because had they found out they would have stopped me going to the dancing, certainly barred me unless I had someone else to go with. There was no way I wanted that to happen. I loved the dancing, made a lot of friends there. It was the only thing I had to look forward to.

'Why the guy had picked on me was something I did not understand at the time, and would never know. But, in the light of what happened later, I became more and more certain that the attacker was the man who would be known as Bible John. Maybe I should have gone to the police then, or even later. But I didn't and, in any case, what were the chances of catching him? All I knew was that I could have been dead.'

So, in the space of a few minutes, the incident began and ended. What happened, of course, begged the question whether Hannah Martin would go dancing to the Glasgow halls again. But she made it plain she would not be deterred.

Hannah had that remarkable property, some might say gift, that is bestowed on the young: the ability to throw scorn at adversity. This might have been just enough to overcome any doubts or fears about what might happen in the future. Naturally, she would be more careful, at least for a while, until the shock of the attack eased. Lightning, it is said, never strikes twice. Hannah was about to find the old adage wide of the mark.

THREE

IN THE BEGINNING

In February 1967, the year following the attack, 17-year-old Pat McAdam, the same age as Hannah, had journeyed to the Glasgow dance halls with a girlfriend from her home in Dumfries, almost 90 miles off. As Pat and her friend thumbed a lift south from Glasgow, a lorry driver named Thomas Ross Young stopped and offered to take them home. Although her friend was safely dropped off, Pat was never seen again. Police interviewed Young but, while he admitted having had sex with the teenager in the cab of his lorry, despite being more than twice her age, he claimed to have left her safely on the outskirts of Dumfries. His explanation appeared to have been accepted because no charges followed then but, much later, the authorities would take a very different view.

There were some Barrowland regulars, perhaps including Hannah, who would have been in the same dance hall as the teenagers that night and while the mystery of Pat's fate merited gossip, few, if any, seemed to have learned the lesson that the Grim Reaper could call on anyone, at any moment, anywhere. Indeed, by the following year, few remembered Pat. But then why should they have? She had been just one more dancer among so many other seemingly ordinary young people. Life was too short to spend it worrying about the fate of a stranger. Yet all were about to be affected in some way by a series of events that would ensnare so many into a web of horror.

In Bellshill, Hannah was growing into womanhood. Perhaps she would never see herself as attractive, yet she had about her a look of pretty innocence that young men found desirable. She was frequently receiving offers of a walk home as the Barrowland bands began their nightly last waltz. On occasions, she accepted but sometimes found herself arriving at Landressy Street on her own, her escort having decided to withdraw his offer after she made it plain she was 'not that sort of girl' and was saving herself for marriage.

There were occasions when she wondered what would happen if Mr Right never came along. Would she miss out? It was an uncertainty caused by the natural impetuosity of youth. In the heart of this 17 year old going on 27, she knew she was doing the right thing, although after the attack by the holy man who failed to prophecy his murderous intentions she had stayed away from the Barrowland for some time.

Early in 1968, a chill crept down the spines of Glasgow's dancing public and it was not one brought on by the cold of a dying winter. A murder – foul, gruesome and disgusting – dominated conversations everywhere but especially in venues such as the Barrowland and the Majestic. It was a killing that had a special significance because the victim was one of their own. And while no one could have known it then, this would be a slaying that would have consequences around the world. To this day, it remains a cloud of shame that hangs over Glasgow, the Green Place.

Patricia Docker was vivacious, a smile rarely far from her lips. She was a woman who devoted herself to caring for others. Her looks and hazel eyes turned the heads of most men, but

27

she saved her love for the joy of her life, her four-year-old son. As a nursing auxiliary at the Victoria Infirmary, not far from the home she shared with the boy in Langside Place, Patricia was accustomed to coping with the grief that inevitably comes from loss. By February 1968, she had to cope with distress of her own, as she was forced to live apart from her husband, a soldier whose duties meant he was stationed at that time in England. It was a situation that placed strains on both but, in the hope of taking her mind off personal worries, her friends had persuaded her to join them at the Majestic for the weekly Thursday night over-25s dance.

She was reluctant to leave her son but, when her parents offered to babysit, Patricia donned a grey coat over her favourite light-tan dress and set off. At the Majestic, there was no shortage of partners eager to hold and be held by the pretty, dark-haired 25 year old. Most might have been content with the Majestic, but for some reason that night Patricia craved a change of scene. No one could remember when or why but, as the evening passed, Patricia gathered her brown handbag and left, heading for the Barrowland Ballroom, where Hannah Martin, long recovered from her encounter with a Bible-quoting nutcase, was among the hundreds having fun.

Dance floors the world over hold a potpourri of humanity eager to impress and the Barrowland was no different. Patricia and Hannah, complete strangers to each other – one an experienced woman, the other still maturing – were surrounded by men anxious to make an impression and not especially concerned about how they did it. All had their own stories. There were bus conductors claiming to be missionaries from Africa, labourers spinning yarns about being movie extras, visiting sales representatives passing themselves off as rich English footballers and civil servants with a neat line of patter from some medical directory they recalled reading somewhere. Other young men tried to sell themselves

28

in manifestly fake accents with tales of being servicemen from Ohio, oilmen from Texas, millionaires, spies, preachers, company directors, ships' captains and members of leading bands. Some of the more astute were already giving false names, knowing how useful this would be should the night end in a sexual encounter resulting in pregnancy.

From among this miscellany, it is evident that Patricia met someone who took a particular interest in her, one that must have been reciprocated sufficiently to persuade her to allow this new partner to accompany her home. It was a journey that would take both across the city, either by taxi or in his car, but one Pat would never complete. Early the following morning, a workman discovered her near-naked body in a doorway just a few yards from her home. She had been battered, raped and strangled.

Police concentrated their efforts to find the killer on the two ballrooms, but especially the Barrowland because it was from there that the young victim had almost certainly left with her murderer. Using an age-old formula that fails more often than it works, detectives questioning the dancers gave little away. To the questions 'What's going on?' and 'What happened?', the police gave the standard riposte: 'We'll ask the questions, you just supply the answers.' The thinking behind this was that by holding back information, the culprit might let slip something relevant to the crime that only the killer could have known. It is a flawed theory, one that rarely, if ever, works, leading to outrageous suppositions that can only mislead and sidetrack. The more facts given to a public generally eager to assist, the more likely they are to focus their memories, and the higher the chances of someone remembering an important, if not crucial, piece of evidence. Astonishingly, it would be nearer to two years before vital information was made public.

And so, as the weeks dragged by without an arrest, snippets of gossip began leaking out. One was that Patricia had been garrotted with her own stockings; another that her handbag had disappeared. Some said one of her dancing partners had been overheard boasting about a relation who had achieved a hole-in-one at golf, while others whispered that she had been seen with a tall, slim man who seemed to drop into their conversation odd words or expressions more akin to those leaving the lips of a priest or minister. But who was to know that if such phrases had been uttered, they had been spoken to Patricia Docker? 'Could he be a Bible basher?' some asked, while others wondered if he was a policeman.

As to his identity and description, plenty of suggestions, and even actual names, were offered. Much would later be made of the name John. It is a common forename, likewise the expression 'picked up a John', which probably emanates from the days of visits by American servicemen. But did Patricia's partner actually offer the name, or was it overheard during a conversation between the couple? Was it simply given by a reluctant witness in an effort to get rid of persistent police questioning? Even now, no one can say. The name John would have appeared on lists of potential suspects certainly, along with names such as Jimmy, Jock, David, Iain, and so on.

The only sure thing was that no matter what forename or surname was put forward as a possible witness, or even killer, during interviews, in each case the detectives would painstakingly visit those individuals, listen to their story and then check it out, though each time a reliable alibi was forthcoming.

There were even some male, and a few female, customers from both dance halls who were positively eager to save the murder team the trouble of tracking them down, turning up at the local police station desperate to give full rundowns on where they had been and with whom. These were husbands and wives, anxious their spouses should not open the door in answer to a policeman's knock and discover some story about a girls night out or a visit to the greyhound track with the rest of the boys had been a lie, and that their partner had in reality been whooping it up at the dancing with a 'fancy man', or the proverbial bit on the side. Again, though, the outcome was the same: a bland, unhelpful statement that gave no clues to solving the murder.

Some would comment on perverse similarities between the cases of the dead nurse and that of missing Pat McAdam just the previous year. Both girls shared the same Christian name, both had been to the Barrowland Ballroom and, assuming the younger of the two had, as most believed, been murdered, then each had been killed in the month of February.

At the time of the nurse's murder, Thomas Ross Young, the Glasgow lorry driver who had admitted having Miss McAdam in his cab, was in prison, jailed in 1967 in Shropshire for 18 months for rape.

There were other topics also being discussed, one highly relevant to the murder. Just 27 months earlier, in November 1965, hanging had been all but abolished, though at the time of the Patricia Docker tragedy a number of hard-line politicians wanted the death penalty to remain for some offences, including cases where murder had been committed during a theft. Whoever had slain Patricia Docker had also surely stolen her handbag and that would have made her killer eligible to swing.

Indeed, law or no law, such was the public fury at the callous way the life of the young nurse had been taken there were many who vowed that if the killer were caught, then even in prison his, or more unlikely her, demise would be just a matter of time.

Hannah herself appears to have been undeterred by the fate of Patricia Docker; it certainly did not put her off visiting the Barrowland. By the autumn of 1968, although the murder investigation, having drawn a blank, had been scaled down, the lingering memory of the nightmare was still one that haunted many dancers. And it was about to become an unwanted stain on Hannah's mind.

Patricia's death had caused revulsion elsewhere in the country but only in Glasgow was there a true sense of loss. To the city's people, this was a personal assault because Pat had lived and worked with them, and it is certain many had used the same corner shops as she, bought dresses at the same department stores and used the same hairdresser's. Often people would be heard telling their friends, 'I knew her face.'

Geography can be a great calmer of emotion; distance soothes and dissolves passions. In Edinburgh, people would have read about the trauma, sympathised with Patricia's family, shrugged their shoulders, wondered what else could be expected of wild, outlandish Glasgow and gone about their business. It was hardly a subject to be talked about by two eight year olds, as they made their way to school each day. To Christine Eadie and Helen Scott, the world was still full of innocence and fun, and the murder of the nurse would in all probability never even have crossed their minds. Yet they would become indelibly linked to it.

FOUR

THE BROTHEL

By April, Patricia Docker's murder was two months old. It had not been wholly forgotten but, recent though it was, the tragic event was fading from the city's collective consciousness, and fading fast. The fact was there were, after all, other topics about which to converse.

Up on the walls of the Barrowland, like dance halls elsewhere in the city, were pinned stark police posters, asking for anyone who might have information about Patricia's last movements to come forward. But it was a faint hope. At that time, a murder that was not solved in the early days tended to drag on, perhaps without ever being unravelled. Today, no killer can feel safe, even many years after the event, thanks to the analysis of deoxyribonucleic acid – DNA – and Hannah's story will demonstrate why.

Claims by scientists that they had found 'the secret of life' were made in a Cambridge pub by Francis Crick and colleagues in 1953, though it was not actually until 1966, two years before Patricia's death, that boffins claimed to have cracked the biological code that allowed sweeping advances to be made in DNA – though such a crime-shattering breakthrough would have meant nothing to Hannah Martin.

Now 18 years old, Hannah was becoming ever more conscious

of her body – although not evidently aware of the attractions it held for the opposite sex. She was not a suspicious or wary young woman, versed in the need to look out for danger or evil, even when neither was apparent. Friends would say she retained a childlike innocence regarding sexual matters, which was odd for one so streetwise in life's material temptations. More cruelly, her detractors would describe her as simply lacking common sense, which was actually far from the truth. If there was a fault, it was that she was too trusting.

Perhaps this was down to the fact that she had never been particularly close to her mother, Jessie – certainly her preference lay with her dad, Malcolm – but at this time she was meeting all the uncertainties that faced her, both physically and mentally, alone. Jessie, long plagued by heart troubles, had died in 1966 at just 41 years old, meeting her Maker never knowing how close her younger daughter had come to beating her into His presence.

Whatever the reality – be it naivety, stupidity or just a sense of wanton adventurism – Hannah would go off to the dancing on her own. In fairness, each time she left home now to catch the Glasgow bus, Malcolm would remind his daughter, 'Now, Hannah, be careful. Think about the girl who was killed. Don't take chances and don't walk the streets on your own.' The bulk of his advice would go unheeded, so maybe he fell into the trap of complacency; he had become so used to hearing Hannah announce she was off to the Barrowland and might not be home at night that he had been lulled into a false sense of security, knowing where she was headed and that she would find a bed for the night on Landressy Street. Had he been aware of what had gone before, such a morally strict man might not have slept so soundly while his daughter was out.

Many of the friskier or more passionate of the couples leaving the Barrowland Ballroom, among them those content with a one-night stand that might consist of mere exploration or full discovery, would head for Glasgow Green, just a few yards away. This huge park, bordered on the south by the meandering River Clyde and on the north by Bridgeton and the Calton, offered privacy beneath spreading trees or in the shadows of the walls of the People's Palace, a giant glass-and-brick structure now largely used as a museum.

The Green had eavesdropped on the frolics of young and old for centuries. One guide to the city proclaims:

> Probably the most important leisure activity associated with the Green is the Glasgow Fair, which was established in the twelfth century and from the early 1800s held on the Green near the present High Court building. The fair originally included sales of horses, cattle and the hiring of servants. In the nineteenth century, it began to attract amusements, such as theatres, circuses and drinking booths. The area has long been associated with the people's struggle for reforms and justice. As at Speaker's Corner in London's Hyde Park, the Green became the place to listen to religious and political speakers debating such causes as electoral reform, trade union rights and women's suffrage. Public executions took place on the Green up until 1865. The women of the east end of the city used the area, including the local wash house and drying green, for washing and bleaching linen. St Mungo baptised Christian converts in the sixth century.

Lovemaking might not be included in the list of officially accepted activities, but it was certainly a prolifically practised one, and still is. Forty years ago, most of the women to be found there were giving their love for free to boyfriends, husbands – not necessarily their own – or in the course of a one-night stand, usually regretted the following morning. Occasionally, a prostitute picked up in the city centre's red-light area around Blythswood Square might be persuaded to take a taxi ride to perform at the Green. These days, it is Glasgow's alternative red-light zone, as hookers feel safer there following a series of murders of sex-for-sale women picked up in the city. The resulting police patrols, supplemented by those of council-employed rangers, might not have put a total stop to high jinks on the damp grass but have seriously curtailed the fun, free or otherwise.

And, of course, Glasgow Green has been no stranger to violence. 'King' Billy Fullerton, the Protestants' champion of the 1930s and '40s, used to dish out early morning hammerings on the Green to challengers, after pacing his bedroom floor throughout the night to work up concentration for the battle ahead. At six in the morning, his pals would call to collect him and march to the battleground to watch King Billy demolish opponents in fist-only fights, then shake hands with them when it was over. When one of his daughters was only 15, she was attacked during a fight at the Barrowland and stabbed in the head. It was said that when police discovered the victim's identity, they refused to hunt the culprit. Eastender Billy, loved and respected to the last, died just a few years before Patricia was murdered.

Hannah's self-determined celibacy would have meant it unlikely she would be seen among the consummating and non-consummating couples, either already busily engaged or heading in the direction of the Green. At this time, she avoided the dark tenement blocks of Risk Street and The Dwellings, which held such frightening memories, and looked for a route that would take her through the rows of Georgian mansions overlooking the area, buildings once so magnificent, home to the tobacco barons who made their millions plying between America's eastern seaboard and the Clyde. By the late 1960s, many of the buildings had sadly gone, too big to heat and maintain; others had been divided up into flats, but their days, too, were numbered. Today the only remaining edifice is the Monteith Hotel, a superbly grandiose structure that retains its aura of superiority.

Whichever route Hannah chose, almost certainly her entry into Landressy Street would have taken her past a building on Main Street that could well have played an infamous but overlooked role in the Bible John story. It housed a business run by a recognised but mostly despised professional man whose nefarious activities had enabled him to buy up other properties in the east end, one of which was a brothel tucked away in a tenement in Dennistoun, a mile away from his base. The existence of this establishment and the name of the brothel keeper were familiar to the police, though, for reasons best known to themselves, they refused to order the owner to close it down. This baffled those living nearby, who constantly and bitterly complained at the brothel's continued operation. A base such as this for a house of carnality could only attract the kind of people ordinary families regarded as 'perverts'.

Landressy Street, the vertical of an inverted 'L' shape, with McKeith Street as its foot, then largely consisted of ground-floor shops with tenements above, in which lived hundreds of working-class families. The majority of the buildings have now disappeared, but there was a strong community spirit in evidence at the time. Many adults had been born there, as had their own parents, and although many were moving out to settle and start afresh in burgeoning schemes, such as Castlemilk to the south, most had grown up there and gone to school together. Kids played in the streets outside, kicking a ball against the doors of the backyards belonging to the shops, often to the annoyance of storekeepers who were convinced they were about to be burgled;

menfolk drank in the same bars in which their fathers had supped and then staggered home drunk on Friday nights; women met in the same corner stores to gossip and complain about the lethargy of the local council in bettering their living conditions or moving them elsewhere. A tragedy for one affected them all. Jemima McDonald, who lived on McKeith Street with her three children, would be testimony to that.

The brothel did not merely attract men during the day, either. Its location gave it an added advantage and at night prostitutes who used it as a base would frequently head to the Barrowland on the lookout for customers, taking the view that if they failed to attract business then there was always the consolation of a dance or two. But those who did 'lumber a John' would invariably take their client back to the Dennistoun base, where there was at least a bed. This arrangement meant both a continuous late-night flow of prostitutes and punters and, worse, from the point of view of those unfortunate enough to have to live amid this prurience, the never-ending arrival in the streets of men directed there for the sole purpose of seeking sexual gratification. It was not unknown for an innocent family to have their door rattled by a semi-drunk asking for the brothel, or for decent women to be stopped in the streets and asked if they were 'looking for business'.

There were, naturally, other brothels in the city that would from time to time be raided and closed. In one particularly infamous episode, the female proprietor, or madam, discovering her premises had been kept under surveillance for several days – during which time male customers had been stopped and made to identify themselves then asked if they had handed over money for sexual services – insisted when arrested that the payment was for nothing else but bowls of home-made soup handed out to the men to restore their energy. She ran nothing more than a café, she said, where the waitresses offered a little extra to diners. Her story failed to convince a sheriff, who fined her, but the following day soup was once again being dispensed as though nothing untoward had transpired.

Customers who had visited the Dennistoun brothel once would occasionally, when they again felt the need for the services of the women, simply knock without making a previous appointment and hope one of the girls was available. But such unexpected calls were discouraged. The preferred arrangement was that punters would first visit the business on Main Street to ascertain which, if any, prostitutes were on offer. A telephone call would then be made to the brothel to forewarn them that a customer had requested the services of either a particular female or any woman. If supply met demand, the male would be directed on his way. If not, he might be asked to return to the business in half an hour, by which time a prostitute would almost certainly have been contacted and asked to make her way to Dennistoun. Time, after all, was money.

This appalling set-up meant sex-hungry men were regularly loitering furtively around Main Street and the surrounding roads in search of the scoundrel who controlled the operation. On occasion, a prostitute might be hanging about, looking for the pimp to collect money or to be given instructions as to where a client had asked to meet her. Additionally, a man, having been unsuccessful in trying to pick up a sexual partner at the Barrowland or in the streets and bars around the dance hall, probably feeling angry and frustrated, might well have headed to Main Street to learn what was on offer at Dennistoun. It was a situation fraught with danger and yet, despite the raids on other houses of ill repute, the Dennistoun knocking shop would, throughout the Bible John terror era, be allowed to remain open and running. This gathering of whores and their seedy clients meant that whenever Hannah stayed over with her aunt, en route she would have to mingle with them – hardly a satisfactory or safe situation for a young girl blossoming into a woman. It would eventually cause the authorities severe embarrassment.

FIVE

BETRAYED

Having survived the attempt on her life, Hannah had convinced herself there was no reason to alter her routine. If she was inspired to change at all, it was to become wary of men who invited her to step out with them.

She had continued her excursions to the Barrowland, still on occasions heading to Landressy Street but always making sure she had company she knew, if not for the entire length of the walk then at least until she was in sight of the familiar tenement where her aunt and cousins lived. Her prudence did not stop her dancing with strangers, but hard as some tried to persuade her to join them on a late-night stroll around Glasgow Green, using every ounce of guile they possessed, none succeeded.

She remained true to what her friends might have thought an old-fashioned, even outmoded, resolution to remain chaste until her wedding night. When she lost her virginity, she determined it would be to a man she had pledged to stay with for life, and he with her. Weeks after the attack by the stranger, Hannah became involved with a man she decided would be the one for her. We will refer to him as Joseph.

Her first employment after leaving school had been working for the world-renowned knitwear company Lyle and Scott in

Glasgow. It was not a job into which she settled and within months she had moved to the then giant Hoover factory at Cambuslang. There were three principal advantages to the move: the plant was nearer the home she shared with her father; it was close to her adored grandparents, Richard and Hannah Martin; and it paid better. Despite what would happen in the not-too-distant future, Hannah remained there for 22 years until she became a victim of a series of lay-offs that would ultimately signal the end of production in Glasgow, the company deciding to manufacture instead in China.

Before becoming involved with Joseph, Hannah had had occasional boyfriends. These were casual flings that never lasted, perhaps due to her age but more likely because of the attitude of Jessie, a matriarchal figure once the front door was closed. She seemed to view her younger daughter's purpose in life as solely to bring about the betterment of the family as a whole. She would use the youngster as a key to unlock a treasure chest.

'The relationships would spring up and then fade after only a few weeks because Jessie could not see that Hannah was desperate to bring feeling, love, into her own existence,' a friend said. 'She'd announce some local young man or other had asked her out and Jessie would ask, "What's he do?" Hannah might say, "He's a butcher," and her mother would reply, "Oh, a butcher, is he? Stay with him, bring him in for a bite of tea and he might bring us a parcel with some meat in it."

'If the young man did so, Jessie would say, "Hannah, you're not to give him up, not as long as the meat lasts anyway." When the parcels petered out, she'd tell her, "Can't you find yourself an electrician? We need these lights fixed," or even, "Never mind what they look like, if they have a trade or can get their hands on things for the house, bring them along and make them welcome. Prince Charmings are for fairy stories, they don't put food on the table or mend a burst pipe."

'She met Joseph after her mother died. Jessie would have been over the moon because at first he was an assistant at a fishmonger's, but he later went to work at the Hoover factory in the next workshop to Hannah. It meant they would see each other every day. She fell head over heels for him and understood, for the first time, what it was like to be really fond of someone. She'd kept all his cards, those he sent for her 19th birthday on 14 December 1968, at Christmas and for Valentine's Day the following February, even taking them out sometimes so she could show them to us. Hannah was so proud. There had been other boyfriends, but this was the real thing as far as she was concerned. He was the love of her life. Some weekends, Hannah would stay at his mum's and his mother got on really well with her. As far as Hannah was concerned, she and Joseph were engaged and would marry.

'Sex was something you just did not talk about, certainly not the act of sex anyway. If you went home with a guy, your pals would be asking you afterwards in whispers "Did he kiss you?" or "Did he cuddle you?" That was as far as it was expected to go. Was Hannah aware of what sex was about, what it involved and what could be the outcome? Did she know how babies were made, because attitudes in the '60s were far less liberated than they are 40 years on? Had she discussed the subject of sex even with close friends? In each case, the answer was probably no. The thing, then, was that you knew a little bit, you knew the word "sex" and you knew what was supposed to happen once your husband and you took off your clothes and climbed into bed, but it wasn't meant to happen until you were married. You were supposed to be a "nice" girl and keeping yourself pure until you were married was sometimes the first and last line of defence when a man tried it on.'

Hannah Martin had saved herself for Joseph, but she was about to discover her investment in maidenly virtue would pay a bitter return. Casually strolling along the street one midweek afternoon, Hannah chanced upon an old friend. Joseph had said he would be unable to take her out that weekend as he had another engagement, which she assumed was probably work, so she asked the friend if she fancied a trip to the Barrowland on the Friday night.

'Sorry, can't,' came the reply.

'You going out somewhere?'

The friend was clearly disconcerted. 'I just can't, Hannah, sorry.'

'Well, come on, you got a boyfriend hidden away?'

'No, it's not that.'

'Well, what is it? You can tell me, I keep secrets.'

'Hannah, I'm going to the show of presents.'

'Show of presents? What show of presents? Somebody getting married?'

'Yes, that's right.'

'Well, who is it? Anybody I know?'

'Yes.'

'Well, who?'

'Look, Hannah, I have to go.'

'When's the wedding?'

'Saturday, the day after the show of presents.'

'So, who's getting married?'

'Don't you know, Hannah?'

'Haven't a clue. Come on, tell me.'

'I'm really sorry, Hannah.'

'What? Who is it?'

'It's Joseph.'

'Joseph? . . . My Joseph? It can't be. We're engaged.'

'He's got a girl pregnant and they're having to get married. Didn't you know?'

'No, he's said nothing.'

'Hannah, I'm so sorry.'

'Not your fault. Thanks for telling me.'

It was the bitterest pill. What distressed Hannah, and would do so from that day on, was that her fiancé hadn't had the courage to tell her the truth that behind her back he had met someone else. While she was keeping herself for him, he had been sowing his oats with another.

'We were engaged and I have to hear from somebody else that he's marrying another woman because she's pregnant,' she would later blurt out to a work colleague. Never did she confront her now former fiancé. 'If he couldn't tell me, then I won't belittle myself by asking,' she said. 'It would sound too much as if I was pleading.' And each day she would pass Joseph by, her head in the air, letting him off so lightly.

The betrayal had a calamitous effect on her. For a while, she found it impossible to contemplate a serious relationship. She continued visiting the Barrowland, the tragedy of Patricia Docker by now more than a year distant, occasionally agreeing to a casual date but never going beyond a peck on the cheek at the end of a meal. She began drinking, now and then heavily and sometimes to excess, something she had never done prior to the break-up. It was drink that would both destroy her and probably save her life.

One night in April 1969, she took the short walk from her home to the stop from which she would take a bus to Glasgow and the Barras. Those who knew her would assume she was heading for the Barrowland, but this was a night when Hannah would break with tradition. All bets were off. She was setting out with the intention of having a good time, getting drunk, casting care to the wind. She headed into the city centre and found herself in the Locarno in Sauchiehall Street. What happened in the next few hours would always remain hazy, but she found herself drinking, knocking back glass after glass, as though expecting to hear at any second the ten o'clock closing bells. She drifted from pub to dance hall.

At the Barrowland, she joined the regular dancers milling about, chatting, arguing, hearing an occasional oath or threat from someone who had already over-imbibed, and not necessarily a male. There was much to talk about. Glasgow, being on the west coast, has a special affinity with Northern Ireland, where the political situation was becoming serious. Discussions at the highest level were ongoing about the possible need for troops to be sent to the province, a particularly worrying development for a deprived city such as Glasgow, where many young men had found joining the army the only solution to avoiding the dole queues. Now they faced the prospect of being called upon to fire shots and, even worse, to be fired at. The atmosphere had not been helped by the election of firebrand Bernadette Devlin who, at 21, became the youngest-ever female Member of Parliament, winning the Mid Ulster seat after standing as an independent Unity candidate.

Others at the dance hall were boasting of their links to the ganglands in Newcastle upon Tyne and London. The underworld had always held a special fascination for Hannah, possibly handed down from her mother, who had ties with families in Glasgow linked to petty crime. Not that that said much because most families in the city at that time had some connection or other with the criminal element.

Newcastle was still reeling from the convictions two years earlier of Dennis Stafford and Michael Luvaglio, who were given life sentences for the murder of fruit-machine cash collector Angus Sibbet. No one in the city doubted the innocence of Luvaglio in particular, and he and Stafford launched appeals against the jury's verdicts. In the meantime, film-makers were showing a marked interest in what had happened and would ultimately use the murder to inspire the making of *Get Carter*, starring

Michael Caine. It would become one of the all-time great gangster films.

There were some who queried how it was that in these cities detectives managed to crack murders that appeared complicated to solve, while in Glasgow the brutal killer of an innocent nurse remained free; however, even though Hannah had slightly more than a passing interest in these matters, her thirst that night was for alcohol rather than questions of law and order.

As she saw it, she had already had more than a taste of injustice, having been bashed over the head by a probable killer and then jilted in the cruellest and most cowardly fashion. As she poured down drinks, she became ever more revolted by her treatment: to have kept herself immaculate while others benefited from their promiscuity was unfair, to put it mildly. As the night wore on, she lost track of her bearings to the extent that she would never know for certain where she ended up.

What she soon realised was that the floor was beginning to spin. She felt giddy, a strange devil-may-care sensation taking over, and suddenly a tall, slim man was holding her, almost carrying her around the floor, nuzzling her neck, his embrace ever more intimate, whispering words that she found difficult to interpret through the haze of levity and offering to give her a ride home in his car.

Hannah was in a dangerous state, near helpless and yet willing in the grip of a stranger at a venue in which another woman had been seduced and later killed. But drink drowned out the danger signals and before she knew it she was in a moving vehicle. When it stopped, she soon found to her horror her clothes awry. It was a sobering and terrifying experience. She realised she had taken part in a sexual act and that her lover was now making it plain he wanted to continue, to the extent of beginning forceful advances. Something told her she should not be there. She would admit to friends that she asked herself in the years that followed many questions: was the man familiar? Were there faint resemblances in his speech, his form, to the stranger who had attacked her near Landressy Street? Did she hear a voice warning her that eternal damnation faced those who transgressed, that in ancient times adulterous women were stoned to death? Hannah would never have the chance to answer these questions.

She knew only that, as they struggled, having had sex once, she was on the verge of being raped. His efforts to pull off her remaining clothing persisted. She clawed at him and they fought. And then she threw up, spewing over the man, his clothing and his car. She heard shouts of disgust, vile curses and oaths, and found herself on the pavement. She thought she could recall the man offering to give her a lift home, clearly as a pretence to induce her to climb into his vehicle. But there would be no ride home now. By the time she dressed and climbed to her feet, the streets were empty. There was no sign of the car or the man who had taken her. Tidying her crumpled clothing, she gulped in the spring air.

Being sick had further sobered her, but she would say she remembered little of her first lover. She told her closest friend that they had had sex once and that he then forced himself on her, insisting on a second helping. But Hannah's reluctance to talk about the experience made her confidante suspect her introduction to sex had been wholly against her will. Had he given a name, she would be asked? She replied that if he had, she could not remember it. She would also say she thought she heard him telling her he worked in the shipyards. John Brown's famous yard was certainly in the news at this time. It had launched *Queen Elizabeth 2* amidst a flurry of publicity in September 1967 but, after a series of catastrophic teething troubles, the liner had only just been accepted by its owners, Cunard. Was it possible a young man would try to impress a girl by boasting he worked in a trade that had brought shame on Scotland? She would say, too, he had told her he was aged 20.

To many, there would be something odd about the details she remembered and those she did not. Wouldn't the one detail any woman would take from her first lover be his name? In territory where one woman had already died – two more would tragically follow – at the hands of a man who had offered to see her home and then ripped off her clothing, she had been the victim of a brutal sex attack while hopelessly drunk. The fact was a desirous lover would give a name; a rapist would not. Maybe the truth was simply that all she could be certain of was that by vomiting she had saved herself.

'She left the dance hall with the guy but didn't know him, although if she saw him again she might have recognised him,' said Hannah's old friend. 'Could he have been Bible John? He could have been. But if he gave his name, any name, she didn't remember it. For sure, being ill over him saved Hannah and she always knew that.'

By the summer of 1969, Hannah was aware that something was wrong. She had missed periods but was convinced whatever was amiss was not serious because, though difficult to understand or accept now, she was certain that it was impossible for a woman to become pregnant as a result of her very first act of lovemaking. As has been shown, being ignorant of sexual matters was not uncommon then. Many bizarre fallacies persisted and Hannah was not alone in believing such a fantasy. During girlie talks, she had been told in hushed tones that 'doing it' for the first time would be painful but after that it would be the source of considerable pleasure. She could recall neither sensation.

With almost childlike naivety, Hannah tried to regard the incident as if it had all been a dream, thinking that if she managed to put it from her mind altogether then the consequences would disappear. She would revert to being the innocent and pure woman who had set out from home that April night. She wanted to neither think nor imagine, and certainly not talk, of her deflowering; in fact, it would be many years before Hannah spoke of her ordeal at the hands of a man who may well have become a mass killer.

'Sex meant nothing to her then,' said a close friend. 'She went into self-denial about the near certainty she was pregnant, seeking to convince herself she could not possibly be having a baby. For a long time, there was no outward sign and when her body did start to swell she started wearing loose clothing to hide the fact. Malcolm was a big, dour individual, a kindly man but very strict, and she was terrified as to what would happen if he found out. It was almost as if she thought that by denying she was pregnant it would all suddenly disappear without him ever learning anything had ever been amiss. It is so easy to scoff and laugh now at what must seem an incredible attitude to something so basic, but that was her genuine belief.'

Perhaps Hannah could be forgiven for being so naive and imagining there was anything that could distract her father from her condition once he had learned about it.

There was certainly enough tragedy and murder to pack the newspapers Malcolm liked to read. James Griffiths and his friend Paddy Meehan were suspected of being responsible for the murder in Ayr of elderly Rachel Ross during a robbery at the home she shared with her husband, Abraham. Meehan was arrested and convicted of the murder, but was later given a Royal Pardon and financially compensated. However, when five detectives went to bring Griffiths in, he went berserk with an armoury of guns, eventually taking refuge in his flat in Hillhead, firing at all and sundry and screeching insults at police, who urged him to abandon his folly. Despite being surrounded, he escaped, eventually bursting into an empty tenement flat in Springburn from where he kept up the fire before being fatally hit when a policeman fired through the letterbox. Griffiths had killed news vendor William Hughes, aged sixty-five, and injured another twelve people, including an eight year old.

Meanwhile, if Hannah was embroiled in her own very private sexual scandal, elsewhere in the world the outcome of another must have left her wondering how some seemed to escape folly while common folks like her had to suffer indignity and strain. That month on Chappaquiddick Island, off Martha's Vineyard, Senator Edward Kennedy's car plunged off a bridge, drowning his young passenger, Mary Jo Kopechne. He survived and was given a legal slap over the wrist in the form of a two-month suspended sentence for leaving the scene of an accident after causing injury. Hannah, meanwhile, was facing a lifetime of punishment.

Mary Jo's tragedy was quickly overtaken by an occurrence of such magnitude that all else paled to nothing. Three days later, Apollo 11 achieved the seemingly impossible by flying three men to the moon. The first steps by Neil Armstrong, Edwin Aldrin and Michael Collins were beamed through television into front rooms all over the world. It was a momentous achievement, but even had the man in the moon handed over a cheese sandwich to his visitors and made a televised speech of welcome, it would still not have taken first place in Hannah's thoughts.

SIX

KEEPING MUM

On Sunday, 10 August 1969, the actress Sharon Tate and six others were butchered by members of Charles Manson's cult, known as The Family. It was an omen that would point to a month washed in blood. On the Thursday of that week, British troops, many of them from Glasgow, were sent into Northern Ireland to keep the warring factions apart, and the coffin makers prepared to work overtime. Saturday came and as the afternoon passed crowds began streaming homeward from football matches. The Old Firm had done well, Rangers winning 3–0 at Airdrie, while at Celtic Park, the Hoops had trounced Raith 5–0. Local fans ought to have been in a good mood later in the evening when the Barrowland began filling up: both had lots to celebrate.

In Bellshill, nine miles away, Hannah, by now four months with child, was preparing to catch a bus for a night's dancing, although she was conscious of moving more slowly these days. Ten miles further south, John McInnes was also looking forward to finishing work and having a night out. In Main Street, Bridgeton, customers were eagerly arranging meetings with prostitutes, who were already doing a thriving trade with supporters heading into the city, buoyed up from watching Celtic and deciding to assuage some of their own energies, even at the cost of a few pounds, before hitting the bars and then the dance halls.

Around the corner in McKeith Street, the slight-framed Jemima McDonald, with naturally blonde hair that she dyed brown, was putting on her make-up and pulling on a frilly white blouse under a black dress before setting off to walk to the Barrowland. Unmarried Jemima, or 'Mima' to close friends and relatives, had known Patricia Docker through bumping into her at the dancing and had quietly grieved for the murdered woman. Jemima's three children were being looked after for the night by her married sister, Margaret O'Brien.

Elsewhere, a tall man was surely patiently glancing through pages of the Holy Bible as he buttoned his shirt and slipped on the jacket of his neatly pressed single-breasted suit. Like the others, he was looking forward to an entertaining night.

At the Barrowland, the band went through a tried-and-tested repertoire while the hall filled up. At the doors, as the sun slipped away and darkness drew in, there were the customary disputes, as drunks demanded entry only to be turned away, rudely jostling other customers, arguing with wives and girlfriends and even becoming involved in the occasional scuffle along the Gallowgate. Inside, Hannah was finding it hard to concentrate, her mind on that night, months earlier, as she scanned the crowded floor, wondering if she might glimpse a face that she would recognise as the one that had shared with her the back seat of a car.

There were no such worries for Jemima McDonald, who knew how to enjoy herself. She drifted away from friends, who saw her dancing and chatting earnestly with a man over six feet tall. It was difficult to be sure under the spotlights sweeping over the dancers just what was the colour of his short hair but most who remembered would later say it had had a light-reddish tint.

Hannah left alone that night but, remembering her dad's advice to be careful, waited until she spotted a couple she knew from Landressy Street heading in the direction of their home and arrived safely at her aunt's house. The next morning, she walked to a bus stop to head back to Bellshill.

As she walked, head down and deep in thought, around the corner in McKeith Street Margaret O'Brien was at first not overly concerned when Jemima failed to reappear. Sometimes her sister would spend the night at the home of a friend, occasionally not returning home even until late afternoon. But as the day wore on, she began to worry; her concerns increased when no word came to say Jemima would be delayed but was all right.

By Monday, there was still no trace. The children were wailing and asking where their mother had gone and Margaret had no alternative but to have the police called in while she went looking herself. It was she, alerted by children playing in a derelict tenement only a few feet from Jemima's close, who found her sister's body. A doctor told detectives she had been strangled with her own stockings and battered. Despite an intensive search of the tenement and the surrounding area, her black handbag could not be found. Was it coincidence that the murder had similarities to that of Patricia Docker? Both had been to the Barrowland and had been strangled, raped and battered, then left near their homes. Each girl's handbag had been stolen and at the time both had been having their period.

The killing had a special significance for Hannah because, like the dead woman, she had been headed for a near-identical destination at the time of her first attack. When Hannah read what had happened, it sent a chill down her spine. She wondered how close she had come to suffering the same fate, and whether after killing Jemima the murderer had returned to the streets around the Barras to collect a car.

Those who had been neighbours to 32-year-old Jemima were outraged, not just because three children had been left orphans, or a deranged killer had been so close to their own homes, but because their fears about the consequences of allowing a brothel to operate in the neighbourhood, encouraging frustrated males to call in the midst of a largely residential area, had been realised. If there were some who felt there were similarities between their situation and that of the sister towns of Sodom and Gomorrah, destroyed by God in a hail of fire and brimstone because the men were sinners, then they kept their thoughts to themselves. That would prove to be a wise decision in light of future events. Shouting biblical lessons at the police in an area where a mother of three had just been murdered would not have been the done thing; however, as the detectives carried out door-to-door inquiries, both the brothel and its owner carried on.

The presence of so many police officers did deter most of the regular clients from visiting, but local people knew that once the hubbub died down and policemen in their confidence-inspiring uniforms disappeared, the situation would unfortunately revert back to normal.

The prostitutes were questioned about their customers and pressured into giving names and descriptions, divulging how often Mr X or Mr Y visited and what their normal calling hours were. The answers, of course, meant that customers themselves received a visit. Most hurried to get to the police stations first, as in the case of the Patricia Docker investigation. The last thing they needed was to return home from work to a cold look from a wife wanting to know why her husband was wanted by the police. Thinking up an excuse on the spur of the moment could prove tricky.

Eventually, public pressure forced the closure of the Dennistoun brothel and, such was the angry outcry, the pimp himself was forced to shut up shop and move on. It was as near as it could be, in the Wild West that could sometimes be the east end of Glasgow, to the good women of Tombstone demanding their sheriff curtail the activities of unscrupulous saloon keepers. But there were many who, even to this day, are convinced the pimp and his set-up were responsible for introducing a callous killer into the area.

None knew of the assault on Hannah, but it raises the possibility of a scenario in which, having been rebuffed at the Barrowland and wanting to take out his humiliation on any woman, her attacker lured her into walking through the dark, near-deserted streets with him. He may have been in the Bridgeton area not because he lived there or passed through it on his way to home elsewhere in the city, but to satiate his lust for violence. It is impossible to ignore this possible motive for his coming close to killing a friendly, innocent young woman.

The members of the murder team were, of course, ignorant of what had happened to Hannah and no one would ever know how crucial her story could have proved in their inquiries. Once more convinced they were frustrated by a wife or mother shielding their quarry, they would be defeated, although it was not for lack of effort. Hannah watched the detectives mingle with the other dancers at the Barrowland and wondered whether she ought to tell them about her own encounter but decided that in doing so she would open a can of worms the lid of which, from her perspective, was best kept firmly shut. Questions, too, would then be asked as to why she had not come forward sooner. And her family would surely be dragged into it. The last thing she needed at this stage was extra trouble.

But should she have come forward? An officer who worked on the hunt for the Barrowland murderer is in no doubt that she could have helped the investigation. 'Two innocent women had died in a very brutal fashion and everyone must have been aware the police were desperate for any assistance. She must have realised from her own experiences what these victims had gone through. There's absolutely no doubt that both the attack from behind and the sordid business in the car would have been of very keen interest to officers in charge of these inquiries because there was every likelihood that the man responsible had his own transport. It appears very possible that both these men fitted the pattern of the killer or if, as some believe, there was more than one murderer, one of the killers.

'At the same time, the attack from behind may well have been the forerunner to a ligature being thrown about her neck. That would be the modus of the murderer and she was in an area of the city where he preyed on women. Perhaps her age and fitness saved her, maybe the blow was not as effective as he intended. Who knows? But the car incident had characteristics that bore comparison with the killings.

'Clearly, this was a man taking advantage of women who had their defences down – in the case of the incident in the car with Hannah, through drink. He was intent on having sexual intercourse at any cost, even to taking a girl's virginity, and then seeking more. Patricia and Jemima had been menstruating and this may have induced in him a sense of disgust in the same way that in some primitive societies they would be looked upon as unclean. Hannah being sick over him and his motor was possibly so unexpected as to take him by surprise and create such a sense of revulsion that he could no longer bear to touch her.

'It is impossible to guess what goes through the mind of such very disturbed individuals. But there's no question of what was the right thing for her to do. Had she explained to the police the delicacy of her situation every sympathy would have been shown and every step taken to ensure her privacy was protected. She must have been especially aware, through having family who lived so near, of the suffering of the McDonalds. It's easy to make decisions more than 30 years on and here was a teenage girl finding herself very pregnant with no mother to fall back on for support and dreading the shame that illegitimacy undoubtedly brought in that era. But, at the end of the day, these were murder investigations and the families of the dead women were entitled to feel that everyone who could help in bringing the murderer or murderers to justice was doing so.'

But the carnage was not yet over.

On Thursday, 30 October, pretty Helen Puttock, aged twenty-nine and a mother of two, went off to the Barrowland with her married sister, Jeannie. Both were aware of the police warnings that a predator was about but felt there was safety in numbers. Like Jemima McDonald, Helen had decided to wear a black dress. Tragically, it would turn out to be an apt choice. Her husband George, aged 28, was a corporal in the Royal Corps of Signals and was based in England. He would next see his wife in a mortuary.

It was remarkable that in the light of the blanket publicity that had followed the two previous deaths, once inside the dance hall Helen had an unexpected and not wholly unwelcome meeting with a man assumed to be a stranger. She had gone to buy cigarettes from a dispensing machine but while it gobbled up her cash no packs emerged. The stranger appeared as if from nowhere, offered his help, then a drink, then suggested a dance: propositions to which Helen agreed.

When the time came to leave for Helen's home on Earl Street in Scotstoun, a five-mile taxi ride, the sisters announced they would be leaving together. Helen's partner for the evening, oozing charm and courtliness, offered to accompany them and they had no reason to turn him down. He had introduced himself as 'John' and, by coincidence, a second man giving the same name joined the trio in the taxi when they hailed it at Glasgow Cross, although he soon left, saying he was catching a bus to his home in Castlemilk.

The taxi headed to Knightswood, close by Scotstoun, to drop Jeannie off. As it sped through empty streets, the women became fascinated by their fellow passenger as he began telling them about himself. He said he had been forced to suffer a strict religious upbringing by a father whose view of dance halls was that they were 'dens of iniquity'. As a boy, he had been made to study the Holy Bible; to prove the lessons had not been lost, he began quoting from scripture, including what would in hindsight seem a sinister reference to the fate of women committing adultery. 'They get stoned to death,' said John.

On a happier note, he repeated from Exodus the story of Moses being set adrift to avoid an edict that all Israelite children should be butchered, only to be discovered in bulrushes by the daughter of the Pharaoh and raised as her own. When they got onto the subject of Hogmanay and the women asked if he would be seeing in the bells, he told them, 'I don't drink at Hogmanay. I pray.'

Religion, especially in the fickle west of Scotland, was an odd choice of subject at any time and particularly during a taxi ride from a dance hall of all places, but Helen and Jeannie felt safe with John. Jeannie had no cause for concern as she waved her sister farewell when the taxi left Knightswood, doubling back towards the city to make for Earl Street. It was the last time they would be able to smile at one another.

Early next morning, a distraught dog walker found Helen's body in a backyard in the same street as she lived. She had put up a fierce fight for her life, it was reported, kicking, scratching and marking her killer, but she had been strangled, battered and raped. She was menstruating at the time. And her handbag was also missing. Word soon leaked out about the religious nut who had been with her and the tag 'Bible John' was coined. It has stuck to this day.

There was never any doubt from the outset that Helen's slaying would be linked to those of Patricia and Jemima, although some police officers doubted that all three crimes were the work of the

58

same man. Regardless of that view, all have, in popular opinion, been laid at the door of Bible John.

So many were affected by Helen's killing and none more than a heartbroken Corporal Puttock, who announced he was asking to be discharged from the army after eleven years' service to look after his children, David, then five, and Michael, just twelve months old. 'This man has ruined the lives of my two boys and myself,' he said. 'For the sake of my two little sons, who loved their mother, I'd ask anyone with information to contact the police.'

Within days, approval had been given for the issue of what the media described as 'the fullest and most detailed description to be released of a man police wish to interview in connection with a murder in Scotland'. The culprit was, according to a police statement, 'between 25 and 30, 5 ft 10 in. to 6 ft tall, of medium build, with light auburn-reddish hair styled short and brushed right'. He had 'blue-grey eyes, nice straight teeth, with one tooth on the right upper jaw overlapping the next tooth, fine features' and was 'generally of smart, modern appearance'. The statement continued:

> He is known to have been dressed in a brownish, flecked single-breasted suit, the jacket of which has three or four buttons and high lapels. There are no turn-ups on the trousers and the suit is modern style. He was also wearing a knee-length brownish coat of tweed or gabardine, a light-blue shirt and dark tie with red diagonal stripes. He was wearing a wristwatch with a broad leather strap of military style. He may smoke Embassy tipped cigarettes. He is known to go to Barrowland on occasions and is thought to go alone. The man is thought to be called by the Christian name of John. He may speak of being one of a family of two, his sister and himself, and of having had

a strict upbringing with a severe parental attitude towards drink. He may also speak of a strict religious upbringing and make references to the Bible. He is quite well spoken, probably with a Glasgow accent, and does not appear to be engaged in heavy manual work. The man could have recently made marks on his face.

Unusual for those times was the issue of an artist's impression of Bible John. This was soon followed by a painting of the suspect by Lennox Paterson of the Glasgow School of Art. When it was unveiled, Detective Superintendent James Binnie, deputy head of Glasgow CID, announced, 'We would like everyone in Scotland to see this painting. Coupled with the description already given, this man must be known. He could be the man next door. He could be the man you danced with some night. He could be the man sitting next to you in church. He could be anyone and we would ask everyone who knows or thinks he knows him to come forward and our inquiries will be treated with the strictest confidence.' Detective Superintendent Joseph 'Joe' Beattie of the Marine and Maryhill Division CID, whose name would become synonymous with the hunt for Bible John, commented, 'We think it's a very good painting of the man.'

The men and women of the division began attending the city dance halls en masse, complaining that skipping around the floors required a considerably higher output of energy than pounding the beat. It was just as well from the point of view of hall owners that the police turned out in force because custom dropped off dramatically. Women were too scared of meeting Bible John, while men were terrified of being accused of being the mass murderer. Some with a passing resemblance to the suspect were questioned so often and cleared that they were eventually issued with cards declaring they were not the killer.

Everyone, it seemed, had his or her own theory as to who the killer could be. One suggestion was that the police should examine closely the Hell's Angels during their monthly forays into Glasgow in search of a rammy and in some cases a woman, preferably willing but on the odd occasion likely to have her protestations ignored. It was pointed out that the mysterious murderer seemed capable of vanishing into thin air after each of his crimes, just as the bikers would disappear south when their night's jolly was at an end. Could Bible John be a biker?

Likewise people wondered if he had travelled from afar to the Barrowland simply to select a victim when the mood took him. Then, once the evil deed was done, hotfooted it until the next time. What, then, did he get up to in between the slayings?

In the middle of what was now a triple-murder inquiry, the morale of the hunters was further lowered by an announcement that while homicide rates in England and Wales were up by 20 per cent, Scotland had seen an astonishing rise of 165.5 per cent. Who knew what the explanation for this was, but with Bible John on the loose there seemed every likelihood that the differential would increase even further.

The police called on nearly 700 dentists in the Glasgow area, asking each to check their records and see whether any of their patients had a dental pattern that matched Bible John's. Not all were happy at what they considered an intrusion into patient confidentiality, but the detectives were convinced the oddly shaped teeth of their quarry were a giveaway. A man could hide what was in his mind, he could cover scratches on his body, but without using some home-made device to rip out a tooth or two he could not avoid showing his incisors each time he opened his mouth.

This last request produced some unfortunate results when men already overly conscious of their appearance found themselves at the sharp end of a police investigation in which a handful who were tall and thin had to account for their movements on the nights of the murders. In one especially memorable case, a young man who had recently joined the Glasgow police was sitting at home about to tuck into breakfast after a particularly cold and galling nightshift pounding the city streets. Colleagues he did not recognise hauled him off to be questioned on the grounds that they had been told by his dentist that his teeth had a likeness to those of the killer. By the time he returned home, his breakfast was cold and the hot-water bottle a kind mother had placed in his bed equally chilly.

And then there was the State Hospital in Carstairs, Lanarkshire. This establishment, steeped in mystery, held at the time, and still does so today, men and women deemed a potential danger because of their mental conditions. They were classed as patients rather than inmates but that made no difference to the public perception. Not all had committed crimes, but the majority had shown imagination in devising methods of inflicting pain and misery. There were killers of children, beasts who tortured and murdered, deranged teenagers, sickening paedophiles. Whenever a particularly awful crime was carried out and there was no obvious culprit, the word 'Carstairs' would be mentioned. People wondered: had the killer been a patient?

Everyone had his or her own theory about who Bible John could be. One suggestion that probably deserved further examination was the idea that the killer was a schizophrenic, suffering from a mental illness that can lead to swingeing changes in a victim's personality. Some believe a major cause is childhood abuse, a subject not given the concentration in the 1960s that it is now. There have been countless examples where schizophrenics have murdered, their victims ranging from total strangers to the closest family members.

What those who worked with the mentally disturbed would discuss privately were the references to Bible John quoting religious passages. Many schizophrenics appear to have an obsession with the Bible, often almost to the extent of allowing biblical sayings to become the rules that direct their actions. To a schizophrenic, 'an eye for an eye' can mean just that. Was Bible John abused as a youngster, in the sense that he was forced to study the Bible until it warped his thinking and caused his brain to direct his actions away from what is looked on as normal behaviour? Certainly schizophrenia would account for what seems to have been the remarkable changes in the character of Bible John, first behaving with immense charm, then brutally and bloodily slaughtering his victims, then vanishing into oblivion, or was it back into respectability?

It is possible this was an ordinary man from the outskirts of Glasgow who chatted happily over the garden fence with his neighbours at weekends, took his wife and children on family holidays to the west coast, had friendly arguments about football with his workmates and went to church on Sundays, then for no clear reason he would suddenly snap and murder in cold blood. A feature of schizophrenia is that outbursts are rare and it may have been that only the man's closest family were aware of his condition. Families will often put themselves at great risk to protect loved ones from being unmasked as criminals. In the case of Bible John, it is a distinct possibility that those around him suspected he was the killer but decided to stay silent rather than face the undoubted shame and humiliation of being associated with a murderous madman.

They would not be alone in making mistakes. It was suggested that a man questioned several times and arrested for rape was found to have a Bible in his car, smoked the same cigarettes as Bible John and had a close relative who had once had a hole-in-one at golf. He was known to have mental problems, but there was not enough evidence against him.

Neither the extensive and intensive dragnet nor a £200 reward succeeded in producing an arrest, although the detectives did say after interviewing a distraught Jeannie that they would like to speak with a man from Castlemilk – 'Castlemilk John', the fourth passenger in the taxi who had hopped out almost as soon as it set off. In light of his sharing the same Christian name as the prime suspect, it was hardly likely he would come forward. The odds of him returning to the Barrowland, or any other dance hall, for that matter, in the foreseeable future were remote indeed. But the significance of Castlemilk was not lost on the folks living on McKeith and Landressy streets. Someone motoring from the Barras – or more likely going on foot, as the car population was not as prolific then as it is now – and heading for Castlemilk would very probably pass through their area. A man seeking a prostitute, for instance. Or simply seeking a woman; any woman.

As Hannah Martin, aged 20, read the newspaper reports and headlines about the man everyone was calling Bible John, her mind flashed back to the incident three years earlier that might have happened on London Road, certainly near to it. She wondered about the stranger who had come so close to killing her. She remembered the biblical saying but, hard as she tried, could not recall the exact words.

But then Hannah had other things on her mind.

SEVEN

THE GODFATHER

As the killer of the three women was becoming a much-talked-about figure, so was another individual whose name was frequently being linked to matters where violence was involved. Arthur Thompson was born in Springburn, Glasgow, in September 1931 to decent hard-working parents, Catherine and Edward. By yet another of the bizarre coincidences that would become such a part of Hannah Martin's life, her mother Jessie was a distant relative of the Thompsons. Hannah and Thompson would never meet, but in different ways both would be influenced by Bible John.

As a teenager, it was obvious Thompson was bigger and broader than most of his contemporaries – something he was well aware of. He enjoyed the profits such a physical advantage brought and one of his first jobs was humping boxes of fruit and sacks of potatoes at Glasgow fruit market, building up muscles that soon had him a night job as a doorman. Among the spots where he planted his feet firmly apart and stared down would-be troublemakers was at the Barrowland. City businessman Morris Mendel had taken a shine to the young heavy and used him to guard his clubs and bars. He also had another task for young Thompson: to help in the disposal of stolen property, mainly clothing. Thompson, though, wanted to be his own man.

First, he had to overcome problems with the law. Officers must have thought him an easy touch when he dropped his keys outside a bank he had robbed in the north of Scotland, a spot of carelessness that earned him a three-year stretch behind bars and a reputation as a bungler – although those who held these views made sure they were aired out of his earshot. Free at last, his liberty was short-lived, as he found himself going down for 18 months in 1955 for extortion. Still, Thompson was a coming man, although it would be a while before he was given the title of 'the Godfather'.

Back in the outside world, he took over a scrap-and-demolition business, using bribery to win contracts and find out which properties were listed to be knocked down. He then branched into security, employing strong-arm tactics to take over at least one thriving shop in Glasgow. He had connections among firearm suppliers and he was one of the first to recognise the fortunes that could be made through dealing in drugs.

Arthur, it was said, used to visit London from time to time to carry out contracts on behalf of the much-feared Kray Twins, Ronnie and Reggie. The story goes that he used some of the money the Londoners paid him to buy a gaming club on Glasgow's North Hanover Street and started up a prospering and totally illegal money-lending racket, charging extortionate sums to customers, many of them businessmen who needed another hundred pounds or so to continue playing at his tables. They invariably lost and found themselves being charged 50 per cent interest a week. Failing to pay was unthinkable. It brought visits from brainless thugs who threatened dire consequences or, worse still, Thompson himself. One man who omitted to pay his debt to Thompson was crucified, nailed to a door as a lesson to others. Among his customers were young housewives married to errant or spendthrift husbands who left them with nothing to feed and clothe their children. To Thompson these women would go, begging for a few pounds to tide them over. Mostly he would take pity on them and pull out his wallet, reminding them when repayment had to be made and how much it would be. The more attractive he would order to call on him 'personally', as he would say, 'so we can sort something out'. This would involve a visit a week later to his club, or to the shed he called his office at his demolition business – the venue was irrelevant. What mattered was that they would be offered the chance to dispense with the interest on the debt by performing a sex act on Thompson or, if he saw them as especially attractive, having full sex with him. But no matter how energetic their performance, when they left they would still owe the original loan.

With the money rolling in, Thompson could afford to pay for prostitutes, but he rarely used them in Glasgow for fear of his wife, Rita, getting to know. In London, armed with the Krays' money, it was a different matter: he had money to splash about and lavish on attractive women. He could pay for the best, but sometimes payment was not necessary, the Twins providing him with a female for free. Thompson's visits did not go unnoticed by the police in the capital, who enquired of their counterparts in Glasgow details about this enforcer from the north, informing them of the fact that he appeared to have a liking for women.

On his home territory, Thompson enjoyed the hordes of smart women who danced at the Barrowland. He became a regular at the dance hall, surveying the talent on offer and passing on lewd comments to the cronies and sycophants, many much younger than himself, who accompanied him and hung on his every word. Thompson's own favourites were those who were married: taking them to bed made not just the women his conquest but also their menfolk, to whom, in his mind, he had dealt the ultimate insult.

He was not the most handsome of men, but his reputation as a kingpin in Glasgow's violent underworld seemed to attract women.

It may have been that in Thompson they saw the power that women sometimes crave and that some believe is to be found in criminals. Then again, his money was a magnet that drew towards him even those professionals who would amongst their own class loudly cast scorn on the idea of associating with a thug.

His success also brought with it the inevitable consequence that gangsters must face. In 1966, Thompson started up his car outside his home on Provanmill Road with the aim of giving a lift to his mother-in-law, Margaret Cameron Harrison. As the car moved off, a bomb planted under the engine blew up, killing Margaret and badly injuring Thompson. He was convinced he knew who was behind the assassination attempt and later that year drove his Jaguar at a van carrying Arthur Welsh and James Goldie, who both died. He was charged with their murder, although he was acquitted by a jury.

Awaiting trial, he was visited in an interview room at Barlinnie prison by his lawyer, who had with him an exceptionally pretty woman in her 20s, with breasts even more substantial than the solicitor's fees. On the pretext of seeing another client in the jail, the legal eagle left both on their own, a move for which Thompson had been well forewarned and was prepared, as was his guest. Later, Thompson would boast he was the first man to have a conjugal visit in a prison in Scotland.

His voracious appetite for women had become a talking point among the criminal fraternity, many of whom looked on Thompson as an enemy. So, two years later, following the murder of Patricia Docker, he was questioned by police.

A former officer remembered visiting him: 'Thompson was an obvious candidate to be quizzed. Family apart, he regarded women as objects for his own personal pleasure and there had been tales circulating that some to whom he'd loaned money and had refused to cooperate sexually when they couldn't pay up had been given a very heavy slapping about. His name was thrown into the hat as a suspect, but at the time so were scores of others whose only crime was to have offended some business rival. It wasn't only him we were interested in, but those who knocked about with him. He made it clear he had nothing to do with Pat: didn't know her and gave the usual spiel about being appalled by an innocent woman's murder. If he knew anything, he said, he would be the first to help the police. No one believed him, but there was no evidence linking him to the murder either.'

Thompson might have felt his luck had run out that year after he was arrested following a burglary on a clothing warehouse and jailed for four years. He spent part of that time at Peterhead prison in Aberdeenshire, at the time used to hold men looked upon as the elite regarding major crime and violence but now predominantly home to sex offenders. While he fumed and paced the floor of his cell, Jemima and Helen died.

Thompson had the perfect alibi but that did not stop police visiting him and asking about the freeloaders and lackeys who had followed him on his excursions to the Barrowland. He was shown the artist's impression of the man the police were also now unofficially calling Bible John and asked to look back and think about whether anyone he knew matched the description and picture. Once more, helpful and courteous to the police as he would always be, he appeared to give the questions considerable thought but announced he was as baffled as they. That would not stop him, however, he assured his visitors, putting the word about that he was in the market for information, which he would instantly pass on should anything useful come his way.

If big Arthur was in any way surprised to find the police visiting him, his shock was nothing compared to that of a gang of council cleaners who found themselves whisked off the street one evening and into a police station to be quizzed about their movements on the night Patricia Docker died. They had been working a late shift, picking up overtime in the area around the

Barrowland, and detectives wanted to know if they had seen or heard anything unusual. They were released along with their brushes and barrows after a few hours.

After Arthur's release, with the Bible John mystery still unresolved, he would be visited once more at a bar he ran in the centre of Glasgow called the Right Half and to which young men were known to call before heading off to the Barrowland. But his vacant expression answered questions more effectively than any reply. Thompson doubtless hoped this was the last time his womanising would interest detectives dealing with murder.

If so, disappointment was headed in his direction.

EIGHT

FAMILY SECRET

Within days of the police releasing the detailed description and rumours of the killer's religious utterances spreading, the expression 'Bible John' had become part of everyday language. Tall, slim men would think twice before uttering an expletive that could be vaguely construed as blasphemous. In churches and chapels throughout the west of Scotland, parishioners eyed preachers suspiciously, looking for a telltale sign that might link any one of them to the killer.

Drinkers in bars and hotels would furtively eye the man sitting next to them, first to see if what lay in their glass was alcoholic, knowing of the suggestion by police that Bible John might be teetotal, and second to check if his teeth were out of alignment. Mothers who had once threatened wayward children with the promise, 'The bogey man will get you,' now warned, to startling effect, 'Bible John will come for you if you don't behave.'

The name was on everyone's lips and the majority wondered if he would kill again before the police triumphed. Of course, as with any murder inquiry, the officers had to contend with the usual raft of nutcases and time-wasters desperate for their moment of notoriety by declaring themselves the killer. Normally, they dry up quickly once it becomes apparent that either their claims have been dismissed or the real culprit has been arrested, but the unsolved nature of the Bible John case meant such foolishness would go on and on.

Two years after the death of Helen Puttock, three children playing by a river at Renfrew, on the other side of the River Clyde from where she had been dumped, discovered the naked body of a woman in the bushes. Some police officers may have wondered if Bible John had struck for a fourth time. Certainly, the killer this time wanted them to think so. The corpse was that of local nurse Dorothea Meechan and beside it lay a note reading:

Mr Polis,
I have killed that woman in cold blood,
Bible John

Richard 'The Snake' Coubrough, the man who was eventually arrested for the crime, would deny being both the murderer of Dorothea and the killer Bible John, but he nevertheless spent 34 years in prison as a result, protesting his innocence every single day.

But not even Helen's murder was enough to persuade Hannah to seek a meeting with the police. Having decided not to make contact after the slaying of Jemima McDonald so close to a tenement where she herself occasionally stayed, it was unlikely she would put herself at risk on behalf of someone for whom she no doubt felt the deepest sympathy and sorrow but who was, nonetheless, a stranger.

If she was aware of the impassioned appeal by a tearful Corporal George Puttock for someone to come forward and perhaps provide the key to discovering the identity of his wife's killer, she remained silent, convincing herself with the same arguments that she had used to stay in the shadows during pleas for assistance following Jemima's death. In fairness, like many, she was confident Bible John had killed once too often and that, having failed twice, the police could not miss their target a third time. In any case, she would have been hoping that by the time she made her next trip to the Barrowland the murderer would be safely behind bars.

It has to be remembered, difficult though it might be to come to terms with, that in Hannah's eyes the predicament in which she found herself was just as traumatic as that being endured by the families of the three victims: the consequences for them would span their lifetimes, as they would for her.

She constantly told herself that her missing periods were the result of stress, or some mystery illness that would eventually disappear, but by the time of the demise of Jemima McDonald she was beginning to wonder if, after all, she really was pregnant. It was now dawning on her that her condition was not going to disappear. It was a cloud that darkened her every day and almost with each hour that passed the force of the burden that lay in her belly became heavier.

When it was reported that Helen Puttock had become the victim of a Bible-ranting lunatic, Hannah's resolve that nothing untoward was taking place inside her was further weakening. While outwardly she continued telling herself she was not having a baby, a persistent voice within her was whispering that she must indeed be pregnant and that there could be no turning back to her life before the calamitous episode in the stranger's car.

Just as it is easy to condemn her for the decision to remain mute over the attacks, it seems natural to criticise Hannah for her attitude to a condition that even the most unworldly of women would not just have recognised but would have very soon come to terms with its inevitable outcome. However, it should be remembered that she lived in a society that would have had little compassion for a fallen woman, and she would certainly have been placed in that category.

Another in her plight, surrounded by family equally keen to dispense with the problem, would have been advised quite frankly much earlier about how to get rid of the baby, but if Hannah was unable to grasp the reality of actually being pregnant, what chance was there of her understanding terms such as 'termination' or 'abortion'? It is impossible not to commiserate with her dilemma. Most women on the verge of giving birth have a married friend, relative or, more importantly, mother to whom to turn to find out what happens next. Hannah felt there was no one that she could ask simple questions, like 'Will it hurt?' or 'How will I know when the baby is coming?' As she saw it, there was nobody in whom she could safely confide her fears without them being so scandalised that they would blurt the news of her pregnancy to all and sundry. And how long could she continue without it becoming patently obvious to outsiders that she was either putting on weight at an alarming rate or was carrying a child?

At the time of Helen's murder, Hannah was still working at the Hoover factory in Cambuslang. Close friends are fairly sure none of her workmates, including her former fiancé, had a clue about her condition, although there was probably some gossip to the effect that for one so young – she was 20 – she was letting herself go. Had there been a regular boyfriend on the scene – and in such communities as Hannah lived it would have been impossible to hide this – then tongues might have wagged more cruelly and, as it would transpire, accurately. But her loose-fitting smocks and dresses became such an accepted garb that when the baby bump grew more noticeable no one thought it odd that Hannah was beginning to fill out her clothes.

One or two, in kindness, had a quiet word with her, suggesting she would look more ladylike in outfits that were more tight-fitting, but Hannah simply replied that she liked the way she was and was happy with the way she dressed.

And at home her father had certainly not noticed any difference in his daughter; she was not in the habit of going about the house semi-naked so to him she appeared absolutely normal. Fooling her dad was easy. She rose early and came home late and, because of the time of the year, most went to work in the dark and the few hours of sunshine had vanished well before they returned. As Hannah made her way between work and home, apart from the lights within the buses she travelled on, she was walking in darkness. And in the chill of that time of year, everyone wore heavy clothing to stay warm, giving them the appearance of having considerably greater bulk. So there was little or no chance of anyone thinking anything was out of the ordinary outside – and within – the family home.

She had also ceased going to the dancing in Glasgow, but then that was hardly likely to attract attention: so had scores of others who had traditionally taken buses from Lanarkshire to the city – mostly the single females who had either decided for themselves to wait until things were declared safer or who had had their minds determined by anxious parents laying down the law and flatly refusing them permission to go. Generally, there was little dissent to these rulings. In Hannah's case, it meant a potential problem was taken out of her hands. Not that a triple murder would have otherwise deterred her sense of defiance: not against her father but the climate at the time that urged caution.

Would Hannah have blithely gone on in her world of make believe until the moment came when pain and a baby suddenly arrived? No one will ever know, as Hannah's predicament was solved for her by a close neighbour and family friend who had kept a motherly eye on her since Jessie's death. We shall call her Joan.

This kindly woman was not the type to pry on the Martin family, but she did by chance regularly meet Malcolm or his daughter. She noticed a slight difference in Hannah's gait and a bulkier look to her shape. Having had a family of her own, she knew the telltale signs and suspected, astonished though she was, that they were there in the girl.

Joan was both baffled and worried. She waited for some days to see whether her eyes had been deceived by a trick of the light or a breath of wind blowing out her neighbour's clothing; she waited, too, to discover if it would be Hannah who would make the first move and pass on news that, in the circumstances, she might not altogether be happy to tell. Joan felt that if she was right then help would be needed, and quickly, but she had first to find out the truth. In the end, there was only one way that could be done.

Greeting Hannah one day, Joan opened with customary small talk, asking about her work, her friends, her father and her health, then suddenly she pointed a finger at Hannah's tummy. 'You're getting a bit on the big side there,' she shot. 'Is there anything wrong?'

For a second, Hannah was stopped in her tracks. Then she burst into tears. The masquerade was over. Years later, she would admit that by the time Joan intervened, she had come to accept she was having a baby and knew that it had been crazy to carry on thinking that such an event was not going to happen.

'I can't believe I didn't tell myself right away that I was pregnant and try to do something about it, seek help, advice,' she said. 'But I was terrified as to what my father would say, what the rest of the family would think and how neighbours would react.' These were the fears that flooded out with the tears.

Joan immediately reassured Hannah. She took the girl, her eyes red, her face covered in teardrops, into her own home, sat her down and asked when the baby was due.

'I think it's January,' was the reply.

'You sure?'

'As sure as I can be.'

'Your father must be told.'

'No.'

'He'll have to know. He'll find out anyway.'

'He'll go wild.'

'Perhaps, but he has to be told and told right away. You cannot hide this from him a day longer.'

'I'm too scared to tell him.'

'You want me to do it for you, Hannah?'

'Would you?'

'OK, I'll tell him. But he's going to want to know the name of the baby's father.'

'I don't know his name.'

'You don't know his name! What do you mean?'

'I think he might have said he was a shipyard worker. But I can't remember.'

'You better tell me what's been going on. I can't believe you thought you could get away with this without anyone finding out.'

Hannah felt better after telling Joan the story of the night she had tried drinking away the memory of jilted love. Her older friend knew a good part of it had to be the truth, but now she too was not looking forward to telling the news to Malcolm Martin.

There would have been no point in putting off the dreaded moment, so Joan called on him when she knew he was alone and told him she had something important to discuss, then broke it to him. She knew it would be a shock, but he was still a young man, just approaching his 47th birthday, and had coped with worse traumas. He had handled sudden death, now he was required to face the shock of unexpected life.

Malcolm sat briefly stony-faced, sullen, silent and hurt. Perhaps this pain came from hearing that his daughter had been abused or because she had evidently been too afraid to tell him herself. He would never say, but when he did react Joan would later tell a friend only that he 'blew his top'. When he calmed down, his first thought was that nobody must know.

Malcolm was unashamedly old-fashioned, in the way he acted and dressed and in his outlook on life. One of his friends noted, 'He was close to Hannah and liked to think that if she had a worry, she would go to him with it. He knew, of course, he could be no substitute for Jessie, but he was the head of the household and the decision maker. This was one situation in which he was simply out of his depth. He wasn't a bad man, but he got it wrong from the very first words he uttered. As far as he was concerned, this was all about what others would think, about the shame and scandal he felt Hannah was bringing. What he should have been concerned about was his daughter, her well-being, happiness, her state of mind. Just as she had for months tried to pretend there was no baby, her father's attitude was that there would be no child in his house. At the time she needed her father most, he wasn't there for her. His thoughts were first and foremost for his reputation and that was wrong.'

Malcolm Martin was no fool. He would have read in the newspapers about backstreet abortionists, often elderly women versed in quackery or one-time medical students booted out of university for reasons mostly of drunkenness, unpaid gambling bills or lasciviousness. Three years earlier, the death of a teenager in Glasgow had been put down to an amateur termination, although the abortionist was never discovered. With enough money and the necessary contacts, finding someone to 'take care of things' was always possible.

The Abortion Act of 1967 had specifically targeted backstreet abortions, ruling a termination could only be carried out by a registered medical professional. Even then there were few conditions in which it was considered necessary, one being that the mental state of the mother would be at risk as a result of having a baby following a sexual attack or rape. Had Hannah come forward sooner, it is highly possible she could have proved that she fell within this category.

There is little doubt among those who knew Malcolm that the idea of an abortion would have flashed through his mind very soon after Joan broke the traumatic news to him. But even though he was no medical man, he would have realised just as quickly that such a solution was out of the question. No one would even contemplate terminating the life of a now seven-month-old unborn child. That would undoubtedly have been murder.

By ordaining that no one should know about the pregnancy, Malcolm had automatically limited the practical options to one. Hannah might have had the child and then gone off somewhere else to live, but her sudden and unannounced disappearance would have posed so many awkward questions from friends and relatives that it was out of the question. To have kept the baby and brought it into the house and explained it as the child of a friend who had died or had found herself unable for a swathe of reasons to look after it was too unlikely a scenario, inviting equally uncomfortable queries. In the end, there was only adoption, and immediate adoption.

Malcolm would contact social workers and start the process, but it was an approach that left him feeling humiliated and shamed. Through all of this decision-making, Hannah was left on the outside, told by her father once choices had been made rather than consulted during the process. There were risks in this, but what Malcolm saw as the consequences were very different to those seen by friends who sympathised with Hannah's predicament. His fear was that the inevitable legal process, involving outsiders, would lead to a leak locally: the secret would be out and shame galloping to his door. But was not the possible effect on his daughter of having the infant she had carried for nine months snatched away almost at the moment of delivery potentially more devastating?

To carry on the secrecy required considerable thought and planning. Hannah would continue at her work almost until the point of delivery, leaving her departure to the very last and explaining away her absence by some sickness. No other neighbour had to find out and as for immediate family not even her grandparents, Richard and Hannah, were told. The mother-to-be would, until the birth, refrain from her frequent visits to their home on the grounds that she was being required to work extra hours. In the event of unexpected visitors to the house, she would make herself scarce. The need for absolute discretion would be explained to the social workers assisting with the adoption, who would no doubt protest confidentiality was an inbuilt rule. Malcolm, however, feared their penchant for gossip and indiscretion and their role would remain a constant worry for father and daughter.

NINE

ARRIVING AND LEAVING

As 1969 disappeared, leaving memories of so many tragedies, Hannah found herself visited by and calling to see a never-ending stream of officials. There were numerous checks with doctors acting on behalf of the adoption authority to ensure all was well. Both Hannah and her father, as her next of kin, sat through lengthy meetings with psychiatrists and psychologists, filled in countless forms and underwent a string of interviews. All of it was well-meant: giving birth for the first time is the most momentous event of any woman's life; having that baby taken away forever represents a pivotal step. Once done, it is done for good; there can be no turning back. Regrets are allowed but not encouraged. Tears expected.

Time after time, Hannah was asked if she was sure about the adoption. The social workers asked if she felt she could cope with the knowledge that her child would be brought up by strangers, who almost certainly would not tell the child about her. They explained that the child would look upon this man and woman as mother and father and told her it would be they who gave the baby a name, not her. 'When your baby cries, they will provide comfort, not you. When it falls and bleeds, they will hug it and kiss the wound better, not you,' she was told. 'At Christmas time, they will give it presents, not you, and it will thank them, not you. If your baby succeeds in life, becomes famous, important, you will never know. When your child is an adult and having a family of his or her own, you will not be a part of it. The infant you pass on the street, the schoolchild playing with friends, the handsome young man or pretty girl you see holding hands and looking lovingly into the eyes of another may be the baby you carried and brought into the world, but you will never know. Is this what you want, Hannah? Decide now because in a few weeks, perhaps only a few days, it will be too late for a change of mind.'

As the time grew near, Hannah surely began to wonder if she was doing the right thing. She must have felt an attachment for the growing baby she had not sensed previously. But, effectively, the choice was not hers to make: Malcolm Martin had decreed what would be and that was it. When she tentatively raised with him the issue of perhaps, after all, keeping the child, he was adamant. 'You don't have a mother behind you, there's only you and me, there's no way we can take care of a wean. You have to let it be put up for adoption.'

Whatever changes might have occurred in her own feelings, she was railroaded into going along with what her father commanded; however, these new emotions strengthened with each passing day and by the time the baby was born there is no doubt Hannah wished she could have kept the child. By then, it was too late. In any case, her father had laid down the law; to have defied him was unthinkable to a 20-year-old girl, largely alone in life.

As with her silence on the Bible John issue, it is so easy to condemn Hannah, but her options were already severely limited because of the secrecy of her pregnancy. If Malcolm said the household could not cope with a youngster, then that effectively barred her from taking a baby home. She would be homeless and jobless and, while not friendless, who else was there to offer shelter to a young woman some would regard as immoral?

Social workers were hardly likely to want a change of mind at such a late stage either. The process of adopting a child is long and convoluted, and for the adoptive parents to have endured the wait only to be told that the birth mother had changed her mind would be devastating for them. Hence a heavily pregnant woman who has said she does not want to keep her child is encouraged to stick with her decision. Hannah had the added pressure of her father agreeing with the social work team.

By January 1970, it was obvious the arrival of the baby was imminent. Hannah was forced to miss work and a note was sent to the Hoover factory to the effect she was ill. Hannah was taken to the Bellshill Maternity Hospital – a careless mistake, as the hospital was staffed by local people, some of whom would know Hannah and her family. Tongues would wag and the secret would be out.

As soon as the bungle was realised, she was instantly removed and transferred to the posh-sounding Glasgow Royal Maternity Hospital in the north of the city, bizarrely named 'The Rottenrow' after the street in which it stood. It is said the name was derived from the area being used in medieval times as a dumping ground for refuse and sewage.

One who entered the world there was Ian Brady, born Ian Duncan Stewart illegitimately at Rottenrow to tearoom waitress Peggy Stewart on 2 January 1938. He would later take the surname of a stepfather. At the time of the Bible John horror, Brady's was a name recognised and reviled, as was his girlfriend's, Myra Hindley, for the sickening wave of murders he had orchestrated, the victims being children, four of whom were buried on Saddleworth Moor near Oldham in Lancashire. Hannah felt a shudder of revulsion as she was wheeled through the same doors Brady had arrived through, newly born, just over 30 years earlier.

At least the deaths of these children had been solved and the perpetrators caged forever. As Hannah went into labour, teams of detectives outside in the city were still sifting through even the most tenuous clues in their search for solutions to this latest spate of madness.

The baby arrived in early January 1970. It was a girl, born without complications and evidently healthy, her appearance arousing in her mother the deepest of maternal instincts and the strongest desire to retain what was hers. It is difficult not to share Hannah's distress at being separated from the child so soon, probably within hours, before the bond between them became too close.

Before entering hospital she had confided to Joan, 'I know I'm going to have to give my baby away, but I'm not going to send him or her into the world without anything. It's a bad enough place to begin with. I know I won't see my own child, but I want to know the baby leaves me looking cared for and knowing when he or she grows up its mother made sure it wasn't given up with nothing.' She had bought a tiny woollen outfit for the babe, which had been brought into Rottenrow with her and handed to maternity staff. It was a heart-rending gesture and those who attended the new mother could see the hurt and distress she was suffering.

There would be even worse to come for her. After the baby had been delivered and nurses were preparing to take her away, Hannah begged them, 'Is it a boy or a girl?' The rule was that a mother who had agreed to have a baby adopted should be told nothing, the theory being that the less that was known, the less it would hurt. It was impossible not to be moved.

'A girl,' she was told.

'Then I want to give her a name.'

'OK, Hannah, what are you calling her?'

'Isobel.'

'Isobel, what a sweet name. Why Isobel?'

'Isobel was the name of my sister. I'm keeping a promise.'

She clearly wanted to talk more, but her fatigue was evident. She would need every ounce of strength in order to cope with the ordeal that lay ahead. As for Isobel, she would remain at Rottenrow until doctors were satisfied she was free from illness and ready to face life in the outside world.

The couple she would in the future call her parents were waiting anxiously. They had simply been told a baby could be theirs, without anything more specific. It would have been a bitter blow for them should their hopes have been raised only for something to change the plans at the last moment. The slighter the expectation, the easier would disappointment be to bear should it come. The legal documents that accompanied Isobel on her way out of hospital stated that the baby's mother had been prevented by her own father from keeping it and that it was in the child's best interests to be given a future with another family.

The birth would be registered in due course, although the space marked 'Name, surname, and rank or profession of father' would remain blank. Hannah would maintain that in all honesty she did not know who he was. But was it a name that would ultimately be provided by the police? Had Bible John become a father?

A few days after the birth, Hannah left Rottenrow alone and returned home to Bellshill, outwardly as though nothing had happened. Inside, she felt wretched, racked with questions. What colour were her baby's eyes? What colour was her hair? Who was to comfort her when she began teething? When would she begin to crawl? When would she take her first steps? Who would be there to see her first laugh? When would she begin to form her first words? Would she cry on her first day at school? Who would take her there? What is in store for her when she grows up? Would they ever meet? What would her new parents be like? She was inconsolable with grief but knew the clock could not be turned back.

The next day she was back at work. Colleagues sympathised with her over her illness but were aware that their queries as to what had been wrong were met with vague looks and not really answered. That first night, lying in bed, Hannah found it impossible to sleep, as she restlessly tossed and turned before abandoning any hope of relief from the torment. Her uncertainties were dominated by the future, but it was the past and its memories that took over.

A month later, in February, Hannah read that a man named Thomas Ross Young, a lorry driver, had been jailed for eight years. He had offered to give a girl aged 15 a lift but stopped at Abington, 35 miles south of Glasgow, on the main west coast route into England, where she was savagely attacked and raped. Hannah hardly needed reminding of that terrible night nearly a year ago when someone had offered her a lift, but seeing the newspaper article brought it flooding back.

'I know what that girl must feel,' she thought to herself. 'I wonder if she's pregnant?' But there were few with whom she could share her thoughts.

TEN

TEA IN THE GRASS

Malcolm's insistence that Hannah give up her daughter for fear of the shame her existence would bring on him was puzzling. His own father had been adopted and so the family had come to know what it was like to feel unwanted. It was strange that he should be so unsympathetic to a woman, particularly one formed from his own flesh and blood, who found herself in the family way before tying the knot.

The relationship between father and daughter was close and loving, as good as either could have hoped for. When Hannah was a youngster, Malcolm had fought her corner and his protective attitude towards her provoked envy in many of her school friends.

He and Jessie had married at the end of December 1945, when he was aged twenty-three and she three years younger, exchanging their vows knowing she was already pregnant. Just seven and a half months later, on 14 July 1946, Isobel, their first child, was born.

Fortunately for the couple, such a relatively short pregnancy and early arrival was not uncommon at this time. The end of the Second World War had seen many thousands of young men sent home, some of whom had neither seen their girlfriends nor slept with a woman for years. It was hardly surprising therefore that, after such long periods of enforced separation, many young men and women discovered they were about to become parents and so hastily arranged marriages followed. If a baby arrived before the ensuing nine months were over, the excuse would be made that the baby was the result of a premature birth.

After Isobel, Jessie had fallen pregnant again. She and her husband had desperately hoped for a son and their prayers were answered with a chubby boy with red curls for hair whom they named Richard. But it was soon obvious something was wrong with the baby. The child's body began developing at an abnormal rate. It is possible he was a victim of the rare Proteus syndrome. The result was tragic and Richard died before he reached his first birthday. His parents were shattered by the youngster's death, but the effect on Jessie was devastating. She had pinned her hopes on having a boy and now he had gone. A doctor called in to comfort her and gave her the best advice he could offer. 'Have another baby, and have it right away.'

So Jessie fell pregnant for a third time. She suffered from heart disease and carrying a baby and giving birth could place huge strains on that vital organ; nevertheless, there was no reason to suspect anything was wrong when Hannah was born three and a half years after Isobel. And there wasn't. Not physically at least. But the child was not the boy the mother had so wanted to replace Richard. She already had a girl and felt cheated. Hannah's mother would always find it difficult to overcome these emotions.

'Hannah was resented from the word go by her mother,' said a friend. 'Isobel was now aged three and a half and the apple of Jessie's eye. There was no room in her heart for a second girl and so Hannah was doomed to take second place throughout her life. The result was that she had a terrible relationship with her mother, turning instead for love to Malcolm, a quiet, thoughtful man who said little but was popular with a lot of the other children because he was not the strict Victorian type their fathers were.

'Jessie loved to go out partying, dressing up and having a good time, and as a result Hannah was often left in the care of her dad. He had a kindness about him and a tolerance for other children who used to play with Hannah.'

At the time of her birth, the family lived in Blackburn, midway between Glasgow and Edinburgh, but they would move to Clyde Place, Bothwellhaugh, where the young girl would spend most of her formative years. Bothwellhaugh, a mile from Bellshill, was known locally as the Pailis, a play on the title of the local mine, Hamilton Palace Colliery. Built up in the late nineteenth century, the village was made up of long rows of terraced homes, with outside shared toilets where bath night involved taking it in turn to climb into a massive metal bucket in front of the coal fire, cleanest first, muckiest last. Up to 2,000 people lived in the Pailis in its heyday, but the closure of the pit in 1959, when Hannah was approaching ten years of age, took away the reason for its existence. Sadly, the move to a new home in Bellshill made no difference to the manner in which Jessie looked upon her youngest daughter.

For reasons that will become apparent, other parents living in the Pailis were not so keen on having their offspring visit the Martin home, but the children themselves were envious of Isobel and her sister. Each week they had something to look forward to that the vast majority of the others did not. It was called the Family Day.

Saturdays, barring some serious occurrence such as a wedding or illness, were reserved for the family. Nowadays, with a car at the disposal of most families, travel is taken for granted; it is even looked upon as a chore. However, for the majority in the early 1950s it was something of an adventure, especially if the family had access to a motor. The Martins were lucky in this respect.

Family Day meant an outing from the Pailis to the nearby

town of Hamilton. As this was an outside treat, from time to time Hannah would beg for a friend to be allowed to join her. The sisters and their parents would take a bus and tour the town's shops, gazing in windows, looking enviously at rows of jars filled with every taste and colour of sweet, at gay dresses and shiny shoes, and then, as a special treat for the children, head for stores where the wide-eyed youngsters could eye up toys and dolls.

The supermarket era had not arrived; instead, Jessie and her band of followers would visit the butcher, baker and general dealer, perhaps get the girls new clothing and, come late afternoon, they'd pile into a restaurant for a sit-down meal. Around six o'clock, lugging packed shopping bags, all would pile into a bus for the journey home. But, alighting, Malcolm would disappear and head off in the direction of one of the local bars, returning sometime between nine and ten in the evening with fish suppers for all. This weekly treat might not sound like much, but it was utopia to the children and well within the family budget. The average weekly wage at this time was £5 2s 3d, while Malcolm's pint would have set him back 1s 2d.

About once a month, the wider Martin family – Malcolm, Jessie, Isobel, Hannah, Malcolm's parents, Richard and Hannah, plus various uncles, aunts and friends – would meet up, usually on a Sunday, for what became known as Tea in the Grass. This was in essence a grand picnic. The contingent would frequently head in the direction of the Trossachs, and the favoured destinations included Loch Lomond, Balloch, Helensburgh and Arrochar, and the appropriately named Rest and Be Thankful, a stopping point with spectacular views.

'As we drove along, Granny Martin would turn to her husband and say, "I think this is a good spot for Tea in the Grass. What do you think?" He'd always reply, "Whatever you think." He never argued or disputed her choice. Her word was law,' recalled an old friend. 'The car would stop at the side of some road, everyone would pile out of the motor and from the boot they would start producing chairs, but first one for Granny, blankets for everybody else to sit on and then the food. It must have involved some considerable preparation because Granny Hannah could put on a full dinner, meat and a variety of vegetables on a plate, and when that had been eaten open tins of custard, which would be poured over cakes or some other delicacy she had baked. You would see others passing and know they would be eating sandwiches while we felt as though we were seated in a restaurant having a full Sunday lunch.

'The meal over, we'd sit around or go play until it came time to have tea, a sandwich, some biscuits and a cuppa. While we were having Tea in the Grass, the menfolk would drift away in the direction of the nearest pub or hotel for a pint and a natter, about the previous day's football probably, or gossip about what was in the newspapers. The invitation to take alcohol did not include the women, and Granny would say, "You let the men do men's things and the women do women's things." A couple of hours later, by which time we'd have had tea and cleared up, the men would return. They always came back cheerier than when they went.'

Family snapshots, taken during Tea in the Grass outings, reveal how seriously these occasions were taken. They show Richard Martin dressed in a formal dark suit, his shirt buttoned to the neck and wearing a tie; his wife in a patterned dress, a cardigan around her shoulders, before a portable table heaped with cups and plates; Malcolm, clearly relaxed, eating as he lies in the grass then squatting on the edge of Loch Lomond to wash his plate; Jessie, dark haired, upright and attractive in a flowing white dress pulled up to her knees to reveal long, shapely legs; and the children, playful and conscious of the camera, eating and drinking with relish.

Buddhists are taught the law of karma, which states that

everything that happens is caused by something done previously; that we are responsible through our own actions for the course of our lives. Do good and good follows, evil and evil will result. In these terms, it is impossible to look at the faces of these little girls and understand why the events that would determine the course of their lives occurred. Their expressions suggest innocence and joy. Some suggest our karma is influenced by the thoughts and deeds of others, which might provide a solution, but the photographs give no hint of what lay in store for the sisters.

Granny Hannah was raised during an age when a woman's home was her castle, filled with starched linens, leaded fireplaces and a kettle always near boiling point. The pictures demonstrate the formality along which the lines of her life ran. She was solid, dependable, respectful and respectable, decrying changes in the world that had brought a relaxation in moral standards. For her to have discovered Hannah's later pregnancy would have been a shattering blow and she would have found it difficult to forgive her granddaughter. She was, in short, of the old school. Visitors to her home, expected or unannounced, regardless of who they were or what their purpose, would have been received with the same deference shown by Arab sheiks. Tea would have been offered and to refuse would have been considered rude. It would not have arrived in a mug but in a delicate china cup, accompanied by a saucer and a plate filled with home baking.

The sisters' granny seemed to them to exist around her stove. Hannah especially would talk fondly and proudly to anyone willing to listen about her granny's soup, her granny's stew, her granny's baking. The truth was, she felt happier, safer and more wanted at her grandparents' home than she did in her own.

All children feel the urge sometime to run away. A mild rebuke, a stern ticking-off, a chastisement for being selfish: the reasons for deciding to flee are myriad. There follows the brief packing of a bag with a favourite comic and toy, and a handkerchief containing a handful of coins. Next, slipping out of the door vowing never to return. So it was with Hannah. She would regularly take to her heels in her younger years, fleeing, often with tears streaming down her face, through the Pailis, determining to walk to Granny Martin's in Cambuslang. A toy would never be found in her pack: she would just take her weekly comic and maybe even a change of clothing.

Sometimes her absence would be noticed. Isobel might tell their parents that her younger sister had left and one or other of the adults would seek her out and bring her home. Sometimes Hannah would hop on a bus to Cambuslang and reach her journey's end only to be told she would have to go back to her parents' house. And when she did return, after being walked to the bus stop and seen safely on board, she would always arrive back at the Pailis with her favourite home-made dumpling that Granny had made. If there was not one ready, Hannah would be allowed to wait until it was baked. She looked upon the dumpling as her comfort against all the ills the world was throwing at her. Best of all, it was for her and no one else – certainly not Isobel.

So, why did she run away? Almost certainly because she had a miserable time at home, her legacy as an unsuitable substitute for her dead brother making her the whipping girl of Jessie, whose eyes, thoughts and love were reserved for Isobel. This glaring disparity in the way the mother treated her daughters was never more terribly illustrated than during Christmas 1956, as Hannah's seventh birthday approached. Malcolm Martin could not help but notice that at this time of year, when thoughts are with children, his wife would devote herself to ensuring a happy time was had by her elder child. That year he finally felt it was time to intervene and, alone in her bed, miserable and in tears, Hannah heard her parents arguing as her father looked over the pile of wrapped presents heaped upon a kitchen chair.

'All this stuff is for Isobel! Where's Hannah's?' he demanded of his wife.

'I forgot.'

'You forgot?'

'Yes, I forgot.'

'Are you seriously telling me you forgot you had a second wean?'

'I can't be expected to remember everything, can I?'

The weeping child would not see what followed, but next morning the pile had been halved. It would make no difference, though; the girl knew she had been snubbed, left out, and that the gifts she was given were no more than an afterthought, an attempt to clear the conscience of her father. She would never know what lay inside their wrapping because she refused to touch them, hiding them away, a woeful reminder of what it meant to be forever second-best.

What happiness Hannah enjoyed emanated from her grandparents, not her parents, and the extent of this was demonstrated one summer when Malcolm announced to Jessie that the family would be taking a week's holiday in Argyll. His choice was a reasonably priced hotel near the then almost derelict Carrick Castle, a spectacular ruin on the side of Loch Goil and one the family had occasionally reconnoitred during Tea in the Grass excursions to nearby Lochgoilhead. It would be a remarkable change of scenery from the Pailis: the backdrop to the deep waters of the loch was a forest through which wound a maze of paths and animal tracks. Malcolm was convinced it was just the sort of spot where the family could bond and the sisters play together, something they rarely did. Hannah took along a school friend and the two youngsters loved the break, but as she remembered how much she loved it she recalled how her mother and Isobel had hated it. What made the break even more delightful for Hannah was the unexpected appearance one day of Granny and Granddad

Martin. To her, the arrival of Father Christmas could not have been more welcome. That day, with her friend and her father, she showed her grandparents around the area, excitedly pointing to nooks and hidden paths the children had discovered.

'It was a very, very happy time,' her friend said many years later. 'It may have been the one and only happy time in her childhood.'

ELEVEN

A NICE LITTLE EARNER

One in three girls is a victim of child abuse. Hannah was that one and her sickening experiences surely helped guide the direction of her life. Experts agree child abuse comes in many forms: physical, when parents or others simply batter their charges until they are bruised or bleeding; sexual, when kids are forced to indulge in acts the purpose of which they are usually unable to understand at the time; and emotional, most often showing itself in a lack or total absence of care and affection by parents. Hannah was certainly a victim but by way of a fourth, more subtle, method: exploitation.

Nowadays, society is conscious of abuse to the extent of sometimes being overprotective. Incidents in recent years, in Cleveland and on Orkney in particular, have demonstrated the horrific damage caused to families by overzealous workers in the caring professions. In the 1950s, when Hannah was a child, abuse was often accepted as a way of life, a part of growing up endured because there was no alternative but to allow it to happen, and many knew no better anyway.

The initial lack of affection that appears to have been shown by Jessie towards her daughter, who she always felt should have been a son, might have been understandable to a degree but with the passing of time it ought to have disappeared. Instead, the mother's affection for the elder daughter, while excluding the younger, would only grow more obvious. As the years passed, Hannah became ever more conscious that she was, in her mother's eyes at least, unwanted. But then her mother found other uses for her child.

Perverts have polluted society in every walk of life, from the excesses of the Emperor Caligula and earlier. As children were at risk in the palaces of Ancient Rome, so they were in the terraced streets of the Pailis. Rife, too, was gossip, innuendo and suspicion. In the marbled corridors along which strode the elite of Roman society, strange desires were discussed openly. In Bothwellhaugh, they were whispered about behind closed doors. No one wanted to be identified as the source of gossip, even if the facts were true, but it was claimed that Jessie was using her youngest daughter for a neat little sideline.

In later life, Hannah would confide that when she was aged 11, her mother had suggested she should sit on the knee of a local businessman. No harm would come to her from this innocent act, said Jessie. The man might simply caress her as a dog owner lovingly strokes his pet. She was to be taken to his place of business, but knew it was not right and ran away.

'Her mother hammered her for not doing what she was told,' said her friend. 'Hannah knew it was wrong and was smart enough to recognise her mother had agreed to let her be abused by a man for money. What was so awful was that the money was to get Isobel a dress for some party she was going to.

'Hannah was too terrified to tell her dad and wondered if he would have believed her, in any case. It would have been her word against that of her mother. I know of at least one girl who used to go to Hannah's house, but when her father got to hear of what Jessie was doing he tried putting a block on his daughter going there. Jessie got the message that her little game was out in the open when the Martin family asked the girl if she would like to accompany them on a caravan holiday to Ayrshire. She knew she would be made very welcome and asked her own parents for permission, but was refused. The disappointment of not being able to join in what seemed a great adventure was made the worse when the girl demanded to know the reason, and none was given. Some years later, the friend's mother told the daughter what her father had said.'

It is probable at the time that Hannah did not fully understand how dreadful a proposal her mother had put to her, but as the years filtered by she became ever more aware of and revolted by it, and it is almost certain that the path she took in life in later years was a consequence of knowing one man at least had wanted to abuse her with the approval and permission of her own mother. The abused would in time learn to use men.

While Jessie's scheme fell flat when the principal performer refused to take part, it did not stop her abusing the child in yet another, more insidious fashion. Jessie's connection with Arthur Thompson was the result of a mutual association with a Glasgow gang known to handle stolen goods. Clutching their loot, shoplifters and burglars would make their way to the base of this group, which operated on a remarkable 'sale or return' basis, an arrangement previously unknown within the criminal fraternity. The home was an Aladdin's cave of treasures, from blankets to bicycles, carpets to curtains, tea sets to tables, even coloured prints to china dogs. Collecting goods was a risky business because no one could be certain an informer had not tipped off the police, who could be lurking in wait, the threat of a cosy prison cell awaiting anyone caught.

Jessie would peruse the items on offer during visits to her relatives in Bridgeton and hand over the asked-for sum, although there would occasionally be haggling over the price. She would then tell those running the reset operation that someone would be along later to fetch her purchases. There was no way she was going to take a chance herself; instead, she would slip Hannah her bus money, tell her to take a day off from lessons at Bellshill Academy, assuring her she learned nothing there anyway, and give instructions as to what was to be brought home.

The girl knew, even at the age of 11, that if she was caught, it might mean being put away for a spell in a home for wayward or wanton children. But the feeling of solitude brought on by being so often ignored or abandoned by Jessie had made her stubborn and independent. As much as she told herself she was being used, she did what was required, mainly because it was a little bit daring. She had an audacious spirit, which would stay with her throughout her life. She enjoyed mingling with criminals. Hearing about the exploits of movie-star gangsters and flashy molls aroused in her an excitement that school books could never inspire, and as the years wore on Hannah found herself drawn ever more to lawbreakers – not cheap thugs with a taste for violence but big-time gang bosses with imagination and verve. These were the people she would come to admire.

Meantime, her mother impressed on her daughter that their arrangement had to remain a secret between them; certainly Hannah should never tell her father. Often the little deceit would be arranged to fool him, with Hannah arriving back from one of her trophy-gathering expeditions at the same time as she would normally have returned from school, having already called in at a close neighbour's and left the stolen goods until the coast was clear.

This set-up involving Hannah became so prolific that the school authorities began to wonder why the child was having so many absences. It was a grossly unfair arrangement, depriving Hannah of an education and condemning her to a future restricted to menial work – one more abuse to add to the list. But at least it was better than sitting on a man's knee to be fondled.

While her peers learned about the outside world, its history and geography, and were shown how to paint and calculate, the increasing blanks against her name in the school attendance register meant Hannah had few interests. She would eventually become obsessed with dancing, but treading ballroom floors would never pay the bills. Much later, Hannah would demonstrate an ability to adapt herself to take advantage of any opening that came her way, earning a steady income in the process, even if it meant partnering criminals. But even when compared with the least intelligent of her classmates, she fared badly. Her school reports were poor, riddled with complaints about absenteeism, urging her parents to ensure she turned up more regularly. Naturally, these comments were never seen by her father. When she did take her seat in class, it was quickly apparent she was so far behind the others that there was little, if any, prospect of her ever catching up.

Eventually, Jessie was ordered to appear before the School Panel, a team representing the school and the education board, and asked for an explanation as to why Hannah stayed away so often. As ever, she had an excuse. 'I have a bad heart,' she said, producing a note from the family doctor confirming what she said. 'Some days, I'm too tired, too breathless, to get out of bed and I have to rely on Hannah to help me get about the house and go for the messages.'

It was true she had poor health, but strangely no one appears to have asked why the task of caring for her could not be shared with the older sister. The upshot was that the situation was allowed to continue as before, although it was suggested to Jessie that she should make a greater effort to reorganise the household so her younger daughter could be at school more often.

Away from the house, Hannah would always be full of fun, trying to see life as a giggle, not to be taken too seriously, an outlook no doubt encouraged by her lack of knowledge as to the pitfalls of life. She had a reputation as a happy-go-lucky girl, but privately she resented the way in which people took advantage of her youthful helplessness. 'I'm the gopher,' she would bitterly complain to friends. 'I go for this and go for that. All I hear is "Hannah will do it . . . Hannah will get it." It's just so unfair. Even when I do what my mother orders me, it's as if I've made a mess of it. In her eyes, I can do nothing right, while Isobel can do no wrong.'

To say that Hannah was treated worse than the lowliest skivvy is not an exaggeration. There is no better example of this, and of the recklessness shown towards her by Jessie, than in the callous disregard the mother showed for her daughter in asking her to collect and deliver stolen property.

When she was aged 12 or 13, a distant family member found himself incarcerated at Saughton prison, on the outskirts of Edinburgh. Prison life then was considerably more severe and restricted than it is now. Under European human rights legislation, prisoners today are allowed to receive mail without it being read by staff, while the censoring of outgoing letters has also been dispensed with. Such laxity did not exist in the 1950s and '60s. Anything an inmate wanted, such as an additional packet of cigarettes, a lighter or extra tobacco, would first have to be vetted by prison staff, though it is unlikely items such as these would be permitted, as they were generally used within the prison as currency. Those in possession of such items had the ability to build up a minor empire.

The prisoner had asked his family if there was any chance of them helping him by sneaking illegal items into Saughton. He was probably aware of what the answer would be. There was no way they were going to jeopardise their own freedom on his behalf. Then a solution was mooted. Why not send Hannah? Adults meeting with inmates were carefully searched before getting anywhere near the visiting room – if anything untoward was found on them, the police were called and, while the miscreant was hauled off, the inmate was deprived of privileges, no matter how much he might protest his innocence. But at that time children did not receive the scrutiny they do now. Streetwise Hannah could probably get a pack or two of cigarettes, or whatever, past guards and slip it to the man in the course of a welcoming hug.

Another advantage to this proposal was that as well as being safer it was actually cheaper to send a youngster to Edinburgh, because her age meant she could travel on the bus half-fare. So while the relative's own brothers or sisters would not contemplate putting themselves at risk, they were content to endanger a schoolgirl. Having worked once, it was a plot that was repeated on a regular basis, prison staff becoming familiar with the little girl who seemed so innocent.

These forays into crime meant Hannah was effectively trained in the arts of guile and trickery. She grew old before her time. An inevitable spin-off from these lessons was that she began organising her own life early on. By the age of thirteen, she had as good as left school; few of her pals can recall her joining them at their desks and lessons before she officially left two years later.

While her friends had to be at home by a certain hour, she had the run of the streets. Hannah almost turned the runs to Glasgow or Saughton into a form of blackmail. If Jessie came down hard and refused to allow her daughter to stay out, then Hannah could simply refuse to carry out her visits. Malcolm was a stern disciplinarian, but it was Jessie who directed her daughters and so others looked, often with envy, at the leeway Hannah was allowed. Friends wanting to stay out later would have to dream up excuses or lies, often relying on the age-old 'my cousin wants me to babysit' and praying that by the time the cousin was next seen the good turn would have been forgotten. There was no such need for duplicity by the Martin girls. They simply came home when they were ready, an arrangement that only added to rumours about what went on in the household.

While good girls her age were tucked up in bed by nine, not so the youthful Hannah, who began spending more time with older girls, including on occasions Isobel. And even at only 13, she was discovering the delights of the dance halls. She looked old for her age and was sufficiently cunning to know how to dress up and look the part of a shop assistant or factory girl of 17 or 18. And she was a natural at picking up dance steps. The Barrowland was her favourite destination and it was no surprise men cast her admiring, even salacious, glances. Had they known they were contemplating tampering with a child whose age would put them behind bars for a long time, they would have acted very differently. But this confident Lolita was innocent of dressing to thrill. She simply preferred the company of older people; many of them would even admit she seemed the most mature in their group, exuding a confidence about the dance floor that belied her years.

But back at the Pailis, she would forever live in the shadow of Isobel, a sad substitute for the brother there would now never be. The girls had little in common other than that as they entered their teens their teeth began dropping out due to a calcium deficiency. At least it gave them something to talk about.

While she received little affection at home, to those outside who were kind to her Hannah could show a remarkable degree of loyalty. She was a faithful friend who looked on those close to her with possessiveness rather than intimacy. All she ever wanted was somebody for herself: she did not take kindly to having to share friends or friendship. In a crowd, seeing a close friend spending time and showing an interest in someone else – Isobel especially – Hannah would noticeably become quiet and sulky and show signs of jealousy. At home, she had to take second place behind her older sister but did not see why such unfairness should continue outside.

This sullenness showed itself in different ways and probably contributed to her attitude at home of 'Why should I care?' By the age of 14, she had become lazy and lethargic, lying about the house on a settee, disputing orders by her mother to run here and there. She would utter the expression 'Aye, later' more often than any other.

'Hannah, go get some milk from the shops.'

'Aye, later.'

'Hannah, take in the washing.'

'Aye, later.'

'Hannah, go to the butcher.'

'Aye, later.'

Everything became 'Aye, later', a pattern that would only be broken when it was time to get ready to go dancing. 'Right away,' she would call. 'I'll be there, don't you worry.'

While her contemporaries were anxiously casting about, seeking work and the rewards of receiving a pay packet, she showed no such urgency, finding excuses time after time to avoid going to interviews, mostly pointing out that her mother's health was worsening and she had to be on hand to help care for her. Her interests were restricted to dancing, music and clothes, the latter being hampered by a lack of money and so she relied on hand-me-downs from Isobel, though even here she would find herself at the back of the queue. That she showed little interest in sex was neither surprising nor, for that time, out of place.

She saw her life as following the same pattern as that of so many others she knew – leaving school, eventually getting a job, having a good time, meeting a man, getting engaged then married, and having a family. The matter of finding out about sex would come in time. When she needed to know, she would either find out by asking her friends or simply by discovering through experience. For now, sex and the way in which babies were made had to wait, generally until after marriage. Until then, it did not feature in the scheme of things; dancing and music were what mattered. And the existence of Granny Martin.

Having been knocked about by her mother for so long and in so many ways, physical and emotional, Hannah came ever increasingly to lean on the old lady with a fondness that was always reciprocated. It may have been in that fondness that she found the goals for which she spent her entire life searching: happiness, security, comfort and love. It was probably the only time when, having discovered something she needed, wanted and could call her own, it was not snatched away by the actions and greed of others. She would spend so many years feeling unwanted, even unnecessary, which must surely have left within her a sense of resentment and bitterness, especially towards her mother. Jessie told her one day, 'When you get married and you've weans, if you have a wee lassie promise me you'll call her Isobel.' Despite everything, Hannah gave her word and would keep it.

TWELVE

DYING FOR A SONG

Hannah was always destined to take second place to her sister. In the normal course of family life, she might have expected to find Isobel a slight favourite – after all, she was the firstborn and was understandably looked on by her parents as special. But Hannah had then disappointed her heartbroken parents by being a girl when they had hoped for a replacement for Richard. While Jessie took hardest the failure to produce another boy, Malcolm seemed simply glad to have been blessed with two pretty girls whom he adored, his fondness for them shining as a lighthouse in a storm, his love never wavering. In time, Jessie was given further reason to pile her attentions on Isobel.

Like most mining communities, there was a special warmth about the atmosphere at the Pailis, even if the houses themselves were dank and vermin-infested. Housewives were forever popping in and out of each other's homes to gossip, sympathise or borrow a cup of sugar or a half-pint of milk. Their menfolk worked, drank, watched football and occasionally fought together, although disputes rarely lasted beyond the end of the following morning's hangover. Even religious differences were few, Protestants and Catholics living alongside one another in relative harmony; jibes that in Glasgow, for instance, might be liable to spark an open street battle were laughed off as nothing more than nonsense. The Martins were among the last to move into the village, and as newcomers they were treated with a certain suspicion, an attitude not sweetened in time by gossip over the way Jessie treated her youngest. But children are the world's greatest diplomats and the girls themselves quickly struck up their own circles of friends.

Isobel herself made a particular friend of a girl named Margaret, whose family had moved to Bothwellhaugh from Glasgow. The youngsters went to school together, played with one another and regularly visited one another's homes. Margaret had an infant sister and regularly babysat for the tot when her mother went shopping or visiting. Isobel was thrilled to help care for the child. One Saturday, when she was aged around 13, she and Margaret were happily playing outside her friend's home when they became aware of smoke pouring from its windows. Neighbours began screaming that the building was on fire and, to her horror, Margaret realised the baby was inside in her cot. Understandably, she became hysterical, screaming, too petrified to move, but her friend, without a moment's thought, dashed into the by now blazing building, ignoring flames and deadly fumes, lifted out the sleeping baby and fled into the safety of the open air and the waiting arms of neighbours and helpers.

In no time, alerted by the emergency services and admiring onlookers, newspaper reporters and photographers were at the scene. Rescuing children from fire always guarantees good copy, but here was the newsprint equivalent of solid gold: a youngster, ignoring peril and the likelihood of death, saving the life of a helpless child. It sounded good and next day her story was splashed across the Sunday newspapers. 'Brave Isobel' read one headline, 'Girl Heroine' another. Photographers persuaded her to pose and the articles also carried a blown-up photograph of the baby. Jessie proudly kept copies of the accounts of her daughter's bravery and would naturally boast of what Isobel had achieved to anyone within earshot.

Some years after the drama, the baby's family moved away. Hannah would often wonder whether the child grew up knowing the name of the schoolgirl who defied danger to save her life, or was aware of the other drama that would involve her saviour.

Like the majority of girls stepping up into their mid-teens, Isobel became, in the words of the song that might have been written for her by The Kinks in 1966, a dedicated follower of fashion. An attractive girl, she dressed to look older in knee-length dresses splashed with giant polka dots – a favourite of the day – and dark two-piece suits, and had her dark hair swept up in a bouffant style. She made friends easily, but, like Hannah's, they were often older because she preferred their maturity, probably reckoning that by mingling with them she would more quickly be gathered into their worlds, with boyfriends, even marriage, following on. It was a desire echoed by many of those her age, whose youthful looks might have prevented such wishes. But Isobel knew how to dress, and dress well. Photographs taken at the time show her as an elegant young woman rather than a teenager. It was not unnatural for her to frequently be the centre of attention, something the younger Hannah would often find difficult to cope with or accept; indeed it may be that as time went on she would feel, if not dislike towards Isobel, then certainly resentment.

One sad story demonstrates why. It is not the sole reason for the lack of warmth between the girls but is an indication of how one viewed the other. One day when she was around 13 years old, Hannah was at home when a party of Isobel's friends arrived. The younger sister was not invited into the group, a snub that left her feeling isolated and unwanted. Nevertheless in the small family home she was able to overhear the conversation, a mix of girlie talk about boys and the young womanly subjects of fashion and make-up. The subject turned to marriage and the relative prospects of the group. Each described the wedding they hoped to have. When it came to the turn of Isobel, one of her friends said, 'When you get married, Isobel, I expect you'll want Hannah to be your bridesmaid.'

The reply cut deeply. 'Will I hell have her, she's too ugly!'

If there were further words, the laughter of the little group drowned them out, as it did Hannah's sobs. Perhaps their youth and ignorance absolve either sister from blame for such a distressing state of affairs, but the same cannot be said of Jessie, who must have been aware that Isobel was set on ensuring Hannah was left out of her circle of friends.

There were other ways in which Isobel showed disdain for her younger sibling, as a close friend of Hannah's remembers. 'Isobel wouldn't be seen in the same thing twice in the same month and having bought a garment or a suit once and worn it, if she didn't like it, it would be cast down, never to be worn by her again. It would be a case of, "I don't want this, so I don't care what happens to it." The cast-offs – although since they were often virtually brand new that might not be the correct way to describe them – went to three girls: first, a relation; second, someone close to the family; and third, Hannah. In that order.

'Hannah was last because Jessie was the one who decided who would get Isobel's things when she was finished with them. The relation had first choice, then the friend, and Hannah got the last pick of what remained. The friend certainly did not know she was getting the chance to wear the clothes before Hannah, and Hannah never commented, but it must have hurt horribly to see her own sister's belongings being offered to others, while she would have the chance with what the others didn't want.

'Isobel didn't seem interested in what happened. She'd just say to her mother, "I got this for the dancing, but I've had it on a couple of times and don't want it any more. Do what you like with it."

The relation would probably wear it and then Mrs Martin would say to the friend, "I think you should have a wee shot of that." But she'd never say – and the friend never ask herself – if Hannah wanted it first. Instead, she'd pick it up and think, "That's great," because the other girls didn't have a lot and they all loved getting really dressed up to go to the dancing, just like the older ones.

'When she was 14, Hannah was bought a brown suit from a department store. To her, it was like a child's very first toy. This was the only new thing she'd ever had that Isobel hadn't worn first. It was Hannah's very own and she would never share that suit. It was sad to see how one sister had so much, yet so little of it ended up with the other.'

Like the other Pailis families, the Martins would hardly be classed as being well off, yet there never seemed to be any shortage of money, particularly when it came to buying for Isobel, who earned modest wages working as a machinist in the Hector Powe factory in High Blantyre. For instance, Jessie was able to buy her daughter an ocelot coat. Standard ocelot coats came with three pleats at the back, so Isobel turned heads immediately as she walked down the street wearing a coat showing five pleats, a clear indication it had been made especially for her and, as such, would have cost a small fortune. So, where did the money come from?

Jessie might have been a good manager, but there was talk along the streets of the Pailis that she had a sideline that took her to Glasgow from time to time, and when she returned her purse was bulging. The suggestion was that Jessie sold herself to the occasional man. No one would ever know for certain, but the rumour only added to the reluctance of neighbours to allow their children into the Martin house without an adult chaperone.

On Monday, 14 December 1964, Hannah was 15. Christmas Day, eleven days later, seemed no different from any other. Friends visited each other's homes for a celebratory drink, exchanged cards, admired presents. Isobel was excited when she awoke the following day. It had a special significance because one of her friends, Jean Caffrey, was getting married and Isobel was among the guests. The elder sister had been looking forward to it for weeks and had wondered about buying a new outfit, but in the end settled for a dress she had worn to the marriage of another of her friends. Of course the fun would come after the wedding ceremony, during the reception that was to follow. Isobel was calling the shots, instructing her sister and her friend to meet her that evening outside a Bellshill pub, after which they would meet the rest of the wedding party in the town's miners' institute, the 'Chute.

After splashing out on Christmas presents, Hannah's friend was broke and her appeals to her mother to give her enough cash for a night out were falling on deaf ears. To add to her misery, she had caught a heavy cold. Hannah was to step from a bus at 7.20 that evening, walk to the friend's home and then the two teenagers would take a five-minute walk to catch another bus for a ten-minute ride that would see them in front of the institute at eight. It was neatly planned, but in the end the arrangements would count for nothing. The friend prepared, half-heartedly, to meet Hannah, but the 7.20 bus came and went and she was nowhere to be seen. Her friend, almost relieved, stayed in for the evening and went to bed early, wondering what the explanation was for Hannah not showing up. The next morning, after picking up a newspaper, she discovered why. Staring in horror at the front page, she read the headline: 'Wedding Tragedy: Three Dead'.

A further report in the *Daily Express* on Monday, 28 December 1964 gave details of the accident. Under the headings 'Policeman's Call Stuns Guests at Reception' and 'Wedding – Then Three Died in Car Horror', accompanying a photograph of a happy couple staring shyly at the camera as they cut their wedding cake, came these words:

The bride and groom smiled happily as they cut their wedding cake. The guests looked on and applauded. But little did Charles Glancy (23) and Jean Caffrey (21) know that their wedding reception was a prelude to tragedy.

An hour later, three of the guests were dead, victims of a car crash at Mount Vernon, Lanarkshire – where the Hamilton to Glasgow road swerves under a railway bridge. Their Ford Zephyr failed to take the bend, struck a lamp standard and rammed the brick bulwark of the bridge.

Robert Glancy (22) of Kerr Street, Blantyre, brother of the bridegroom, and Anne Caffrey (20) from Whinpark Avenue, Bellshill, sister of the bride, were killed instantly.

Isobel Martin, another guest, died on her way to hospital and Michael Glancy (24), another brother of the bridegroom, was taken to Glasgow Royal Infirmary. His condition last night was 'comfortable'.

The young couple were married in a Bellshill church on Saturday morning. They had breakfast afterwards at a local restaurant and then went to a reception at the bride's home in Whinpark Avenue, Bellshill.

It was from there that the Glancys and the two girls set off to return a borrowed car.

Behind them they left 16 wedding guests celebrating. They were to rejoin the party later.

The report went on to say that the reception had been interrupted by a policeman calling to break news of the horror.

In the Martin house, around four that afternoon, Malcolm, Jessie and Hannah had been relaxing. As her parents, their appetites sufficed by another huge meal, nodded off in their chairs before the coal fire, Hannah was in her room making preparations for going out that evening, wondering what the others would be wearing.

There was a knock at their door in Clyde Place. Jessie answered the door to a policeman, who asked for her husband. The adults knew something was wrong, but the police officer would say only that there had been an accident and he had been asked to collect Mr Martin and take him to the police station at Bellshill. He had no other information. It was a white lie, but an understandable one. Malcolm was actually being taken to a mortuary in Glasgow, where he would be asked to look at a body lying on a slab and confirm it was Isobel. He would later say he noticed only a bruise on her forehead, but few believed the damage to be so slight.

As he was being helped back into a car, an officer asked how old she had been. 'Eighteen,' Malcolm replied, fighting back tears.

Around nine that night, the family re-assembled, this time joined by others, including the grandparents. It was left to Malcolm to formally break the news, but before he did so a doctor arrived to sedate Jessie.

It would later emerge that Robert Glancy and Anne Caffrey had died when they shot through the car windscreen as it came to a catastrophic halt. Isobel, in the back seat, was catapulted into the driver, who was crushed against the steering wheel. When horrified locals reached the carnage, she was still alive but ambulance crew were later forced to concede they had lost the fight to save her.

Some reporters covering the tragedy had taken the trouble to look in their newspaper libraries and unearthed the fact that the Isobel Martin who had perished so dreadfully was the same heroine who had rescued the baby from the blazing house years earlier. It gave them an excuse to publish a fitting tribute to her – a photograph of the child whose life she had saved. It appeared among black-and-white shots of the wrecked car, a high-speed tomb in which so much hope had been wiped out in a tick of time. Other journalists had the thankless task of calling at the homes of relatives, seeking photographs of the victims and a few details about their lives. One or two discovered the true reason for the deaths. The mission had not been to take back a borrowed car; rather the four young people had leapt, happy and laughing, into the Ford to take a ten-minute journey to Bridgeton, where they would collect a guitar for one of the guests to help provide the entertainment that night. They had died for a song.

The next day a particular friend of Hannah's felt she ought to pay a fleeting visit to the Martin home to express her sorrow and then quickly leave to allow the teenager space in which to grieve in privacy. She was surprised at how she was received. 'Hannah was there all right and I'd expected her to be down; she wasn't. Her mother said, "Oh, that's good you're down for Hannah. Just you stay where you are, don't bother going up the road until it's time for you to go." Hannah wanted to talk about what I got for Christmas. It was an odd reaction and I never really understood it. I had the feeling I was more upset over Isobel's death than Hannah.'

Three days after the accident – on 29 December – two black cars gently nosed their way from the Pailis, following a hearse carrying the coffin in which Isobel lay. Hannah sat dry-eyed in the lead vehicle with her parents. The cortège was headed for Daldowie crematorium on the outskirts, to the south-east of Glasgow, but this was a tricky journey for the undertakers. Daldowie is close to the bridge – still in existence – at Mount Vernon where the teenager and her friends had perished, and care had to be taken to ensure their route stayed well clear of the spot, which still showed scars of the impact. While other families in Bothwellhaugh were struggling to clear their Christmas debts, the Martins had an additional sum to find: the cost of their daughter's funeral. It worked out at £52 19s 10d – over £700 today.

A couple of nights later, families all over Scotland, indeed Scots the world over, would be raising their glasses to toast in 1965. Hogmanay is traditionally the highlight of the Scots' festivities, a time for fun, drunkenness, singing, roistering and partying. Earlier in the month, Hannah and her friend had been invited to a Hogmanay party in the Parkhead area of Glasgow. The friend, still grief-stricken and shocked over the accident, had wanted to stay away, fearing the emotions aroused by the celebrations of others would resurrect too many recent memories. Out of courtesy, she asked Hannah, 'Do you think we should go out?', expecting, and hoping, her friend would respond in the negative. She was taken aback to receive the word 'Aye'.

The party was to be at the home of a young man who had been given permission by his parents to invite a group of friends, provided it was over and everyone had left by eleven o'clock, at which time the adults would be returning from a local bar where they were to warm up in preparation for seeing in midnight. The fun was in full swing when the young host's absence was noted, but it was assumed he might have stepped outside with a girlfriend. But he was still missing when his guests left, Hannah and her friend among them; in fact, he had felt a headache coming on and had gone upstairs to his bedroom to lie down, hoping that when he awoke it would be gone. Only he never woke up. Later that night, his parents discovered him dead in bed. The cause was later discovered to have been a brain haemorrhage.

How deeply did Hannah mourn the sudden loss of her sister? It is likely Isobel never realised the hurt her position as mother's favourite caused the younger girl. Among those who were friends with both were some who recognised a jealousy in Hannah when she felt her sister might be monopolising a girl she herself regarded as one of her own particular friends. After the accident, she singled out a handful in whom she would place her trust from that day. Perhaps Hannah felt that with Isobel no longer about she might now garner a mother's affection and be given the love that she had craved for so long. If this was the case, she would be sadly disappointed. From then on, Jessie's near contempt for the flesh and blood she had brought into the world would no longer be a latent barb. She would chastise her daughter blatantly in front of friends, not bothering about the embarrassment she caused Hannah or those around her. It was deeply hurtful to a teenager whose journey through life appeared marked not with milestones but with heartbreaks.

Isobel's ashes were buried beneath a rose bush at Daldowie's Garden of Remembrance and a month after the tragedy Jessie insisted her surviving daughter dress up and, with a friend, accompany her on a sad pilgrimage to have their photographs taken at the spot.

Malcolm in particular was heartbroken by her loss. He would sit quietly in his chair before the fire, gazing at the embers while his eyes filled with tears. The others understood, but realised words would have been an intrusion into his sorrow. Families who have suffered the sudden death of a loved one display their emotions in differing ways. Some set up shrines in bedrooms, others simply move away.

Comforted by neighbours at the Pailis, the Martins may well have been happy to stay on at the mining village, but the terrace at Bothwellhaugh could never be the same. In any case, the decision as to whether or not to remain was taken out of their hands. The closure of the pit had created a cancer that spread along the village streets. Once thriving, the village was now dying; old life was moving on and there were no new arrivals to take their place.

Hannah, so close to the unexpected deaths of two young people, hardly felt the chill of the January winds that opened 1965. She knew other pastures beckoned but cared little, blaming her mother's coldness for her feeling an outcast. And so, as the months moved on, so the remaining families began moving out. The Martins were among the final five families to leave a ghost village. Once four now three, they would find themselves making a short move just along the road with their belongings to Rockburn Crescent in Bellshill. They would be glad to go, finding themselves in their last few weeks in Clyde Street boxed in by empty buildings where vermin scavenged, haunted by eerie sounds and unhappy memories. As the last removal lorry disappeared, the Pailis waited for the arrival of bulldozers.

For the Martins, once moved, nothing was too different because so many of the Pailis folk were settled in around them. The new neighbours were by and large the old neighbours. Friendships continued. Scandals and gossip also.

Nowadays the spot where families lived, loved, sang, sobbed, drank and died lies beneath the waters of a 200-acre artificially made loch, part of the massive Strathclyde Country Park. Those who remember it see it almost daily as they journey on the M74 motorway just south of Glasgow, the streets where boots once clattered on their way to work now coated in silt and travelled only by creatures of the water.

The change of surroundings did nothing to lift the gloom that had fallen over Jessie with the death of her daughter. That, coupled with a long-term weakness of the heart, had understandably left her irritable and feeling continually unwell. With the arrival of 1966, it was clear something was seriously wrong with her. She had difficulty in sleeping and was forever on edge. Neighbours would say Jessie, during her bad days, was 'a bag of nerves'. It was not meant cruelly, but the fact remained that much of her feeling of irritability was taken out on Hannah who, at 16, with years of abuse behind her, had the mental toughness of someone much older. She was not aware of it, but some of her mother's vices were rubbing off on her. More and more, Hannah was unconsciously learning to use others to her own advantage.

Meantime a doctor prescribed for her mother the sedative Nembutal. As the months passed she would come to be more and more dependent on the drug, using it from time to time as a means to block out the memory of Isobel in her coffin. Malcolm would warn her, 'You're taking too many of those things,' but he was at work during the day and the task of looking after his wife was left to Hannah and one of her young friends. Frequently, when Jessie had taken an excess of Nembutal, the teenagers would walk her up and down the living-room floor, at times almost carrying her, her limp legs dragging as they struggled to force her to come to life before Malcolm arrived back from the local steelworks.

It was understandable that once her father was home Hannah sought freedom from a house in which there was so much gloom. She was, by now, a regular traveller to the Barrowland, dancing to the hits of the time.

In November, Jessie's heart was unable to carry on and she died peacefully. There were some who wondered if her reliance on Nembutal had led her to overindulge. But then the answer was irrelevant. If taking it in ever-increasing quantities brought relief from the distress of an existence that seemed barren through the death of the daughter on whom she had so doted, then why should she not seek salvation by whatever means? At the end of the day, it was her life to do with as she pleased.

The same undertaker who had taken care of the arrangements for Isobel was again asked to provide their services. And yet again the sad cortège headed to Daldowie crematorium, once more avoiding the Mount Vernon railway bridge. The bill was £59 7s 4d. In less than two years, the Martin family had been halved.

Hannah's friends joined her to sympathise, some travelling a few yards, others many miles. Among them there were those who were surprised by her apparent lack of sorrow. They would go home to their families, saying how they had seen few signs of heartbreak and no tears. In fact, Hannah would admit only to her very closest friends that the death of her mother brought with it a sensation of relief. It could not erase the stain of the businessman's knee, or being cast into the role of a prison smuggler, or having to behave as Fagan's apprentice. Even when Isobel was no longer around, she could not escape the feeling she was still second-best, this time to a ghost. But with her mother gone, the fear, hanging over her shoulder, that abuse might return was gone.

What would come to surprise those who knew her well, and even Hannah herself, was that she would keep the pledge she had given her mother. Admittedly, the circumstances under which the baby was born could hardly have been envisaged when the promise was given, but she kept her word. It would be more than three years before she was called upon to fulfil her vow, but to her huge credit not once did she seek to renounce it.

THIRTEEN

BIBLE JOHN

As she stared out of the window of the bus during her journey to and from the Hoover factory each day, Hannah often wondered about her daughter. Just as Jessie had insisted, she had given the child the name of her sister, Isobel. It is not the name she is now known by but one we shall continue to use. It was difficult for Hannah not to look into a pram and wonder if the tiny being inside was the child she had carried. Or, as time went by, see a mother struggling with bags of shopping in one hand and a boisterous infant in the other and be tempted to call out 'Isobel' to see whether there might be a response. She knew, of course, it would have been a useless gesture. The odds against the couple who had adopted the baby choosing the same name as her must have been phenomenal.

She wondered too what had become of the outfit she had pressed into the hands of the nurses who had been with her when Isobel was born. If only she had been allowed to hold the baby, even for a second. But that had been out of the question, according to the social workers with whom she had talked in the lead-up to the birth. To have taken the tiny bundle of blood and flesh just once and then let it go for all time would have been traumatic and potentially damaging. In addition to the emotional stress this would have caused for the mother, the danger would have been that she refused to hand the baby back; an unbreakable bond might have been established in that mere moment. The friend who accompanied Hannah to Rottenrow had been allowed a brief hug but had been requested not to display emotion or go into detail about the baby's appearance to the mother.

The subject of the birth was not discussed with her father, a fact that was a relief to him probably even more so than to his daughter, because it was Malcolm and not Hannah who was ultimately responsible for Isobel being adopted. Now that sister Isobel was gone, as was Jessie, along with little Isobel, instead of a family of five the house was home to just two. He had had to build a new shape to his life, one without the routines of marriage, one allowing for loneliness. It had been different for his daughter. Since her schooldays, Hannah had all too frequently been used to being on her own, which was why outings with the rest of the family meant so much to her. Now, in her 20s, she was, often without being aware of it, using others to help create her own pleasures.

The search for Bible John continued but with the operation, of necessity, scaled down. When social workers had asked Hannah for details of her baby's father, she had said he was a shipyard worker aged 20 and did not know his identity. Both they and Hannah's friends thought it odd she had not remembered his name, or evidently asked it, because that was usually one of the first details any woman would seek from a sexual partner. She said nothing then about having been very drunk, nor of her having been an unwilling participant in that first sexual act or of the attack three years earlier by a stranger with an unholy interest in the Bible. Hannah was always convinced that man was Bible John, a killer lurking around the Barrowland in search of prey, and she had come close to being his first victim.

As time went on, a growing number of police officers engaged in the investigation into the three killings would suggest there had been more than one murderer, that Bible John was in fact at least two people. No one could ever be certain if that was correct. But it was only much later, when she confided to her closest friend what she could remember of the night Isobel had been conceived, that Hannah admitted it had taken place amidst a blur of emotions clouded by drink and she believed one of those two was the man who had so cruelly and without feeling taken her in his car.

Now, on top of all else, she had to live with the knowledge that she had in all probability given birth to the child of the man known as Bible John. That only added to a determination if not exactly to seek revenge on men then to at least use them in the way others had used her. She felt even her own father, in his lack of compassion, had taken advantage of his parental hold over her.

For a time after Isobel was born, Hannah went into a shell, turning down invitations to join her friends for nights out. But as time passed, she emerged and went back to her old routine of hopping on a bus to Glasgow. Many of her friends were envious of the freedom she had to choose her own pursuits. Malcolm never appeared to intervene in her private life and as time went on would happily loan her his beloved Austin Princess so she could drive herself and chums to the dancing in Glasgow. Despite its memories, the Barrowland remained her favourite destination and she thought nothing of going alone, although she frequented the other Glasgow dance halls, too. There were always enough single men on the lookout for a partner. She knew a good number were probably married and seeking a sly evening, or even night, away from a wife and family. Then there were the sales representatives, spotted a mile off by their appalling chat-up lines and oh-so-blatant attitude of being cocksure. The ones to be wary of, she knew, were those who made it too obvious they were single. Having held onto that status, the men were unlikely to want to relinquish it.

That was not to say she spurned romance or abandoned herself to remaining a spinster. Having experienced motherhood, Hannah felt suited to it. When friends became pregnant, she encouraged them to enjoy the sensation, even the physical discomforts that it brought with it. It may have been that she relived her own pregnancy; certainly, she fell in with the hype of it, enjoying being present to hear the excited questions from others as to when the baby was due, what it would be named, or details about the buying of tiny clothes in preparation. One friend in particular was perplexed at how Hannah was able to predict the many feelings and emotions she experienced as the birth of her own child neared. But she would never know the truth. When the friend's firstborn came into the world, to be followed by others, Hannah lavished affection on them, wishing she could have imparted it to Isobel. The child was in her thoughts constantly. She knew she had a little girl somewhere, but where, she could not be certain. However, the one thing of which she could be sure was that she would never have done to her daughter what her mother and then her father had done to her.

'Other close pals had babies,' said a friend, 'talked about them and showed Hannah their babies. She would praise them, tell them how gorgeous the weans were, say all the things the proud mothers wanted to hear, but she never mentioned her own child, even when someone would ask her, "Hannah, isn't it time you settled down and got married? You'd make a really good mother. You're a natural." She never talked about what she'd had to do. And that must have been a terrible, awful hurt. Being a mother who had to be childless left a massive gap in her life.'

Throughout the '70s, in between the dancing and nights out with friends, there were occasional boyfriends, but Hannah concentrated her affections on her grandparents, Hannah and Richard, and her energies into making comfortable the home she and her father shared at Rockburn Crescent, Bellshill.

'For many years, while Hannah was working at the Hoover factory, she would come out of her work and go straight to her gran's. It was on her way home, but even had it been in the other direction it would not have made a difference,' said an old friend. 'She loved being at the old couple's, putting her granny's fire on, making tea, doing the housework, something she had been forced into doing when she was young at home and hated as a result, but she took a genuine pleasure in doing it for her granny of her own free will.

'Sometimes on a winter night, she would go straight in the door, grab a blanket and sit at the fire, and Granny would produce whatever she had cooked for tea. And then she would maybe get into bed with her granny to watch television. When her granny was old and bedridden, Hannah would arrive and hop right into the bed with her granny. Yet, despite her fondness for and closeness to the old couple, her grandma and granddad never knew she had the baby.'

When the old couple died, Hannah was given a cushion cover, black with a peacock embroidered upon it and made over 100 years earlier by another of the grannies called Hannah. She had passed it down to Granny Hannah Martin. It missed a generation and then came to Hannah, who promised it would be handed on to the next in the family to be christened Hannah. It was a gift so precious she would find it hard to part with it, as her friends would come to discover.

Hannah would never know it, but Isobel was living only a few miles away with her new family. Obviously her adoptive parents did not know the identity of the baby's mother but at an early stage in the adoption process had asked whether there would be a possibility of the natural mother seeing her child and recognising him or her. Identity was one more reason why Hannah had not been allowed to see Isobel. Now Hannah wondered if she stared directly at the youngster, would she know her? It might have been the case that, as time went by, mother and daughter did pass on the same side of the street, waited in the same queue, stood side by side at the same shop window. But neither knew it. It was just as possible that the baby's father looked at Isobel without knowing she was his child, danced with Hannah or stepped aside to allow Isobel and her new parents to pass by.

The youngster was raised in a happy household. She had not been handed to her new parents directly from the Rottenrow delivery room. They were allowed a handful of visits to begin the bonding process, to see whether they appeared comfortable with the baby, and it was soon clear they were overjoyed in her presence.

So, a few weeks after her birth she was carried to her new home to join her new parents' other children. She remembers a very happy childhood in a house filled with laughter and love.

The mother and father, who had brought another human being in to be a part of their own lives so she might be spared loneliness, both worked so the family had a healthy income, a major proportion of which went on the children, who were spoiled but in a kindly sense. There were bedtime tales, outings, birthday parties, toys, games, friends, pretty clothes, fireworks and the annual call from Santa. Isobel had books and beads, dolls and dimples, a mother and a father to kiss her goodnight and to welcome her to each new day. She felt warm and protected and safe, unaware of the evils that lie in wait for the trusting and unwary. It was just as well: a deluge of horror was about to fall on the lives of so many innocents.

FOURTEEN

RESURRECTION

The police knew at least one maniac was still on the loose. Bible John – or however many other men might fall under the moniker – had last struck on Earl Street in October 1969. Then disappeared.

Faced with a situation in which a number of serious or violent crimes, clearly the work of the same serial offender, are followed by a long period of calm, detectives customarily make a number of reasonable assumptions. Each involves thankless routine checks intended to help answer the question: 'Where has he (or, in a handful of cases, she) gone?'

Perhaps the target, in committing the last known offence, had been injured and would therefore lie low for a while to recuperate. (This was almost certainly the case after Bible John's altercation with Helen Puttock, who would have left scratch marks on her assailant.) Another likely cause for sudden long periods when nothing is heard is that the miscreant is in prison. Detective teams therefore began poring over every spell of incarceration handed down after Helen's killing. Perhaps the killer left the area completely, which meant the gathering of information from a raft of sources, particularly informants, on surprise disappearances. Or maybe he had died of natural causes, so a search of the register of birth, deaths and marriages would be required.

The many thousands of hours of dull, regulation checks threw up some names, but none could be linked sufficiently strongly to the murders to merit the men being arrested and charged. Among the names was John McInnes, who was questioned more than once, as his regular attendance at the Barrowland together with a certain similarity in appearance to the painting of the suspect put him in the spotlight. Indeed, the police asked him so often if he was Bible John that he used to make jokes about the fact in his local bar. He took part in identity parades, but Helen's sister Jeannie failed to pick him out. Joe Beattie, known as 'The Flea' to colleagues because criminals never knew when they'd turn around and find him on their backs, was never convinced McInnes was the man, or one of the men, he sought.

Some of McInnes's friends wondered if the laughs and gags hid his true feelings about being a suspect; around the time of the police inquiries, his marriage went through a bad patch. In 1972, he and his wife, Ella, would divorce.

So Hannah, possibly keeping to herself vital clues about Bible John, danced away the weekends at the Barrowland, often having her feet flattened by those of a plain-clothes cop not too subtly getting the conversation around to whether she had been there on any or all of the nights of the murders. She would never know it, but McInnes's story would bear a strange similarity to her own.

Meanwhile, as her daughter learned to crawl, then walk, then pick up a few childish steps that she gaily practised with her parents and step-siblings, the detectives pounded on, their steps slowly losing the initial spring, before dragging. Bible John, it seemed, had vanished. Gradually, the thieves and muggers, fraudsters and thugs who had enjoyed a relatively easy time while their pursuers were off in search of a more deadly quarry found themselves once more being harried and cuffed as the murder squad diminished in numbers.

By late 1971, the dedicated team had been spread far and wide, although it would never capitulate. Occasionally, an arrest would throw up suspicion and a petty thief or drunk would find himself being asked where he had been on the nights of the murders. Two detectives who arrested a man caught arguing with a woman learned from her that his name was John and that he had picked her up at the Barrowland. They took him to a nearby police station, handcuffed him to a radiator and called Joe Beattie, who took one look and said 'the nearest yet' and ordered them to release him.

A beat policeman chased and caught a shadowy figure spotted relieving himself in a backstreet near the Barrowland. When the suspect grabbed a brick, the bobby thumped him over the head with his truncheon so hard that he needed hospital treatment. At Glasgow Royal Infirmary, a doctor ordered handcuffs to be removed from the patient, who promptly leapt through a first-floor window and disappeared into the night.

In each case, the man had given the same address. He would eventually be traced and made to stand in an identity parade along which Helen's sister slowly walked, up and down, before announcing she had never seen any of those in the line-up before. The suspect was cleared and sent home to be the long-time butt of jokes from pals about being Bible John.

'I hope they catch the bastard,' he told them.

Among senior police there were those who would not be turned from a belief that all three women had died at the hands of the same man – the opposite view to that of Joe Beattie. Thus it was that suspects were measured in terms of all three deaths. If they were unable to provide suitable alibis for two of the nights when the killings took place, they were ruled out by being able to show they were somewhere else on the night of the third. This

Hannah (left) as a child, with her older
sister Isobel

Jessie, Hannah's mother,
at Tea in the Grass

Malcolm Martin,
Hannah's father

Hannah was always close to her
grandparents, Richard and Hannah

Isobel Martin, who was
tragically killed in 1964

Hannah, aged 15, with a friend at
the remembrance tree at Daldowie
crematorium, following her sister's death

Coverage of the accident
in which Isobel died
appeared in the *Daily
Express*

AT RECEPTION

Wedding —then 3 died in car horror

Express Staff Reporter

THE bride and 'groom smiled happily as they cut their wedding cake. The guests looked on and applauded.

But little did Charles Glancy (23) and Jean Caffrey (21) know that their wedding reception was a prelude to tragedy.

An hour later three of the guests were dead, victims of a car crash at Mount Vernon, Lanarkshire — where the Hamilton to Glasgow road swerves under a railway bridge.

Their Ford Zephyr failed to take the bend, struck a lamp standard and rammed the brick bulwark of the bridge.

Charles and Jean cut their wedding cake.

Wave goodbye to

QUOTE

—Mr. Mrs Grace Mills, celebrating her 100th birthday yesterday at Spelthorne Lodge, Sunbury-on-Thames, Middlesex:

THE ingredients for a long life

The Barrowland Ballroom in Glasgow

Police photofit of the man believed to be
multiple killer Bible John

Patricia Docker, the first victim of Bible John,
and his second, Jemima McDonald

Helen Puttock,
murdered after taking a
taxi ride with
Bible John

Detective Joe Beattie, who said he would know Bible John if he met him

Bible John suspect John McInnes, whose body was later exhumed

Arthur 'The Godfather' Thompson leaving a Glasgow nightclub in 1959. A decade on he was questioned by the Bible John murder squad detectives and later by police investigating the World's End killings

World's End murder victims Helen Scott (left) and Christine Eadie

The passport photograph of Hannah
Martin taken so she could make trips to
Spain as a drugs-money courier

John Healy, the man with whom
Hannah fell in love, 2002
(picture courtesy of Mike
Schofield, *The Sun*)

Hannah with friends

The last photograph of
Hannah taken shortly
before her death in 2002

Extract of an entry in a REGISTER of DEATHS

(Section 37(2) of the Registration of Births, Deaths and Marriages (Scotland) Act 1965)

DG 1012138 CE

DEATH Registered in the district of					District No.	Year	Entry No.
Bellshill					566	2002	605

1. Forename(s)	Hannah Keir Cowan	2. Sex
Surname(s)	Martin	F

3. Occupation	Sales Representative

4. Date of birth	Year	Month	Day	5. Age	6. Marital status
	1949	12	14	52 years	Single

7. When died   2002 December Tenth 1630 hours

8. Where died   Monklands District General Hospital Airdrie ML6 0JS

9. Usual residence (if different from 8 above)
40 Simpson Way Bellshill ML4 1TH

10. Cause of death   I(a) Hepatic encephalopathy

          (b) Metastatic liver disease

          (c) Unknown primary malignancy

          (d)

     II

Certifying registered medical practitioner   A McIntyre

11. Forename(s), surname(s) and occupation of spouse(s)

12. Forename(s), surname(s) and occupation of father	13. Forename(s), maiden surname, surname(s) and occupation of mother
Malcolm Keir Cowan Martin Steelworker (deceased)	Jessica Anderson (ms) or Martin Housewife (deceased)

14. Signature of informant, how qualified to give information and address

(Signed) Hugh Martin   Uncle

4 Oakmount Jerviston Court Motherwell ML1 4BS

15. When registered	Year	Month	Day	16.
	2002	12	11	(Signed) A. Millar
				Assistant Registrar

17.

18.

Extracted from the Register of Deaths

on   Eleventh December 2002   *a. Millar*   asst Registrar

The above particulars incorporate any subsequent corrections or amendments to the original entry made with the authority of the Registrar General.

Warning

It is an offence under section 53(3) of the Registration of Births, Deaths and Marriages (Scotland) Act 1965 for any person to pass as genuine any copy or reproduction of this extract which has not been made by a district registrar or assistant registrar and authenticated by his signature. This includes any photocopy made by any other person.
Any person who falsifies or forges any of the particulars on this extract by knowingly uses, gives or sends as genuine any false or forged extract is liable to prosecution under section 53(1) of the said Act.

Hannah's death certificate

might have led to the murderer of one escaping capture because he could prove he did not kill the others.

Even the one-time spate of crank calls and good-faith tip-offs had almost dried up. The painting of Bible John had been circulated everywhere in the world where it was thought Scots might be seen and this resulted in a call from Hong Kong. The information was followed up but brought nothing.

The trail had not merely gone cold; time had blown over Bible John's tracks. And so the years drifted on. By 1977, thoughts had turned to other headlines. In March, some Scots had watched in horror as two Boeing 747 airliners, belonging to KLM and Pan Am, collided at Los Rodeos Airport in Tenerife, killing 583 men, women and children. It still ranks as the world's worst plane disaster. Weeks later, in bars and at workplaces, people enthused over the prolific exploits of Red Rum, who won the Grand National for an unprecedented third time. Then in June came what would initially be seen as Bible John's resurrection.

Bakery worker Frances Barker, aged 37, a petite, respectable, fun-loving redhead, went for a night out in Glasgow with friends on 10 June and vanished. She had flagged down a taxi to take her home to her top-floor flat on Maryhill Road, but the alarm was raised when Frances, a good, conscientious worker, failed to turn up for her job at the City Bakeries. Police made their customary checks, and there were those among them who wondered whether her disappearance was down to Bible John. Those fears increased with the discovery of her body two weeks later. A farm worker spotted what seemed to be a bundle of old clothing in undergrowth near Glenboig, Lanarkshire, a few miles east of Glasgow. When he investigated, he had to fight back nausea. What he had found was a woman's body. It would turn out to be that of Frances. Her hands had been tied behind her back, she had been strangled and her pants stuffed into her mouth. There were elements of the Bible John murders, but what made detectives sit up was the fact that, as with the earlier killings, the victim's handbag had been stolen.

The net closed around dozens of known sex attackers, a normal move by police, aware that this type of criminal is notoriously prone to repeat offending. Among those taken in for questioning was Thomas Ross Young, the man who gave a lift to young Pat McAdam before she disappeared. He was discovered hiding in the flat in Crow Road, Glasgow, belonging to his ex-wife, Annie. The detection team was convinced they had Frances's killer, and enthusiastically – Young and some of his friends would later argue too enthusiastically – produced a damning piece of evidence they said had been found in a hiding hole at Annie's flat. It was a powder compact that had been given to the dead woman by a local store in appreciation of her good and regular custom. How did it get there? The police said he could only have taken it from his victim. Young argued it had been planted. He was a sex fiend, of that there could be no doubt. But had he strangled Frances Barker? Was he the killer they called Bible John?

The latter was ruled out when it was learned Young had been in jail at the time of Patricia Docker's death, but of the former, despite the father of four protesting his innocence, he was convicted and jailed for life. He was packed off in handcuffs to Peterhead, Aberdeenshire, bitterly complaining at the unfairness of the Glasgow High Court jury's verdict in October that year. It is unlikely Young has ever heard of Hannah Martin or her daughter. But he has a part to play in their story.

In August 1977, a month after Young had been arrested, pretty Anna Kenny, aged 20, devoted to her family and they to her, had gone for a night out to the Hurdy Gurdy Club in Townhead, Glasgow. She was a woman who would tell her folks where she was going when she went out and at what time she should be expected home. Her parents began worrying when she was late because the Hurdy Gurdy was just a short taxi journey from her home in the Glasgow Gorbals. They then contacted friends in case she had decided on the spur of the moment to spend the night with a pal and had been unable to get a message home.

By the following morning, 6 August, the family was frantic and headed down to her workplace to see if she had turned up. She had not. The next step was the police.

The pattern seemed all too familiar: a pretty young woman, a night out, perhaps an invitation to see her home. Now there was no trace. She could be anywhere. Customers at the Hurdy Gurdy recalled seeing Anna but could not recall her leaving. It was as if she had been there one moment and was gone the next, though some of her friends believed they remembered her saying she was heading off to get a taxi to the Gorbals.

Searches were made of derelict buildings, wasteland, garages, industrial sites and even the Forth and Clyde Canal, despite it being in the opposite direction to the one she would have taken. But the hourly reports to her devastated family brought nothing. Other Scottish police forces were contacted and given a description of the missing woman, then counterparts in England, in the unlikely event of her having decided to quit Glasgow for good. They too, sadly, could not help. Anna, it would seem, had disappeared from the face of the earth.

Eight weeks later, while posters showing Anna's face still hung in police stations throughout the city, and while music fans were continuing to mourn the death in August at his Graceland mansion of 42-year-old Elvis Presley, came further bad news.

Hilda McAulay, a divorced mother of two, was a regular at the Plaza Ballroom at Eglinton Toll in the centre of Glasgow. The 36 year old had been hoping her forays into the city dance halls might help her meet a new husband. On occasions, she had visited the Barrowland, where it is almost certain she would have known, by sight at least, Hannah Martin.

On the weekend night of 1 October, Hilda had been enjoying herself in the city but half an hour after midnight decided it was time to leave and headed home to Maryhill. Many of the thousand or so dancers had the same idea, and it was easy to lose touch with friends in the throng heading outside. So when her friends managed to make it through the door but could see no sign of her, they had no reason to think anything was amiss. Perhaps she'd been able to get a taxi right away, or someone had offered her a lift home.

Next morning, the body of a woman was found in bushes beside a caravan park in Langbank, Renfrewshire, 20 miles away and near a spot used by courting couples. She had been brutally attacked, undressed, strangled, tied up and her handbag stolen. It was a sickening sight, even to police officers and medical personnel accustomed to witnessing the results of violence. But this was different. The corpse had clearly, after a fierce struggle, been neatly arranged so that having been defiled the humiliation would continue after death. 'You'd think somebody had laid her out to take a mucky photograph of her,' one officer noted to colleagues.

As a result of her belongings having been stolen, there was nothing at the scene that could be used to identify her and so newspapers were asked to print a description. One of those who read it was Hilda's mother, Martha, who broke down, then called the police.

It is doubtful whether neighbouring police forces sympathised with their colleagues in Glasgow over the fact that either Bible John had resurfaced or they were facing the nightmare scenario of having another sex killer on the loose. The last thing senior detectives wanted was advice from counterparts elsewhere, however well meant. This was Glasgow's problem. But would it remain so?

Two weeks later, as detectives were still vainly trying to

persuade the majority of the male dancers at the Plaza to come forward and identify themselves, Helen Scott and her friend, Christine Eadie, both 17, went out for a Saturday night at the World's End public house on Edinburgh's historic Royal Mile. Some witnesses would later remember simply seeing the girls in the crowded bar, others thought they had spotted them talking with two older men. One or two believed they had even seen the teenagers leaving with a couple of men. No one could be sure, but what was certain was that neither made it home.

The following day, Christine's body was found 12 miles to the east of Edinburgh at Gosford Bay, Aberlady. Her clothes had been ripped from her, she had been battered and her panties stuffed into her mouth. She had then been tied up, raped and strangled. And her handbag was missing. It was an appalling discovery, but there was worse to come.

Six miles to the south of Aberlady, near Haddington, lay the body of Helen. This pretty youngster, not long out of school and hoping to become a children's nurse, had too been beaten, stripped naked below the waist and her panties stuffed into her mouth, then tied up, raped and strangled. Like her friend, her handbag had been stolen.

One death was a near carbon copy of the other, except that the knots used to tie up the ligatures around the girls' wrists and necks were different. There were obvious similarities with the murder of Hilda McAulay, but it would take a quarter of a century for anything to be done about that fact.

Now, it was the turn of detectives from Lothian and Borders Police to deal with terrible death. While they set to work trying to trace everyone who had been in the World's End pub, 50 miles away in Glasgow Thomas Ross Young was standing trial for the slaying of Frances Barker.

If there was little action on a possible connection with Hilda's death, the team investigating the World's End murders, as they would come to be known, quickly wondered if there was a link to Glasgow in the shape of Jessie Martin's friend Arthur Thompson.

Years earlier, the Godfather had invested in a holiday home at Seton Sands, close to the spot where Christine lay. If Arthur and his family, including his son, young 'Fatboy' Arthur – himself later to become a murder victim when he was shot dead outside the family house in Glasgow in 1991 – were not using the wooden chalet, friends with cause to keep their heads down and stay out of the limelight for a few days would frequently bunk down there, feeling safe because it was unlikely that the police in Edinburgh would know of them. But it was difficult for Arthur senior to stay out of the limelight. His trips to London and even to Ulster were well documented by Special Branch and a number of forces, and had even reached the files of MI5. While sudden death or murder might not be unknown to the Godfather, the killing of two innocent teenage girls was not for the likes of him. Young Arthur, on the other hand, might be a different proposition, as far as the thinking of some police officers went.

At 18, he had a reputation as a hell raiser and bully. He was a young man who liked to show off and who was into drugs, and it was reasonable to speculate that he and a crony might have picked up the girls in or near the pub and taken them in the direction of Seton Sands, but then decided not to accept 'No' for an answer and simply gone berserk when the girls refused to cooperate.

Two detectives made the journey from Edinburgh to meet with the Godfather and were surprised by the polite reception he gave them. But it was quickly evident he and his son had cast-iron alibis for that weekend. There was no way they could have been involved in the killings and Arthur even pledged that should he hear anything that might help the inquiry, he would ensure it was passed on.

'Nobody should be allowed to get away with doing that to those wee lassies,' Arthur told the officers. 'I'd string up the bastards who did it myself, if I caught them. What must their poor parents be going through?' They were sentiments from the heart. Arthur had two daughters of his own, one of whom would die young from natural causes brought on by drug abuse, her supplier literally having to flee for his life from her outraged father.

The World's End murders sent a chill through Scotland. Fathers insisted on accompanying their daughters everywhere, causing chaos with courting arrangements. But, like the Bible John saga, the police would realise early on that they were up against it. There were clues, but no one matched to them.

While officers continued their thankless task, seven weeks later on Friday, 2 December 1977, nurse Agnes Cooney set off for Glasgow from her aunt's home in Coatbridge, Lanarkshire. She worked in a children's home in Bellshill, the same town that was home to Hannah and Malcolm Martin. Twenty-three-year-old Agnes and a group of friends went out together most weekends, often ending with a party in someone's house. They were a happy bunch, able to smile and joke and even crack the occasional gag about the murders. 'Don't get picked up by Bible John!' they laughed.

On that occasion, they were looking forward to a night at the Cladda Social Club on Westmoreland Street, in the Govanhill area of Glasgow. These days, it is known as the Up 'n Down Club, but the fare is the same as it was that dreadful night: dancing and music, with a predominantly Irish flavour, and perhaps the chance to meet a young man. As midnight approached, Agnes left the club, evidently planning to hitch a lift back to her aunt's. It is possible she succeeded; only the driver did not stop when he reached Coatbridge.

The next day, Agnes had not made it home. She never would.

On the Sunday morning, a farmer discovered her fully clothed body at Caldercruix, five miles east of Coatbridge. She had been tied up before her killer had launched a frenzied knife attack. Pathologists announced after the post-mortem that they had found 26 knife wounds. There was no trace of her handbag.

The detection teams working in the various localities of the murders had little time or desire to celebrate the onset of a new year. They no doubt fervently made wishes that the killing spree was over; as 1978 went by, they might have begun quietly congratulating themselves that their wishes had been granted.

But with the finishing post – if not an arrest – in sight came news of another violent death. The victim was 17-year-old factory worker Mary Gallagher, who, like Helen Scott, had hopes of becoming a nurse. She had been taking a shortcut through side streets in Springburn, in Glasgow's east end, to meet friends when the killer struck, dragging her into a tenement close, where she was stripped, raped, strangled with her own trousers, then stabbed and abandoned on nearby wasteland. Scientists who microscopically examined the scene for clues they hoped might lead them to the murderer found tiny semen stains on her body. The traces were carefully stored away. Locals were quizzed and known sex offenders taken in and questioned, but Mary's killing joined a growing list of unsolved crimes.

Why was it, asked victims of house burglaries and minor violence, that police in Scotland seemed unable to catch petty villains, never mind mass murderers? Perhaps they ought to have sought guidance from officers in the United States, where David Berkowitz, the dreaded Son of Sam suburbs gunman, and Ted Bundy, who killed and gnawed on his victims' bones, were safely behind bars.

Yet while discontent among the public rumbled on, the list would grow. Anna Kenny's devoted family had never ceased in their search to find her or given up asking the police how their inquiries into her disappearance were progressing. Eighteen months after her final smile, as she cheerily waved goodbye to those she loved to enjoy a night of innocent fun, Anna's body was found. Two shepherds discovered human remains at Skipness on Kintyre and dental records confirmed they belonged to Anna. Her killer had taken her 100 miles away. Had he murdered her there, or somewhere else? The body was so badly decomposed it was impossible to tell, but pathology tests indicated she had been tortured, sexually assaulted and strangled. She had been tied up, too. And her handbag was missing.

Ten despicable deaths, then, to investigate in almost exactly ten years from Patricia Docker's killing in February 1968, through Jemima McDonald, Helen Puttock, Frances Barker, Hilda McAulay, Christine Eadie, Helen Scott, Agnes Cooney, Mary Gallagher and Anna Kenny. Only one investigation, into Frances's death, could be claimed as solved, but even that was being disputed as a miscarriage of justice. Hannah Martin had narrowly escaped making the total add up to eleven. She surely had links to the first three; she would also have a role to play in the remaining six.

FIFTEEN

CONTINENTAL POSES

When she was eight years old, little Isobel – we'll give her surname as Martin, in tribute to Hannah – would encounter the first signs of discord between the couple she knew as her mother and father. As is normal for all children, she and her siblings would raise their voices to one another from time to time in shows of temper, frustration or tired tantrums. So when they listened as their parents argued, sometimes hearing a swelling in the timbre of one or the other's voice, they were not unduly distressed. They were still loved and fed, still had their same friends; there were presents for birthdays and handkerchiefs to wipe away the occasional tear. They reasoned these matters did not affect them, so gave them little if any regard. In innocence, children take everything for granted, forever expecting life to continue on an even keel, uncomplicated by the emotions that disrupt the lives of adults, who make the decisions that lead to change, sometimes subtle, sometimes calamitous. Isobel would not have realised her parents were beginning to fall out of love, but as time bore on she knew their disagreements were getting more serious.

Isobel's parents were becoming unsettled. This was a time of much change in Scotland, where the dominance of labour-intensive industries was fast being forced to give way to the march of science. Men were being replaced by machines, with trade unions fighting against the flow and thus drowning.

In Isobel's home, it was her father who seemed more inclined to take a 'wait and see what the future brings' policy, while her mother believed they should bow to inevitable change and move on to pastures new. She had seen friends move away, sometimes great distances, and even though these new environments had not always brought success she believed the family should follow.

For whatever reason, Isobel clearly remembers being told one Sunday morning – when the man she knew of, and still refers to with love, as 'Dad' was away at his work – that things were not as she had always assumed: that she had been adopted.

'Adopted? What does that mean?'

'It means somebody else was your mother.'

'But you're my mother.'

'Yes, but you were born to somebody else who could not keep you.'

'Why?'

'I don't know. Maybe she had no money and thought she couldn't give you all the things she would have liked you to have.'

'Who was she?'

'I don't know.'

'Why not?'

'Because nobody told us.'

'Where is she now?'

'I don't know.'

'What does she look like?'

'Like you, I expect.'

'Why did she give me to you?'

'She didn't know we would be your mother and father. Nobody told her where you would go or with whom. All she was told was that you would go and live with a family who would love you and look after you.'

'Did she love me?'

'I'm sure she did.'

'Will I see her?'

'Maybe, when you're older.'

There were a hundred questions the little girl wanted to ask, but her mother probably felt she had already, by saying anything, said too much.

Isobel remembers her father coming home that day. 'He had been against us moving somewhere else because he knew, for instance, how much we enjoyed our schools and how close we were to our friends. Mother was very restless, while he thought it was too much of a gamble to go where she wanted to be.

'When he came home from work, she took him to one side and said she had told me I was adopted. He went off his nut, telling her she had no right and demanding to know why she had said it. She just said it was because she thought it was time for me to know, but his view was that it was too early, that it could have waited till I was older. But it didn't matter anyway because now it was out and nothing was going to change the fact. It had just come right out of the blue. At the time, I couldn't work out why my father was making such a big issue of it because, as far as I could see, they were still going to be my parents and nobody knew anything about the other woman.

'In any case, I didn't really understand what it was all about. It never really played a big part in my life. Things just went on, for a time anyway, as they had before. I was very happy and the subject wasn't raised again or talked about. It seemed to me it would never be an issue.'

But it would.

While the trauma of the truth visited and left the mind of Isobel, two others with links to that little corner of Glasgow life were discovering the cruelty of life's realities. In Stonehouse, John McInnes, the man who poked fun at suggestions he might be Bible John, was finding how little solace a crowded dance floor and a busy bar could bring to a man beset by loneliness. His wife and their two children were gone and his trips to the Barrowland were now few and far between. In the early '70s, he had been able to sense the gossip behind his back and had become paranoid, convinced each of his dancing partners was a police officer in drag. So his trips to the dance hall had gradually become fewer, leaving him morose and full of self-pity, his hand now more accustomed to holding a glass than the arm of a pretty partner.

Below the dance hall, on the floor of the Barras market, could be found the stall of Edward 'Wee Eddie' Cotogno, a man who, but for his appearance, might well have fitted the profile of the dance-land murderer. He had known Thomas Ross Young, by now languishing in jail with no hope of release. Wee Eddie had a variety of daytime jobs, including working as an optical technician and distillery security guard. But at weekends he would leave his Dumbarton home and head for Glasgow to set up his stall selling photographic equipment. It was a lucrative sideline, but his motive in being there was not only to make money; the equipment attracted amateur snappers, among them a fair proportion interested in photographing women in what some would politely describe as 'Continental poses', others hardcore pornography. These customers would be encouraged to persuade wives, girlfriends and even relatives to strip off at widower Cotogno's sordid studio, a dingy attic flat in Dumbarton.

Local businessmen paid handsomely to be photographed with the women, sometimes even in the act of having sex, and Cotogno could double his money by charging the amateurs to click merrily as couples sported on a grimy mattress. One of the 'models' most often asked for was a girlfriend of a married friend. Her speciality was to appear fully dressed and to gradually undress while a fur coat protected her modesty. But that too would eventually be draped over the back of a chair.

Sometimes the amateurs would hang about Cotogno's stall before heading off for a few drinks and then making for the Barrowland, where, with luck, they might score with a not-too-particular woman who would agree to meet up the following day to have a portrait taken.

One day in July 1979, Wee Eddie told a family member he had a meeting with an acquaintance. Hours afterwards a policeman on early morning beat duty spotted smoke coming from the flat. He managed to force his way in but would often wish he had not. Inside, lying on the mattress, now blood-soaked, lay Cotogno's bludgeoned body. On top and around it were scores of photographs of a naked woman. The detectives would quickly track her down, but finding the killer, or killers, proved beyond them.

The murder would enter the files as one more unsolved crime. Had Eddie been a lawyer or politician, then the degree of effort made to discover who had taken his life might have been more noteworthy, but he was just a sad old pervert with nothing much to lose. The photographs, samples of Eddie's hair and his clothes, including a sweat-soaked shirt, would be kept and stored away. His customers faced awkward knocks on their doors and difficult questions, but none had committed an offence and for a quarter of a century Eddie would be filed and forgotten.

SIXTEEN

THE GIRL WITH RED HAIR

Hannah was 28 when Isobel discovered she had been adopted. It was an age by which the majority of the friends with whom Hannah had grown up were married with families. Of course she too had a family, but one she could not talk of. Some of these friends were on their second spouse and now if they accompanied her on a girls' night out, instead of asking the permission of their parents, had to consult husbands or boyfriends and arrange babysitters.

By 1978, however, the dance craze of years earlier, when Glasgow could offer 11 ballrooms – more even than London – and 64 other dance halls, had slowed from a quick to a slow foxtrot and now almost to a stop. Where once the girls had twirled around the floor, now they sat at home, feet up, watching others do it on television, and the hall owners realised there was more money to be made by laying on rock concerts and covering the dance floor with seats rather than French polish. Bums rather than boots now brought in the money.

Occasionally, a big-band leader would drop by with his entourage, but the days when strangers locked eyes across a crowded room and fell in love were largely in the past. Hannah was still being asked out, though the memory of being cruelly jilted remained bitter. How, she would continually ask herself, could she be sure the nightmare of 1969 would not happen a second time? She knew the answer, of course, and it lay in her own hands: it was never to become so involved that she could not walk away in an instant. Love 'em and leave 'em, she told herself. Maybe that was a recipe for a relationship built on distrust, but she already carried one torch that would not go out and did not want to fall in love and be hurt again.

It was years after the birth of Isobel before Hannah began a serious relationship. It was one for which her friends more than her had high hopes of a permanent match; nevertheless, as with previous liaisons, she set out to get as much from it as she could, in every sense. The man who began regularly knocking on the door of the Martin household was a divorcee, who we'll call 'Arthur'. They would become lovers, as would most of her boyfriends, but also good friends, often the key to genuine happiness.

'Hannah never paid a lot of attention to what a man looked like, which was probably just as well,' said her old friend. 'Some of them would have struggled to get a rosette at Crufts dog show. If a man wanted to impress her, then he needed to show her a good time. Arthur got the message. They were forever out together – dinners, concerts, drinks – but she loved going to Shawfield, the greyhound racing stadium in the east end of Glasgow, because Arthur wanted to impress and in his book the way to do that was by showing off.

'So he would give her lavish amounts of money with which to bet. If her gamble won, great; if not, then there was more cash where the last lot came from. This, frankly, was the attraction to Hannah: the money and the places he could take her. It was as near to buying affection as you could get and Hannah went along with it. She used him: used him to get money; used him to buy her clothes, to take her places she wanted to go. Maybe some might have criticised her for it, but after what others had put her through she was entitled to ask herself, "What do I want?" and then go for it.

'She really liked this guy and let her hopes be built up, although she never loved him. But nothing happened and it just fizzled out. This time she might have been disappointed but she wasn't heartbroken.'

At the time this affair was in its opening sequences, another was coming to a tragic end. John McInnes had been brought up in a strictly religious Brethren family in which his mother Elizabeth had made it plain to him and her other children, Hector and Netta, that sex and drink were the tools of the Devil. That he liked to drink and dance, idle time away in bars playing pub games, gamble, visit the occasional brothel and steal was totally at odds with how he had been raised. Yet while he was no angel, he would never lose the love of his family, whose forgiveness did them credit. Like Hannah's mother, he had known the cutting grief of a baby's death: he and Ella, a nurse when they married in 1964, had a son and daughter, but they had lost another child at birth and the memory hurt.

As in any village, there are those who will believe anything for no other reason than that it gives them something to talk about; so it was with his claims to be top of the list of police suspects in the Bible John investigation. 'I am too clever for the police,' he told one local. 'They think I don't know, but they follow me everywhere, hiding around corners and constantly checking up on where I go. I've waltzed with more cops than the star turn at a policeman's ball. They used to hand out cards at the Barrowland to men they'd checked out and decided were in the clear which said, "I'm not Bible John", but they wouldn't give one to me.'

The truth was that had police a shred of evidence on which to take McInnes into custody, they would have done so. No senior officer would risk his job and pension by letting a triple-murder suspect run free in the hope of tripping himself up. So his tales made him a local personality but, as time went by and he was still free, people began doubting his claims to be a suspect and his reputation as a minor celebrity faded. With no wife, no status and no prospects, depression took over. There were stories around Stonehouse that he had tried to kill himself.

Maybe they had been just that, stories, but what happened in 1980 was no gossip's tale-telling. McInnes climbed into the attic of his mother's house, slashed his arm and bled to death. He was 41. He was interred in the village cemetery alongside another family member, with room left in the tomb for his mother to eventually join him there. Maybe, like Hannah Martin, Patricia Docker, Jemima McDonald and Helen Puttock, he had become a victim of Bible John.

John and Ella McInnes had divorced in 1972. Ten years later, as Scots servicemen put their lives on the line in the Falklands War, another marriage came to an end. Isobel's parents had to break the news to her that they were splitting up. One parent moved out of the family home and the other remained, with Isobel. Often adults are more traumatised by the ending of a marriage than children, putting too much emphasis on the effect of a divorce on youngsters. Certainly Isobel seemed to be relatively unaffected.

'I was very happy, even though a lot of things were going on around me that maybe the grown-ups thought would cause me upset. But the parent with whom I remained was as kind and loving as anyone could ask for. I was no different from any other schoolgirl, sometimes going out of my way to seek attention. But I don't recall ever feeling I was missing out or wanting for anything because my mother and father no longer lived together, and the fact that I had been adopted was never raised or considered relevant. Frankly, even after my mother and father split up, I still looked on them both as my parents and there was no reason to do otherwise. Some of my friends had come from broken homes so being adopted didn't make me a different person.'

The parting of the ways of Isobel's natural mother and Arthur created little interest and so, as Hannah entered her 30s, she had more or less abandoned hope of starting a second family.

Then she met a man who we will call 'Peter'. Despite her resolve, she would become heavily attracted to him, but he would take a course that would leave her in turmoil. Early on in their friendship, Peter confessed he had a wife but said the couple only stayed together for the sake of their children. His version of the set-up was that it was an open marriage, where each partner could go his/her own way, unafraid to start up relationships and not embarrassed to be discovered in compromising situations by acquaintances.

Her grandparents by now dead, Hannah would be free to go out with Peter most nights of the week and sometimes to a caravan in the vicinity of Dunoon, or even on holidays to east-coast resorts. Just as she had been determined to use Arthur for her own needs, so she began falling in love with Peter with the same intensity, although the depth of that love would never match the devotion she had felt, and always would, for Joseph.

'She and Peter had a great relationship,' said a good friend. 'She was like a kid again. They were in their 30s but would literally play together, having a very adult candlelit and romantic dinner and then walking hand in hand to some children's play park, where they would jump on swings or roundabouts, pushing one another, giggling and laughing as though they had not a care in the world.

'Hannah thoroughly enjoyed her times with Peter but some of those closest to her wondered about him. For as a married man, even one with the very open arrangement he said his wife allowed him, he appeared to have an incredible amount of freedom. Although he had said the marriage was held together only for the children, he never seemed to give them any time, whereas it would have been expected that he and his wife would have shared their care. No one wanted to say anything to Hannah because she was so fond of him, but some of us wondered if his talk of being bound by a wedding ring was an excuse to avoid having to explain to Hannah why they could never marry.

'She, on the other hand, evidently held nothing back and told Peter about Isobel. He clearly asked if she knew where the child was and when she said she did not but often wondered about her daughter, he took matters into his own hands and did a very stupid thing. He announced to her that he would find Isobel. Hannah pleaded with him not to do so, telling him no good could come of it even if he was successful and trying to get through to him that she had lived long enough without knowing the truth and had in time come to accept she never would. But he saw it differently.

'Maybe he was trying to help, maybe he was trying to show off, maybe he just wanted to learn the truth of the matter, but he came back one night and told her he had traced Isobel. Hannah could not make up her mind whether she wanted to know what he had learned but in the end asked to be told. Peter said he had traced her to Hairmyres Hospital in East Kilbride and that she lived in the town and had reddish hair.

'Hannah said later she let out a gasp when she was told about Isobel's hair. She believed the man who was the child's father was Bible John and the police descriptions of that man gave him as having light auburn-reddish hair. One of the witnesses who had seen Jemima with the man presumed to be her killer said he had short red hair.

'Now, the whole episode came back, making her go over and over again in her mind what had happened in that car. But she could never picture the face of the man who made her pregnant. Peter said he would carry on making enquiries until he found out where Isobel lived, but Hannah begged him to do nothing further. She thought too many ghosts had been dug up.

'But he had sown the seeds of curiosity. What mother could have simply left it at that? Hairmyres Hospital was only 12 miles from the house in Bellshill where she lived with her dad, a 20-minute car journey. She started making excuses to travel to East Kilbride and would hang about the hospital hoping to glimpse the girl with red hair Peter said was her daughter. It was a crazy thing to do, scanning every head that went into or came out of Hairmyres. Each time she saw red hair, she wondered if it could be Isobel. And, of course, she never saw her. When she asked Peter where his information had come from, he refused to tell her. Their relationship would never be the same after that.'

Maybe Peter had acted in good faith and without malice, hoping to impress Hannah by telling her he knew of her daughter without first checking out the information for himself and then approaching the girl to discover her feelings. It was stupid and cruel. Worse was allowing Hannah to go off to search in vain, knowing it could only end in heartache because long-lost Isobel did not live in East Kilbride, did not work at the hospital and did not have red hair. But his words would act as a strange and near tragic augury.

However, among those who knew Isobel there were those who would in the years to come notice a similarity, if slight, between her pretty face and that of the man painted by Lennox Paterson.

SEVENTEEN

SUGAR DADDY

After the disappointment of the fruitless search for Isobel, Hannah's affair with Peter began to lose its impetus. The spark that had once fuelled such happy times began to dim; that it would burn out altogether was inevitable. However, her sadness about the failed relationship was tempered by the fact that her father's health had begun to deteriorate.

By 1988, Malcolm was still only 62 – a comparatively young man in modern terms – but like so many other men in areas such as Lanarkshire, where he had spent his life, his health and chances of reaching old age had been destroyed by working in coal mining and steel making, industries where workers inhaled dust, filth and fumes for half of the day. She had given up her work at the Hoover plant to take care of him, and did so with love and diligence as his life drew to a close. Considering that he had deprived her of that which should have been a great comfort as the years passed, it was an extraordinary sacrifice on her part yet never once was she heard to complain. Others might have asked that he be taken into hospital, because the onset of cancer had left him with a dreadful neck injury that required daily dressing. Cripplingly short of money, she applied for a disability living allowance and was, as is customarily the case at the first try, rejected. Encouraged by friends to appeal the decision, she did.

In November 1988, Malcolm finally surrendered in hospital to lung cancer, the third most common cause of death in the UK after heart disease and pneumonia. On the day he died, Hannah walked up to his hospital bed to see the eyes she loved so much open with a startling brightness.

'Oh, Jessie, I knew you'd come,' he said. Hannah did not disillusion him or destroy his happiness. She had gone there to tell her father that she had received a letter informing her that the appeal for disability living allowance had been successful. But she decided the news could wait. Hours later, he died.

Like his wife and older daughter before him, his final journey was to the Daldowie crematorium. Now Hannah found herself alone and, as a result of giving up work, in dire financial straits. Something had to be done.

She began scouring the newspapers in an ever-more-frantic search for something that would provide an income. In the early days after the death of her father, she had made tentative enquiries about returning to Hoover, but in her heart of hearts she knew the prospects there were grim. From 1979, when the factory employed around 4,000 people, the ever-worsening economic recession, combined with increasing competition, had caused a series of lay-offs and pay-offs. By 1992, just 360 workers remained there to hear the news that the factory was to be shut down. There was little demand for a woman with few skills and her situation became ever more desperate.

Hannah and Malcolm had lived happily in a maisonette in Bellshill, which they had decorated and furnished assiduously, but perhaps because it held too many sad memories she decided to move out to Simpson Way in Bellshill. Admittedly, her new home had a front and a back door, but the house was in a poor state of repair and needed a considerable amount of work done to it. To make the move even more costly, none of the carpets, curtains and fittings were suitable, which added to the bills and meant her having to dip into meagre savings that would, in time, disappear altogether.

'Moving to another house had not been a good idea,' said her close friend. 'They had everything at Rockburn Crescent and the place in Simpson Way was frankly too much for her to take on by herself, especially without money. She had a hard job putting it all together and because there was never enough money, she never really ever got there and made it into the home she wanted. Hannah was only just managing to keep her head above water.'

It was then she spotted a tiny advertisement that would change the course of her life in so many ways. Kays, the mail order company, was looking for representatives in the area to find potential clients. The job involved knocking on doors in designated streets and persuading the householders to agree to have the catalogues sent twice a year.

It sounded interesting work and Hannah made a telephone call in response to the advertisement. Within weeks, she was on the payroll, with a basic wage of £88 a week. She needed to supply ten names per day of willing participants, and each customer above that number would qualify her for a bonus, as would the successful placing of the first order by the new customer. There was the added perk of a little car to get her around, which she could use for her own purposes. Hannah set herself a daily target of 15 signatures and in the early days found meeting that number relatively easy. She also discovered that there was an additional bonus from the work, one the manager at Kays had not mentioned and probably not considered. She got to meet men, lots of them.

At most of the houses on which she called where couples lived, even if the wife did not answer the door it would be the woman who decided whether to become a Kays customer. But where there was no woman involved, she put on a pleasant smile for the gentleman, who invariably would be living alone. If he invited her indoors, all the better. But she was sufficiently wary, remembering what had happened on those dark nights near the Barrowland Ballroom, not to allow her defences – or anything else – to drop too far.

'She was a very, very good saleswoman,' said the close friend. 'Hannah had a knack of knowing the right things to say, when to smile, when to sympathise, when to listen and when she was wasting her time. She railroaded an old school friend into helping her out and the friend said later she found it one of the most soul-destroying, miserable jobs anybody could possibly do. But in order to retain the car, she had to keep the job and that meant filling her quota of customers.

'She would be sent areas, streets and lists of people living there who weren't financially blacklisted. During the days and nights – usually the nights because that's when most people were at home – the pair of them would arrive at one end of a street, park the car and Hannah would tell her, "You do this side and I'll take the other." Sometimes her helper would protest, saying, "I'm not a flipping salesperson," but Hannah would just tell her, "Anybody can do it. Here's what to do. Knock on the door or ring the bell and when they answer it give them everything, all the patter, straight away. If you can't get their attention in the first ten seconds, you've lost the sale, so get right in there immediately."

'There were times when Hannah felt like a beggar, knocking on doors. She was good when her mood was up, but it was hard to persuade her to make a move and get door-knocking when her mood was down. From time to time, she would miss a day and then work double the next day, trying to sign up at least 30 customers. That was even more soul destroying. And if the weather was against you, if it was pelting with rain or snow, or if it was damp with clinging fog or howling with wind, people didn't want to open their doors, and when they did they wanted rid of you as soon as possible. But she must have liked doing it because she stuck with selling catalogues for more than ten years.'

In the early days, Hannah found the work relatively easy, talking her way to her quota with no difficulty. But being bright and successful would be her downfall. She was asked to move into areas of Glasgow where the streets were littered with abandoned furniture and broken glass. Doors were covered with graffiti and signs of repairs, few windows retained all their glass panes and dogs howled their annoyance at intruders. Selling there was tough, too tough at times, and pals convinced her she needed to change her job to one where her wages were not dependent on the whims of a housewife who was in a good mood if the children were behaving or her husband's horses or football team had been successful.

'You'll need to try to get something else,' they urged.

'I'm not going back to a factory,' said Hannah. 'I don't want to get in somewhere one day to find it closing down the next. I want something that gets me out and about with some freedom.'

The answer, it appeared, came in an advertisement that sought people who would call at pubs, clubs and hotels, emptying cash and tokens from fruit machines. She knew it was exactly what she had been looking for and was obviously disappointed when she was told the post had been taken. 'That was made for me,' she sighed. 'Something like it won't come along again.'

So she carried on with her catalogue selling. Now and again, she would encounter a quiet road that offered driveways, well-kept gardens, trim lawns and shining motors. It was as she went up and down one such street that a small, portly man opened his door, heard what she had to say and invited her inside. He became her customer that night, her lover soon after and her long-time sugar daddy. Hannah would come to use him as others

154

in the past had used her. She had only to flash her green eyes in his direction and he was hers for the taking.

'I can use my eyes to do anything, make anybody look at me, and he's so easily hooked,' she would tell friends. 'I can make my eyes sparkle at him and he thinks he's the most important person in the world.' Certainly, the effect she had on him initially was devastating and he begged Hannah to give up work and become his full-time mistress, living in a luxury flat he owned. She knew it would not work out in the long run; he, on the other hand, believed they were in a loving relationship, with genuine feelings for one another.

'She knew she was in it for what she could get from him and for a time it must have seemed ever so easy to her,' remembers a friend. 'She could telephone him and say, "I've got no cigarettes," or "I've seen such and such and it costs £200," and in the early days he would turn up and put that sum of money through her door.

'Hannah would stand in her bedroom, peering through the side of the curtains watching him as he drove up, walked to the door, knocked, got no answer and left. She didn't even bother acknowledging him. There would come a time when she became dependent, in order to pay her bills, on what he would give her. She certainly got a lot out of it at first. He thought they were having a relationship, but Hannah's view of it was different. He was there to help her out. It meant having sex from time to time, but she didn't enjoy it. She would say, "I can get him finished before I need to do anything." He could be so gullible.

'She took him for a lot over time and would actually get a laugh telling her friends how easily she could con him. He had bought her a beautiful leather coat and one night while they were at a Chinese restaurant together Hannah told him how she was so disappointed to find, after he had bought it, that there was a matching leather hat. When he asked how much it was, she told him it was £100 and so he handed that sum over to her. The hat, said Hannah, as she told the story, had actually been £50.

'She'd go through a Kays catalogue with him, pointing to items and asking, "Do you like that?" or "Isn't that lovely? I'd love that," which was a hint for him that he was just unable to refuse because he was so besotted by her.

'After a time, though, he began to cool and that's when she had to work for it. Instead of her promising to meet him somewhere and not turning up, as she had done, it was he who let her down. Hannah was anxious at the thought of all that money and all those presents disappearing. She would then spend days trying to get through to him on the telephone, he not taking her calls or responding to messages for him to get in contact. She would resort to going to the home of a pal and using their telephone so he wouldn't recognise the number, or even getting the pal to make the call for her, though that almost backfired because on one occasion, having taken a call from the friend, it was she whom he asked for a date. The friend, thinking of all the goodies he had heaped on Hannah, was tempted to take him up on it.'

Eventually, this lover would drift into oblivion. But, as Hannah was to discover, someone else was waiting and together they would decide the fate of many others; others who were at this time (around 1990) creating a venture that would mushroom into one that would have a major effect on thousands of Scots.

This woman, who had most probably come face to face with Bible John, who would unwittingly and unknowingly play a role in the horror of a host of unsolved murders, was on a door-knocking, catalogue-selling route that would lead her into the most successful drug-smuggling racket the country had ever known. As yet, Hannah had never heard of Gordon Ross or Billy McPhee, Trevor Lawson or Manny McDonnell, Tam McGraw or John Healy. But around the time she was slogging about the streets of Lanarkshire and Glasgow, a copy of the catalogue under her arm, dreaming of a lost daughter and better times, others were also buying and selling, only the returns were more lucrative and the risks higher than her sore feet and influenza.

In 1989, Gordon Ross and Charles 'Chick' Glackin, inspired by talk of get-rich-quick schemes in their native Glasgow, had pooled their savings, bought a third- or fourth-hand Volkswagen Golf and driven it to Dover, where they boarded a cross-Channel ferry to Calais. Disembarking and clutching a cheap map of Europe, they motored across France, through tiny Andorra and into Spain, where they headed for the coastal resort of Malaga on the Costa del Sol, so popular with package holidaymakers.

Malaga was a favourite target of Scots intent on sitting in the sun, putting themselves through the pain barrier for a quick tan to impress neighbours and workmates. It was also the centre of a thriving trade in Moroccan hash. In no time, Ross and Glackin had stowed away 40 kilos in the seats and were on their way home, literally sitting on £100,000. The enterprise ended at Dover when a Customs search uncovered the contraband and the pair were each jailed for three years.

Back out of prison, the two friends were undaunted by their earlier failure and in 1992 were back in Malaga, where they met up with a Mancunian known as 'Big Ted', who was one of the principal suppliers of hash along the coastal region. They were determined to try another run to Glasgow in an even-more-heavily packed car and set off, despite warnings by Big Ted of the dangers of trying to cross mountain passes in a clearly unsafe motor. Forced to turn back and admit defeat, they met with Big Ted again, who sympathised with them and then arranged to have their supplies smuggled into the UK by lorry. Realising the foolhardiness of persisting with the 3,000-mile round trips between Malaga and Glasgow, the smugglers sought help in their native city.

Others came into the enterprise, thinking up ways of making the racket more successful. It was decided that the cars would be used to shuttle between Malaga and Disneyland Paris, where they would be met initially by transit vans and later by buses into which the hash would be loaded then driven back to Scotland. By now the operation had really taken off, but changes would be necessary after two of the cars were stopped entering France packed with hashish.

Three male Scots caught – William Hassard, John Lyon and John Templeton – were each jailed for three and a half years, while a woman who had taken the place of a fourth was also arrested but escaped thanks to an audacious plot in which a passport belonging to a lookalike was smuggled to her. Even that setback did not deter the gradually growing gang, but as the venture became more lucrative, its very size brought with it new problems into which Hannah would find herself drawn.

Had Hannah but known it, her catalogue area had at one time been so close to the street where her daughter lived that the two women could easily have bumped into one another. No one can ever say whether that happened; however, what is certain is that the strange story Peter had told about her daughter and the hospital almost took on a tragic reality.

In 1993, Isobel was aged 23, and it was a miracle she survived to reach her 24th birthday. There had been boyfriends, flirtations, crushes and brief romances, but such was her happiness at home that she was content to remain in the embrace of her family. Love, however, and marriage, lay around the corner.

She had begun a new job, and while she enjoyed it hugely and was getting to know her new colleagues some noticed she appeared unwell. Isobel brushed away their worries, anxious that her new employer should not think she was a malingerer, even though she admitted to herself she felt ill, experiencing a tightness in her lungs and nausea. She carried on, but her breathing became increasingly difficult. Finally, she collapsed.

When she recovered, she told concerned colleagues she thought she had asthma and was sent home. In bed that night, she began sweating profusely and felt so weak she was unable to stand. The following day, she could only crawl around the house and it was evident that what had been imagined as a bad dose of influenza was something considerably worse. The family GP was called. The doctor took a blood sample and hurried off to have it tested. Forty minutes later, he returned with an ambulance, emergency checks having shown severe deficiencies.

Isobel was taken to Hairmyres Hospital, where, years earlier, Peter had told Hannah her daughter was to be found. She was given a blood transfusion, but after a series of tests doctors declared they were unable to find the cause of the problem. They told her she appeared to be on the mend and sent her home, where she promptly fainted and had to be returned to Hairmyres. She remained there for nine days, her condition gradually worsening, while just a few miles away the woman who had given her life struggled for survival in a different way, seducing a portly businessman and selling mail-order catalogues.

On her ninth day in hospital, laboratory tests revealed the nature of the mystery illness that had baffled the Hairmyres staff. Isobel had fallen victim to a rare disease, where antibodies produced naturally to attack germs become treacherous and instead turn on the kidneys and lungs. When she began coughing up blood, the doctors knew that kidney failure was inevitable. She was transferred immediately to the larger Monklands Hospital, with its specialised kidney unit, 15 miles away in Airdrie. Next morning, doctors carried out a blood-purification procedure called plasmapheresis, though an inevitable process had already begun and within weeks her kidneys had failed. This was a major catastrophe. One possible outcome of this was the need for a kidney transplant. Isobel was given dialysis, which does the filtering and cleaning work normally done by healthy kidneys, until her body showed signs of recovery, aided by oxygen, steroids and chemotherapy.

It was a long process and Isobel was to remain in hospital for many months, during which time she would have cause to ponder about her natural mother. The disease is frequently hereditary, and earlier in the treatment process doctors had needed to know the medical history of Isobel's family, including whether the disease had struck previously. It was also thought at an early stage that a transplant was inevitable and doctors had asked if a blood relative would be able to provide a match, were he or she willing to make the sacrifice. They said that if this was not possible, it might mean Isobel needing to spend an ever-increasing part of her life hooked up to a dialysis machine.

In reply to the nurses' questions about any history of kidney failure in her family came the reply, 'I don't know.' Staff were at first inclined to think their patient's lack of interest was caused by her condition, which left her tired and lethargic, but once she was able to gather her thoughts and reveal the truth, it left the medical team with a major headache should a transplant be required.

It also gave Isobel food for thought. 'For the first time in my life, being adopted became relevant and I began thinking and wondering about who my natural parents had been. I wondered what they looked like, where they lived, how they were and why they had given me away. It was at that point that I kind of thought about them and began to ask myself if they thought about me. But I'd grown up without them and once the doctors told me a transplant would not be needed, they faded to the back of my memory. I'd never known them and now there would be no need to find them.' But there would be. Later.

EIGHTEEN

DEL BOY

Her past had dealt Hannah Martin more than her fair quota of unhappiness, but she could still enjoy a joke. An amusing quip could come in very useful when trying to persuade an undecided customer whether to sign up for a catalogue, and often it proved the key to being invited inside instead of having the door closed in her face.

She had learned, as she tramped the bleak Glasgow streets, when to introduce humour and when it was time to be sympathetic, although there were occasions when she found it difficult not to break out in laughter at some of the hard-luck stories she was forced to hear. The case of the wedding dress was one such situation.

Calling one night early in 1994 on a house in Nitshill, a notoriously violent area to the south-west of the city, an attractive, brown-haired and buxom middle-aged woman answered the door wearing the uniform of one of the emergency services. After explaining why she was there, Hannah was invited to step inside, offered a comfortable seat and a coffee. It was quickly obvious that here was a sure customer, her host indicating that her working pattern often meant shopping had to be done at a rush, whereas having a catalogue would allow her to choose clothing in particular at leisure. Asked if she had children, the woman replied in the negative. 'I don't have a husband either, although I've been married three times,' she went on to tell her visitor.

'Perhaps fourth time lucky,' suggested Hannah, with a smile, looking up as she completed the agreement form for her newly found customer.

'Oh, no, I don't think so. Not with my luck.' It was a remark that begged explanation. There was no doubting she was in the mood to talk.

Recognising a fellow female whose relationships had brought pain and hurt, Hannah was content to hear her out. 'You've had bad luck with men? I know the feeling.'

'Not this feeling, I guarantee it.'

'Go on.'

'My first husband discovered religion after we'd been married four months. He went out boozing with his pals one night and announced when he came home he'd decided he wanted a career change. I asked what sort of new career and was told he wanted to see the world as a missionary. I thought it was the drink talking and that he'd have forgotten all about it when he woke up the next morning, but he hadn't.

'Next thing I knew, he said he was sorry, he'd made a mistake and was joining a religious order. He said he wouldn't stand in my way if I divorced him, so that's what I did on the grounds of unreasonable behaviour. While we'd been courting he could think of nothing but sex and having a good time, and he ended up a monk, preaching somewhere in South America.

'I waited six years before chancing marriage again, meeting somebody I thought was a really nice chap at a singles' club in Glasgow. He was a hospital porter and had a great sense of humour, and a roving eye. I didn't mind that because there was no indication it went further than that. Then one night, for a laugh, we went with some friends to a gay bar in the city centre and saw this character dressed up to the nines in an evening dress. He had on a wig, make-up, earrings, the works. It was obvious he was a man; I don't know what he'd stuck down the front, but they were enormous.

'My husband couldn't take his eyes off them. It was embarrassing. Next thing he had the transvestite, or transsexual, or whatever he was, sitting on his knee and they were snogging. My husband kissing another man! I couldn't believe it. Our friends thought it was hilarious.

'After we got home, all he could talk about was the gay bar and what a wonderful place it was and how we must go back. I told him, "It's disgusting and so are you," but his mind was made up. Every time we went out, we'd end up there, or at some bar where men were dancing with other men and women with women. He used to make some excuse to leave me on my own and I'd see him all over some character covered in stubble and mascara. I told my parents, and my dad – who was in his 60s, bless him – said he'd knock it out of him. But all that happened was that he walked out and I got a letter from his solicitor asking for a divorce. So it was good riddance.

'Somebody suggested I should go for counselling and I joined this group for people who'd had marital problems. We'd sit around talking about them and how they'd affected each of us. One of the guys seemed really sympathetic towards me. He told me his wife had gone off with one of his friends. Naturally, I was wary, but I thought he was a kindred spirit, a fellow sufferer.

'The inevitable happened. I fell for him, he moved in with me and we got hitched – just a quiet registry office ceremony, nothing flashy. One night we were having a sort out when I came across my dress from the first wedding. I was all for chucking it away but my husband said it was so pretty we should keep it. Well, things went along fine, or so I thought.

We went everywhere together, even when I did the shopping and bought clothes. I used to boast about him, and one evening after a friend and I had been out for dinner I told her I wanted her to come home to meet him. When we got in, it was late and he wasn't up, so I thought he must be asleep and was apologising when he flounced down the stairs, bold as brass, wearing a wedding dress. He even had my tights, make-up and jewellery on.

'My friend burst out laughing and I burst out crying. It was so humiliating. I asked him what the hell was going on and in front of my friend he asked if we thought he looked pretty. I was screaming at him to get out and trying to belt him with my bag, and anything else to hand; he was trying to fend me off and kept telling me not to damage his dress. My friend was rolling around on the floor, in tears through laughing.

'That night I wanted to kill the bastard. He got the message and cleared off, taking the dress. The worst for me was the shame. I realised he was just a pathetic fairy. Marry again? Not me, dear.'

Hannah left the house wondering if she had been dreaming. She had heard some crazy stories lately, most recently one on the news about an American called John Wayne Bobbitt. His wife, Lorena, had complained he was selfish because he refused to give her an orgasm, so one night, while he was asleep following a row, she used the kitchen knife to cut off the end of his penis. She drove off and threw it from her car window but police, called to her screaming husband, found it and surgeons stitched it back on. In the courts, Lorena was found not guilty of malicious wounding. Hannah wondered what might have happened to the man in the wedding dress had he been Lorena's husband.

She was still laughing inwardly at the story of the dress the next night when she arrived at Thornliebank in Glasgow to track down more business; however, her cheerfulness soon withered as it began to pour with rain. This was more than an early spring shower, she thought, as raindrops dripped down her neck and she found herself wading through puddles.

Arriving on Clova Street and knocking at the door of a corner house, she wondered if she was seeing things. The man who stood before her was the double of one of her television favourites, David Jason, Derek 'Del Boy' Trotter in the popular comedy series *Only Fools and Horses*. Short, dark-haired and pleasant, this homeowner was clearly impressed that someone should come calling in such weather and invited her in. And so it was that Hannah was introduced to Graeme Mason, unsurprisingly known to his pals as 'Del Boy'.

In light of subsequent events involving Hannah and Mason, it is impossible to reconcile their apparent views of one another; however, there is little dispute about that first meeting. Mason remembers his initial reaction: 'I was at home one evening, it was chucking it down with rain outside and I was doing the dishes, or something of that nature, when I heard a knock at the door. I wasn't expecting anyone and when I opened it, there stood this woman looking extremely bedraggled and soaking wet through.

'I asked her, "Are you selling something?" and when she said yes, she was from Kays catalogues, I said, "Well, I'm not going to buy anything, but if you want to come in and try persuading me otherwise, then in you come." I was into the selling game myself at that time, flogging curtains, I think, and so I suppose I had a certain degree of sympathy for her. She was a sort of sales soulmate, I suppose. In she came, and I told her to go and get dried in front of the fire, while I offered her a cup of tea or coffee. But she said she drank neither, only juice, so I got some for her. I even gave her a towel to dry her hair. She told me her name was Hannah and she came from Bellshill. We had a chat about selling and how she was doing. That was how it all began.'

Hannah would later recall her version of events. 'Graeme Mason was all chat and asked me in. In next to no time, he signed up for the catalogue. Because he was talkative and friendly, I asked him if he could get me some other names, and he said he would. He got me the details of his daughter, a friend of his by the name of John Balmer and someone else, so with that one call I'd almost made half of my quota for the night. It was a great start and we spent a bit of time gossiping and asking about one another.

'Then he asked, "Why don't you come back round here when you are finished?" So off I went, feeling good and thinking that when I got back to Bellshill I'd tell everybody I'd met Del Boy Trotter. When I'd done enough calls, I went back to his house and he asked if I'd like to go out for a drink with him. I said I didn't drink but would be happy to go with him to the pub. And off we went.'

The sellers of curtains and catalogues called in turn at a couple of local drinking houses, the Thornlie Arms and the Cuillins Bar. Both were owned by John Healy, regarded by friends as a hard-headed businessman and by enemies as simply a hard man, a gangster, someone who should not be crossed.

Brother-in-law to Thomas 'The Licensee' McGraw, Healy had a fearsome reputation. It would be said of him when, in the future, he disappeared from the area that lawlessness broke out within it and only ended with his reappearance. He knew Mason well and, as it would emerge, had recruited Del Boy for a business venture of which Hannah would become a part.

That night she and Healy – fit, muscled and, she guessed, in his late 30s – were introduced. They exchanged polite pleasantries and he seemed impressed when it was explained how she made a living. He recognised she and Mason had only just met and the publican left the pair on their own. Hannah thought Healy masculine and interesting and was instantly attracted to him but, much later, when asked, would deny the extent of what developed into a firm friendship.

As they talked, she showed a natural curiosity when Mason explained that he salvaged goods for a living. 'What do you mean by that?' she asked.

'Well, I buy up stock that's been salvaged or saved from something like a fire, or from a company that's gone bust and the stuff has been left to rot. I sort out the good from the bad. Selling on the good stuff at a real bargain price to some wholesaler, or even somebody running market stalls, is dead easy. It's astonishing how quickly you can dispose of damaged stock.'

'You do this from your home?'

'No, no, I have premises in Shawlands, not far from here.'

That evening, when they returned to Mason's home in order that Hannah could collect her car and drive back to Bellshill, he once more invited her in for coffee. As they chatted, for the umpteenth time that night she could not avoid a fascination with the physical similarity between Mason and the television character whose nickname he had been given. Even the patter of the pair had a quirky similarity.

Hannah, no stranger to a white lie in order to make a sale, recognised in him a fellow con artist. Each in turn boasted of the tiny tricks that were the difference between success and failure. Mason was enough of a realist to know that she had the advantage of her sex. 'I know I have good tits and sometimes I don't mind letting potential customers have a wee feel if it gets me a sale,' she told him.

When he heard this, he knew it was time to pounce, to learn whether there was a double meaning to her words. 'It's late, cold and wet outside and a long way to Bellshill. Why not stay the night?'

'On your couch?'

'No, in my bed.'

'You married?'

'Not any more.'

'OK,' said Hannah. And that night, within a few hours of setting eyes on one another, she and Del Boy became lovers.

'What about tonight?' Mason asked the next day, as she was dressing and preparing to set off back to Bellshill.

'What about tonight?'

'Well, are you coming back?'

'You want me to?'

'Of course, or I wouldn't have asked.'

'Then I will. I'll drive over and drop off some clothes. I need to sell today, so I'll try getting the quota during the day otherwise I'll need to make up the difference tonight.'

'I'll see if I can get you a few more names.'

'That would be brilliant. The sooner I have them, the quicker I can call it a day.'

A couple of weeks later, while checking her home in Bellshill was all right, Hannah called on a close friend and told her she had met someone during her rounds and moved in with him.

'Is this permanent, Hannah?' she asked, seeming surprised at the speed at which the relationship had taken off.

'I dunno. We'll see how things go.'

'What about your house? You'll need to have somewhere to go if it doesn't work out.'

'Well, I'll probably sublet. I told him I'd look you up and he's suggested we go out for a meal,' said Hannah.

'Great. Let me know when it's arranged and we can meet up. What's he like, what's his name?'

'Del Boy.'

'Del Boy? What do you mean, Hannah?'

'You'll see when we meet him.'

Her friend was not especially impressed either by the meal, at a pub restaurant, or by their host, who had invited a pal along to make up a foursome, perhaps hinting he might get lucky if he played his cards right. It would soon become apparent this would not to be the case. Later on, Hannah drove her friend home in the little Corsa car that came with the Kays job.

'Well, what do you think?' asked Hannah.

'What the hell are you doing with him?' came the reply.

'I don't go for looks,' Hannah told her.

'Well, that's obvious.'

'But he's got lots of money and he's getting somewhere.'

'What do you mean by that?'

'Oh, he has a salvage business and he's working on something very big that's going to make him very rich.'

'Well, what is it?'

'I can't say, he's sworn me to secrecy.'

'OK, have it your way. All I can say is I hope you're right and you don't end up getting hurt because I'm afraid I don't trust him.'

Hannah said nothing. She had been embarrassed by Mason, who had dominated the conversation during the meal, belittling her contributions; yet while she knew she did not love him, and never could, she enjoyed their kisses and cuddles, and being with him. She had reached an age and situation where it was virtually a case of 'any port in a storm', even if the quayside rails looked to be pitted with rust and unreliable.

Hannah would end up retaining her home and renting it to someone she knew, an arrangement that did not ultimately work out satisfactorily, leaving her with debts to settle. According to Mason, after she was comfortable in his bed and his home, she had raised with him the issue of her house in Bellshill. 'She was afraid that by leaving it empty and unoccupied it would become derelict. Once we became lovers, she suggested "I'll sell my house and move in with you," but I told her absolutely no way. "Keep your own place going," I said, "and it means you will always have a place to go." There was no way I wanted her relying on me to supply her with a roof over her head. That would have been like a millstone around my neck.' In fact, the house would later become useful in a way Hannah could never have envisaged.

The house was one of the subjects they discussed as they lay in Mason's bed, but it was talk of his involvement in 'something very big' that caused her to hang on his every word. From as far back as she could remember, she had been fascinated by gangsters and the secretive, violent world in which they operated. Hannah would not see herself as a criminal, but she had an admiration for those who dreamed up grandiose and at times brilliant schemes for making money and took huge risks to put them into operation.

This also explains the continuation of what was otherwise seen by those who knew Hannah as a most unlikely involvement with Mason. He had told her that very first night in his bed about a plot that was growing from small beginnings into a massive money-making crime, one guaranteed to make millionaires of all those connected to it. It involved, he said, buying hashish in Spain that was produced from cannabis plants in the Rif Mountains of Morocco, shipped across to the south of Spain late at night in motor boats and then hidden in warehouses until it was sold. A Glasgow gang had arranged to buy huge quantities and smuggle it back to Scotland.

'How is that done?' she had asked.

'Oh, in cars and things like that.'

'Isn't it risky?'

'No, I've made sure all the angles are covered. If anybody does get caught, then they are looked after.'

'You've made sure?'

'Yes, I've organised all of this.'

'You're the, sort of, brains behind it all?'

'Yes, that's right. It's my idea, I worked it out. I run it and I tell the rest of them what to do. Everything is sorted, believe me. It will get bigger and bigger. But I don't want you talking to anyone about what I've told you. It's top secret. I don't want word getting out to the police.'

'But you've told me.'

'Yes, but I know I can trust you.'

As the days and nights passed by, there would be more pillow talk about his hash smuggling. He entranced her with tales of making so much money that it was necessary to launder some in order to ease suspicion.

'Launder money? What's that?'

'You take money you've made from a crime, put it into some legal enterprise and then what is produced is clean and legitimate and nobody asks awkward questions as to where it came from.'

'And you do that, too?'

'I do everything.'

Mason knew he ought not to be talking about the drug conspiracy. But the fact was that, having started, he became so impressed by his own bravado he was unable to stop himself.

It was in the bedroom that another secret emerged. Each would later have their own version of how they performed sexually. Mason's view of Hannah was, 'OK, I suppose, she did what I asked. There was nothing especially unusual or quirky about our sex. She wasn't especially enthusiastic but definitely enjoyed what we did.'

One night as they prepared for this enjoyment, Mason lay back his head on the pillow, watching Hannah by the light of a bedside lamp as she undressed, slowly staring at her gently swaying breasts and her belly. When she climbed into bed beside him, huddling under the sheets, he said to her, 'You've had a baby.'

She sat up suddenly and, even in the dimness, he could see

a look of total astonishment on her face, even the beginning of tears. 'How do you know that?' she whispered.

'Look, you have stretch marks on your abdomen. I've been married before and have had a family, so it's not hard to work out the reason for the marks. Don't worry, it's not a big issue. This is something in the past and if you don't want to talk about it, then so be it.'

After a pause, she replied, 'Yes, I had a baby girl a lot of years ago.'

'So, where is she now?'

'I don't know where she is. There were reasons why she had to be adopted after she was born.'

'What do you know about her?'

'Nothing, nothing at all. In fact, it's been a big disappointment to me that she's never bothered to try finding out who her mother is, to look me up and come to see me.'

Mason felt this was a bizarre comment. As it seemed to him, here was a woman in her 40s admitting she'd never bothered trying to find out about her daughter but complaining it was the fault of the daughter for not trying to trace her.

'Who's the father then?' he asked.

'I don't know.'

'Well, how did you get pregnant?'

'Look, it's best you don't know because it's not something I've ever talked about except to somebody who is a very close friend. I have suspicions about who the father might be but, believe you me, you don't want to be told. I think we should drop the subject.' It would never be raised between them again.

While Hannah's relationship was only just beginning, Isobel had recovered from the nightmare of coming close to death and returned home. It had been a terrifying experience. When she was well on the road to recovery in hospital, doctors had explained the potentially disastrous nature of the rare illness. Now she wanted only to get on with her life and would soon meet a young man with whom she would fall deeply in love. It was purely coincidental, but the mother and daughter who had never set eyes on one another had each at around the same time found a man with whom they felt their respective futures lay.

NINETEEN

LAUNDERING

Each night, Hannah listened to Mason's boasts about the exploits of the smugglers and how they accepted his orders; however, only a part of the story was true. While he was heavily involved, he was by no means the leader and, in reality, his function was not unlike that of Hannah's in her younger years when she had complained of being a gopher.

Others would agree that this was Mason's role: a gopher, used by the others. The plot needed a smooth talker and he was recognised as having that talent while not being the type to relish taking risks. He had been recruited by John Healy, who had reservations about his reliability but reckoned, so long as he was kept from the front line, he could be relied upon to do what was asked; he was a player but would never wear the skipper's armband.

A month before that wet night when he and Hannah had met, Mason had gone to an auction in Glasgow and bought for £12,000 a Mercedes minibus once owned by a now-defunct travel company. He paid in cash and used the name 'Balmer'. Alterations made to the vehicle cost another £8,000 and once again Mr Balmer paid for the work in cash. Soon after, the bus made its initial run and when it returned to Glasgow from Disneyland in Paris it brought back not just a party of youngsters but also a fortune in hashish.

In June, Mason, once more under the guise of Mr Balmer, was again the front man when he travelled to Carlisle to pay £52,000 for a larger coach. It was Balmer yet again to whom an invoice for modifications costing £20,000 was made out. Of the buses or of Balmer, Hannah knew nothing.

She settled into her comfortable if not ecstatic relationship with Mason, but she could not help feeling embarrassed at the way he would put her down in the presence of others. Also, his bragging about being a business big shot and hard man about town made her cringe – so much so, she was ashamed to invite friends into their company.

They would often visit one of Healy's pubs and would frequently chat with him. He made his admiration for Hannah obvious, asking how her catalogue sales were coming along and encouraging her when things were not going well. 'I don't know how you can go out there in all weathers and be nice to people who are rude,' he told her. 'I'm not scared of hard work, but I prefer having the sun on my back when I do it. You should take this lady on holiday, Del Boy. She deserves one.'

It was more than just a casual pleasantry, although she did not realise it. Nor at that time did Mason, and neither thought much more about it.

But Hannah thought of Healy constantly, even though she realised he was ten years her junior, married with children and, as she would tell a friend, 'way above my league'. Mason's work in buying the coaches and paying for them to be altered to fit the requirements of the smugglers brought him into frequent contact with Healy and sometimes, even when Hannah had gone along with him to the Thornlie Arms or elsewhere, he would make an excuse and the two men would be seen chatting quietly in a corner, ensuring no one else could listen to the content of their conversation. It was often clear from the way they spoke when they returned to her that the subject of Mason and her going on holiday had been raised again, this time with serious intent in mind.

At the Spanish end of the operation, the hash had to be paid for and that meant getting money out there, which was not as easy as it sounded. Single men heading overseas were regularly stopped at Customs, and checked and searched. In 1994, Healy himself would be found to be in possession of £170,000 and his claims that it was to buy a pub in Alicante failed to prevent it being confiscated.

The answer was for those unlikely to attract suspicion or attention to act as couriers and who was more likely to fall into this category than families flying off abroad on package holidays. Each year the resorts of the Costa del Sol saw Scots arriving in their tens of thousands. Why should some not be well rewarded for carrying an additional package that would be collected from them as soon as they reached their hotels?

And so, as the summer began drawing to a close, Mason suggested he and Hannah had earned a break. 'How about going to Spain for a wee holiday?'

'Where in Spain?'

'Somewhere on the Costa del Sol, Malaga perhaps. I'm told it's really pleasant, lots of nightlife. We'll get a good hotel.'

'I'd love to, Graeme, but I don't know if I can afford it.'

'Don't worry, it's on me, or at least my sideline. Look on it as a working holiday.'

'What do you mean by that?'

'Well, if we take something over with us, we'll get the holiday for free and a few quid for spending money.'

'Take what?'

'Just some money.'

'What sort of money?'

'Money that's to be laundered, like I told you.'

'How much are we taking?'

'About £150,000.'

It was more than she'd ever imagined. When she expressed worries about being caught, he assured her that all she needed to do was to claim she was simply going on a spending spree and might even use it as the deposit on a property in Spain.

Shortly after midnight a week later, in mid-August, as they were about to go to bed knowing that in the morning they would be making for Glasgow Airport, there was a knock at the door. When it was opened, two men stood there, one of them John Healy. He handed over a bundle, wished them a happy holiday and left.

Mason had warned Hannah about the delivery. They had been waiting for it and their suitcases were still open. Inside the bundle was £150,000 in cash.

'Just hide it in the bottom of our suitcase, nobody is going to find it,' he told her and began stuffing money into pyjamas, shorts and a toilet bag. She watched in astonishment.

'Call yourself the brains of this outfit,' she mocked. 'Nobody in their right mind would stash money in that way!' She carefully began to repack his bag, placing the notes in rows inside clothing so neatly folded that unless it was lifted up and shaken vigorously it would not reveal its contents. In her own case, she even packed her brassieres with wads of money. 'Even if they have a really good rummage, they'll find nothing,' she told him when she had completed the task. 'Now, let's get to bed.'

The following morning, all went smoothly. Arriving in Malaga, they were waved through Customs checks, but Hannah noticed that both at the Glasgow check-in and when the time came to collect their luggage in Spain, her travelling companion was sweating profusely. 'I hope he doesn't lose his bottle,' she thought to herself. 'He'll land us all in trouble.'

At the Hotel Alle in nearby Benalmádena they checked into

their room, locked the door, opened the shutters to allow in the morning sunshine and began removing and checking the money. When they were certain all £150,000 was there, it was placed in a plastic carrier bag and hidden under their suitcases in a wardrobe. Mason made a telephone call, simply telling the person at the other end of the line the name of the hotel and their room number.

'Come on, let's go out and catch the sun,' Hannah said.

'I can't, I have to wait for the guy who's coming to get the money.'

'Was that him you spoke to?'

'A friend of his.'

'Why didn't you say we were going out and find out what time he'd be here?'

'Look, I'm not leaving it in the room. I'm sticking here till he turns up.'

'When will that be?'

'Hopefully sometime tonight.'

'And you're going to wait until then?'

'Yes. Nip down to the bar and get me a few drinks.'

'There's no way I'm going to spend the holiday cooped up in here. I'll get you the drinks, then I'm going out for a look around.'

'OK, I'll see you back here for dinner.'

So off she went for a stroll along the seafront, thrilled not just at being there but still tingling with excitement from what she had done. She realised she had calmly walked through Customs checks, almost certainly risking a long stretch in jail, and had not batted an eyelid. 'You never rattled a tosh, but he did,' she told herself, admitting that being part of a gang of smugglers was giving her a real buzz. But then this was the same woman who, years earlier, had been attacked by a man she believed was a killer and yet went back for more.

That first day Hannah felt like a schoolgirl, excitedly wandering about shops and market stalls, stopping eventually for a cool drink in a bar just off one of the main roads leading to the beach. It was nearly deserted, most of the holidaymakers either in the sea or under beach umbrellas. She was content to sit alone until a voice in a familiar accent asked if she had just arrived.

The man seated at the next table was tall, with hair that appeared to have been turned near white by weeks in the sun, and she reckoned him to be in his mid-50s, although he had obviously looked after himself well. No beer gut hung over his trousers; there was no puffiness about his face. He wore light-coloured slacks, sandals and a white shirt open at the neck.

'Yes, does it show?' Hannah asked. 'You surely haven't just come today.'

'No, I live here, at least most of the time. When the season ends, I go home for a break.'

'And where is home?'

'Glasgow.'

He told her he had run a pub in Shettleston in the east end of Glasgow, but a decade earlier had sold up and bought a bar in Malaga, hitching a ride on the package holiday boom, and as a result now owned a second. The man, who we shall call 'James', asked Hannah about herself and was surprised that her travelling companion had opted to remain indoors, although she had not revealed the reason why.

He pointed out the best shopping areas, the best eating places and who to go to if she wanted a prime spot on the beach, even when it was crowded. Eventually, she told him it was time to return to her hotel and he offered to walk with her in case she had lost her bearings. 'If you're on your own, just call back at the bar and ask for me,' James said. 'They'll call me. I'm the owner.'

She sensed he was interested in her and began to regret that

Mason had made the trip with her. Back at the hotel, the collector had still not arrived, so she wandered off once more, tempted to return to see James but deciding against doing so.

That evening, as they were dressing for dinner, there was a light knock on the door. Mason brought two men, neither of whom Hannah recognised, into a short hallway leading into the bedroom; Mason went to the wardrobe, handed over the carrier bag and was given an envelope in exchange. Hardly a word was spoken before the visitors left.

'Let's have a drink,' said Mason. At the bar, she asked what the envelope contained. 'It's the money I forked out for the holiday,' he told her. 'There's a bit extra. Let me know if you're short.'

According to others in the smugglers' gang, the envelope and subsequent envelopes contained £2,000 in cash. It was to repay what had been laid out for the holiday, with the remainder split between them. Mason maintains he gave her money, but her friends say Hannah told them a different version of events.

'She was ripped off by him,' said one. 'He probably used his very sharpest sales patter to trick her out of what was rightfully hers. She had to use her money when they went for drinks or meals. Once when they went to a factory producing china ornaments – she paid for the coach journey there out of her own pocket – she spotted this magnificent coach with footmen and horses and absolutely fell in love with it. It was the sort of thing she could never have afforded in Scotland, but in Spain it was much cheaper and she set her heart on having it. Since she paid for the trip to the factory, she did not have enough for the ornament and asked Mason to help, but he turned her down. She'd have adored bringing it home and giving it as a gift to someone and told me she was so disappointed.' During that first holiday Hannah did not bother to press the point over money.

The next morning, when she assumed Mason would be joining her on a walking tour of the town, she was surprised to hear him announcing he would be remaining at the hotel. 'There's no need,' she protested. 'They've collected the money. Come out and enjoy yourself.'

'That's what I intend doing by lazing around and having a few drinks,' he told her.

So off she set again, searching for bargains and keepsakes and inevitably ending up in the same bar that she had stopped at the previous day. She did not ask for James, but hardly a quarter of an hour had gone by before he was there, placing another drink at her table and sitting next to her. She found him easy-going and could find no hidden agenda in his conversation. When he invited her to lunch she declined, excusing herself by saying she had arranged to meet up with her companion. But the next day, when the pattern was repeated, she agreed; he took her arm gently as they strolled inland to a restaurant tucked away in the backstreets, with wooden tables and seats and filled with locals.

As they talked, she almost forgot about Mason. When they had eaten, she asked James to set her on the road back to the hotel, where she found her partner happily seated in the shade, a glass in his hand.

'Been shopping?' he asked.

'I don't have any money,' was the reply.

'Remind me to give you some when we're in the room,' he told her. But she thought to ask would be to waste her breath.

The next day, the pattern was repeated again, but it was nearer to dinnertime when she arrived back. 'Where've you been? I thought you'd got lost,' Mason told her, as she opened the door of their bedroom.

'Oh, I did. I went window shopping and lost track of time.'

In fact she had once again shared lunch with James, and when it was over he drove her inland, expertly manoeuvring his little car around tight winding corners to a roadside fruit shop that doubled as a bar, where they had a soft drink. On the journey back, he stopped and they kissed before he drove to the three-storey apartment block that he called home far from the beachfront. Inside the shutters were closed and the floor cool and smooth.

She sat on a settee while he made them coffee, then they each removed their clothes, lay on the floor and made love. If he noticed the signs of childbirth on her body, he said nothing. Afterwards, she showered and he drove her to within a hundred yards of the Hotel Alle. He begged her to meet him the following day.

That night after dinner, as she and Mason watched the never-ending procession of holidaymakers meandering along the seafront, she thought about James and wondered why life had been so cruel to her. It could have been her and James, Isobel and grandchildren strolling past, she mused.

They met each day for the remainder of the week but only once did they return to his apartment, as he had to help run one of his bars due to a staff illness. At their final meeting, he pressed into her hand a slip of paper with a telephone number written on it. 'I want you to call me when you come back,' he urged, but she wondered whether her heart could handle so much anticipation and sorrow at parting. There would be more visits to the Malaga area but not to the little bar off the main drag, or the apartment with the cool, smooth floor.

John Healy was clearly impressed when she and Mason called on their return to report that all had gone well. As soon as they were back at Thornliebank, she set about making up for the days she had lost, selling her catalogues with a gusto that surprised even her best friends. But then Hannah needed the car supplied by Kays and could not afford to lose it, even though she sometimes struggled to find money to put petrol in the tank.

Despite her lack of funds, she was a smart dresser, always looking businesslike and efficient, traits that Healy liked. One night, he asked her if they could have a word in private: he had a proposition for her. Among his assets was a grocery store to which was attached an off-licence. In order to sell drink, he needed a licence holder, someone whom a court and the licensing authorities would look on as being of good character. He wondered if she would be willing to go to court and apply on his behalf, adding that he would happily pay her to do so. Hannah agreed but insisted the reward was paid directly to her, although friends believed it was inadvertently given to Mason with a request for it to be handed on. By the time he did so, a 'commission' had been deducted.

There were more trips to Spain; in all, Hannah would make seven with Mason, carrying between them a total of around £1,050,000. Each time their cover – that it was a family holiday – had to be preserved. She realised through listening to conversations involving Mason, Healy and the collectors that others were doing similar work, but she had little concept of the sums involved overall. In fact, up to four couples were needed to carry sufficient cash to buy hash to fill the bus on each of its runs.

She more and more looked forward to the holidays, usually being given only a week's notice, sometimes even less; on occasions they would arrive at Malaga Airport not knowing which hotel the tour company would take them to. Hannah had no qualms about carrying money: emerging through the arrivals door into the Spanish sunshine clutching a fortune gave her a thrill of near orgasmic sensation. Although once she did stop to think how close they could be to disaster.

They had been on a bus journey around Fuengirola when a man snatched her bag. Hannah leapt off the bus and ran after him screaming, 'He's got my bag!' There were other people around who grabbed him and retrieved it, but the thief ran away. Hannah was asked if she wanted the police called, but she said no. As she got back in the bus, she realised how calamitous that incident might have been. If it had happened as they were arriving from the airport and the bag held the money, how would she have explained that to the people back in Glasgow, or to the Spanish police?

Mason, who had a long-standing heart problem, was not as confident as Hannah. 'Sometimes the sweat lashed out of him,' she confided later to a friend. 'When we got there, he was in such a state he took to the bedroom and refused to come out until the money had been picked up, and that might not be done for two or three days. He was a nervous wreck, terrified in case something went wrong. I had to run up and down, getting his breakfast and taking drinks to him. Then I'd leave him on his own and go touring around the shops. Sometimes I'd have a quiet chuckle at the thought that there he was alone in the room, probably dehydrating and hungry, while I was out and about in the sunshine.

'On one of the trips, we arrived at the hotel in the early evening and for once I took a drink. It knocked me out until the next morning, but when I woke up he was still lying on the bed, out for the count. He was snoring when I closed the door and went off for the day.'

Some among the smugglers were concerned that Mason might crack under the pressure of carrying so much cash and they didn't really trust Hannah either, realising his verbosity would almost certainly have led him to reveal to her more details of the operation than she needed to be told. The organisers intended the plot to be run on a 'need to know' basis and there was no requirement for either of them to have all the details at their fingertips. One of the collectors was especially concerned. An Irishman, brought in from the Ulster troubles because of his ability to instil discipline and, if necessary, fear, was wary. He had been appalled to hear that money sometimes lay for days in hotel bedrooms before being picked up. In 1996, he was instructed to visit the couple at the Sunset Beach Club Hotel in Benalmádena and deliberately reached his destination early. He had been told that in order to add to the guise of it being a family trip, they had brought with them a young relative of Mason's who was still at primary school. The Irishman hung about reception and heard the number of the room they were allocated. This is his account of what followed.

'They had got into their room just seconds before I knocked on the door, although they had been warned I'd be turning up to collect the cash. We almost arrived simultaneously because they hadn't even had time to turn on the bedroom light. The blinds were drawn to keep out the heat and make sure the room was cool.

'Graeme said, "Are you the man for the collection?" and I could see the outline of a woman standing behind him. I realised that she was Hannah Martin, although I'd never met her or she me. She came forward and said, "I'll turn on the lights," but I told her not to.

'"It's OK," I said, "I'm only here for the bag, no need to switch them on."

'At that point, she beckoned a third person to come forward – I hadn't noticed there was anyone else in the room – and a boy stepped into the dim light. He had a bag on his back and Hannah helped him take it off. The boy had carried it all the way from Glasgow, taken it into the plane as hand luggage. It had been lying in the luggage locker with something like £150,000 in cash in it.

'Hannah handed the bag to me and asked, "Do you want to count it?" The money, I knew, would be in sterling, in £10 and £20 notes, and counting it would take some time. I didn't want to do it at the hotel, so I said, "No need, I know it will all be there. I'll take the bag, but don't switch on the lights." I didn't really want them to be able to recognise me and I them, so if something went wrong we could honestly say we'd never seen one another. It was so dark inside the room I didn't even see Hannah's face, I just heard her voice and saw her outline. She seemed to be the one in charge, the one making the decisions.

'I met them once more, again in 1996, when they arrived in Benalmádena with another load of cash. I had a couple of other collections to make before reaching their hotel and by the time I did so they could only have been there an hour. I got reception to connect me to their room and Hannah answered. When I got to the door, she came and again I told her not to turn on the lights. I could see past her, Graeme lying flat out on the bed. "He's drunk," she said. "He gets in a helluva funk each time we do this. I don't know what the fuss is all about." I had the feeling she despised him for his weakness.

'I wasn't happy with the involvement of either of them, for different reasons. One pretended to be sharp but wasn't sharp enough, while the other gave out the impression of taking nothing in but missed nothing.'

Graeme Mason, though, remembers the courier arrangements differently. 'We went abroad with money seven times. It wasn't my idea that Hannah should go as a courier, that suggestion came from somebody else. I was totally against her coming with me, but the man who gave the orders said she would have to go, and go she did. She had her holiday paid for and I gave her spending money, but we had very different ideas about how to spend the time once we were abroad.

'To me, a holiday is a holiday. I like to relax and enjoy the sunshine. She wanted nothing more than to trek around markets and shops from morning to night. She knew how to spend money as well and was continually asking for more. We'd say goodbye in the morning outside the hotel and then meet up at night for dinner, each of us doing our own thing.

'I told her nothing about the real reason why we were making these trips to Spain. But she missed nothing.'

TWENTY

THE SAFE HOUSE

Isobel's recovery from serious illness was spurred when she met a young man who confronted her with the realisation that having stared at death she was now facing a new variety of life. She had known the love of a family, but her feelings for this newcomer produced an emotion she had neither experienced nor imagined could exist for her. It was a sensation she had read about in books and had watched being created on the cinema screen, where it was customarily accompanied by armies of violins, choirs of angels and gentle breezes. Now, she had discovered a love that drove her into a private cocoon outside of which no other existed.

The couple's belief that one had been created solely to bring joy to the other was, she was convinced, wholly mutual. Each meeting was as if it was the first, each parting the beginning of despair until the hurt of separation should end. She did not ask for time to think it over when he proposed marriage because her thinking had been done long before and she knew the answer. The ceremony itself was, as far as she was concerned, the start not just of the rest of her life but of life itself, and when it was over she settled down to share love's fruits with a man to whom she happily devoted her every waking second.

Just a few miles away, Hannah too was settling into a mould she could not have dreamed of in the recent past. Suddenly, she was involved in some major, even massive, crime. She knew it was against the law to carry such sums of cash abroad and realised the magnitude of what she was doing by the very scale of the amounts. From time to time, Mason, for all his boasting, could become furtive and secretive. Hannah was curious by nature; quietly, she told herself to take note, listen and remember.

While Isobel was cementing her marriage, Hannah accepted, with regret, that her future lay not with James and the unknown in Malaga but as the mistress of Del Boy. In time she might become more than that, but for the present she decided to plough the weary furrow that had led her this far.

In John Healy she found a welcome ally. He had liked her from the start, not least because she showed her true colours and genuine links to the east end of Glasgow by pronouncing the heart of that area as 'Brigton', sidestepping the customary tendency of non-locals to use 'Bridgeton', as the spelling suggested. He had also been impressed by stories reaching him from others involved in the smuggling intrigue as to how calm and composed she was when gliding through Customs checks in Glasgow and Malaga, while her companion Mason was frequently seen in a profound sweat. Healy made a point of being polite and pleasant to her whenever they met. He found her never-ending slog about the streets selling catalogues both amusing and commendable, knowing how tough and unrewarding it could be. He was irritated a little by the lack of encouragement shown by her lover.

One night, she confided in him the details of a money-making idea she had. 'I came across it when I was browsing around the stalls at the market in Benalmádena,' she said. 'You fill a little wicker basket with a variety of things that might include chocolates, a miniature bottle of wine and a glass, perfume maybe, or even an ornament and a little toy, a teddy bear perhaps. The punters love things like that. They make great presents, the sort you can give at any time of the year. I watched them at Benalmádena go like hot cakes and it was the tourists, especially the Scots, who snapped them up.'

'That sounds great, you should go for it,' he told her. 'What's Graeme say about it?'

'I haven't told him yet,' she admitted.

When she did, he was sceptical, even dismissive. 'You'll never make anything out of that,' he said. 'How much are you going to charge? Where will you get the stuff and how are you going to sell them? Take it from me, and I know from the salvage business, everybody will try ripping you off. You'll put in a whole load of hard work and make nothing from it. I wouldn't bother, if I was you.'

But she had already done her homework. 'I can buy what I need from a cash and carry and I've asked about taking a stall at the Barras market. As for price, I won't know until I've worked out how much the stuff to go into the baskets will cost.'

A week later, the floor of the house in Clova Street was carpeted with miniature teddy bears, Mason grumbling as he tried to pick his way between them. 'You'll never shift that lot,' warned the super salesman. But having made up hundreds of baskets, she loaded them into her car and set off to the Barras, where every one was snapped up in hours. Customers even returned seeking more and when she told them she had sold out they pleaded for her to return the following week.

As the coins rolled into the tin box where she kept her takings, she could not help but look about and wonder at the ironies life brings. This was probably close to the spot, in the shadow of the Barrowland dance hall, where just over a quarter of a century earlier – although to her it seemed like last night – a devil in human form had made her pregnant. She had to fight back tears as she remembered the day of Isobel's birth. How she would have loved to have given one of the bears to her, to have watched the child's face when she tickled her nose with one of the tiny toys. It all seemed so cruel, an affront to creation, that such a monster could have instigated the sheer beauty that is a newborn infant.

When next she saw Healy, he asked how the venture had gone and appeared genuinely pleased when she told him. Others seated around the bar began chuckling when she described Mason cavorting between the bears. One broke into a version of 'The Teddy Bears' Picnic', cheekily adapting one of the closing lines to fit as he sang to wild cheering and hoots of laughter: 'See Graeme gaily gad about, he loves to curse and shout and if he steps on 'em, doesn't care'.

The target of the fun did not appear overly amused and the impression was that he did not like Healy complimenting her on any job she had done, or the fact that she still went out and sold catalogues. In fact, after hearing of her Barras success, the publican had taken her to one side and told her, 'If you come up with more business ideas, Hannah, but haven't got the cash to get them under way, come to me and I'll back you.'

She would later complain that Mason, especially after a few drinks, tried to humiliate her in front of others and there had been one occasion, she said, where Healy had looked him in the eye and told him, 'She's the class act here, not you.'

Despite his deep involvement with the smugglers, and the importance of the tasks given to him, Mason was not entirely trusted by some of those in the plot. There was never any suggestion he told tales, except to Hannah, or was other than loyal to those who took him into the racket, but what was a cause of concern was that from time to time he took his drink in a bar that was looked on as the base for a rival group.

The success of the Spanish hash runs depended on as few people as possible being in the know. Rivals would dearly have loved to scupper the operation in order to take it, and the accompanying wealth, on for themselves. It only needed a careless word in the wrong ear and the project would come crashing down. Mason was looked upon as a good talker, but he boasted and enjoyed the kudos that over-emphasising his own role brought. Others in the gang felt the less he knew, the better. This worry would at times lead Healy to call on Hannah at Clova Street when he knew Mason was elsewhere, even propping up Healy's own bar.

'He liked to run ideas past me,' Hannah later claimed to a friend, 'sounding me out on what I thought of something or other. He was especially interested in finding out what I thought when it was being proposed that he delegate something or other to Mason. What had he told me of what was going on? Was he still as reliable as he had been when it all began? How was his health, because it was known he had heart problems? How did he treat me in the house because it had been noticed that, from time to time, I'd go into a shell such was the degrading way he'd speak to me? Did I want to leave him and go back to my own place because if that was the case, they'd help me remove my belongings? But I said I'd stick it out for the time being.

'I liked John so much I didn't want to leave because that would have ended my connection with him. Whenever he was there, I always seemed to be laughing. Of course, he was a ladies' man, that was no secret, but he flattered me and I enjoyed hearing nice things said of and to me. It was only he who kept me going through the insults I had to put up with from Graeme Mason. Had it not been for John, I would have walked out much earlier.'

There had been an ulterior motive in asking if she intended returning to live in Simpson Way, Bellshill. The very nature of a criminal's life requires him, on occasion, to disappear, usually to avoid the unwelcome tap on the shoulder signalling that a police officer wishes to offer him hospitality in one of Her Majesty's prisons. Gangs in Scotland have arrangements with gangs in England to offer sanctuary should the need arise: a man might be on the run from prison and need to lie low until some arrangement can be made for him to leave the country altogether, or he might simply want to avoid another criminal element wishing him harm.

'Safe' houses are not restricted to the world of spies and the security services. There are more run by law breakers than law keepers, but absolute discretion and secrecy must be guaranteed. Such had become Hannah's reputation for dependability that her home was used to hide out criminals. It was a favour asked of her by someone for whom she had the highest regard. Men would arrive late at night, clutching bags of basic foodstuffs, and occasionally she would turn up to ensure they had what they needed until it was time to move on. They never stayed long and to have asked questions would have been rude.

One further sideline was put her way but by whom she would never reveal. Motors used in the commission of crime needed to be cleansed of clues that could lead to the identification of the occupants. From time to time, she would be seen washing and vacuuming unfamiliar vehicles until they were almost restored to the condition they had been in when they left the factory. For this service she was well paid, around £100 a time, a lot more than a professional car valet would expect. At least once she received £500 for scouring a car in which, she would later admit, she had found bloodstains. Again, Hannah knew better than to ask questions, which is what made her such an asset.

For all her earning capacity, her friends noticed she rarely seemed to have money. 'Where it all went I could never work out,' said one. 'She had nothing to talk about in the way of jewellery or clothes; she even made garments for a long time. Her very occasional ornaments or pieces of jewellery ended up getting lost at a pawn shop when times became really tough for her. Once or twice she splashed out on classic stuff. She had a cashmere coat and a military-type one out of Arnotts that were maybe a bit more expensive than she could afford, but she wore clothes that she had from years before, suits and stuff like that. She tended to buy from shops like Planet and Monsoon, items she knew would make up into an outfit.

'We suspected the money she made from all the little jobs she had went into Clova Street and on Mason and his family because it certainly didn't come back to her home or into her bank.'

In fairness, when others suggested to him that Hannah must be 'coining it', Mason would tell them, 'Look, she knows how to spend money. When we go off to Spain on holiday, she's out from morning until night touring the shops and looking for things to buy. She might make it, but she knows how to get through it too.'

At the end of January 1996, Hannah sat at Clova Street watching morning television news when an item turned her blood cold and then sent her scurrying to the nearest newsagent's shop. She bought a copy of *The Scotsman*, it having been made plain to her by Mason and his fellow conspirators that the tabloid newspapers were not to be trusted. This is what she read:

PERMISSION has been granted for the exhumation of the body of the man police suspect of committing one of the Bible John murders. Strathclyde Police are now finalising details for the recovery of the corpse of John Irvine McInnes from Stonehouse Cemetery in Lanarkshire.

The move comes after forensic tests linked the man to the killing of Helen Puttock after a night at Glasgow's Barrowland Ballroom. She was one of three women murdered in Glasgow in the late 1960s. Last night, a Crown Office spokesman said: 'I can confirm that the fiscal has now obtained the necessary judicial warrant and the police have been advised.' A spokeswoman for Strathclyde Police said the force was now trying to finalise details for the exhumation.

It is understood Mr McInnes, who committed suicide in 1980, was linked with the killing after DNA found on Helen's tights was tested against DNA from members of his family. Police have mounted a round-the-clock guard round his grave in case souvenir hunters try to break pieces from the headstone.

The possibility that the man who had fathered Isobel was Bible John had been a knife continually cutting through Hannah. She blamed herself for not seeing, in the darkest and most dank basements of her memory, the face that must have shown strain, passion, relief and cruelty in the act that sparked life. Now, the rebirth of the Bible John story jolted her into reliving that terrible night.

For what seemed the millionth time, she urged her brain to throw out a clue that might have existed but had stayed dormant. But the frustration of recognising that she would, in all probability, never know brought only tears.

Over the years, the stories, rumours, had persisted, a new name cropping up from time to time. One had been that of a man who lived not far from her aunt in Bridgeton. Locals said he was a strange character who hung around the dance halls, the Barrowland in particular, not for the dancing but to watch the girls. There had been times when his pestering of young women had resulted in their menfolk throwing punches and he producing a razor. It was said that he would mingle with dancers on the crowded floor and sneakily grope females, blaming some nearby innocent when they turned angrily to protest.

This individual had fathered children, one of whom would

become a notorious Glasgow criminal. He came under close suspicion after the second murder, that of Jemima McDonald, and it was thought his movements may have been monitored by the police. But then he vanished. Rumour had it that he had upped sticks and moved to London, never to return. Hannah had heard of him and thought she knew who he was.

Now, could it be that her attacker had been this man, John McInnes, who had lived in Stonehouse, only five miles from Bellshill? His name meant nothing to her and when photographs of McInnes began appearing they stirred nothing within her.

On a February dawn, the police threw a tent around his grave and began digging through ground frosted so deeply that they had to bring in drilling equipment. In the process of exhuming McInnes, they also had to dig up the coffin of John's mother. When his coffin was finally recovered, his remains were taken to a mortuary in Glasgow's Saltmarket – by coincidence a short walk from the spot where Bible John was said to have danced with his victims. DNA samples were taken from bones and hair to be compared with that discovered on Helen's tights.

The police anticipated this operation, so distressing to John McInnes's relatives, would be over in three weeks, but the tests carried out in Scotland proved nothing. It might have been expected that in the light of the hurt the exhumation had caused the proper procedure would have been to end it there and then. But a decision was taken to have the results checked by experts at Cambridge, then yet again by scientists in Germany. Was all this to heap blame on a dead man? Whatever the thinking that led to the delays, the three weeks became five months before it was formally announced that there was no evidence to link him to Helen's murder. The body was reburied, but for Hannah the reopened wound could never heal. She did not know it, but ahead lay an even worse ordeal.

TWENTY-ONE

THE DECEIVERS

About the time members of the family of John McInnes were learning that their appalling trauma had been a waste of time, Hannah Martin was making a discovery that would have a deep and lasting impression on her and, as a consequence, on others as well.

She was still living with Graeme Mason on Clova Street, but the affection she had felt for him after their initial meeting was fading fast. He had dragged her down so many times in the presence of others that she now thought of him as cheeky and derogatory, delighting in ridiculing her while they were in company. She never showed the hurt that swelled within her, but hurt she was. Hannah had felt like this many times in her life and remembered each occasion.

Mason, she was sure, did not like hearing Healy compliment her on the small tasks she carried out for him, or that she continued selling catalogues; in fact, she was convinced Mason was jealous of the publican. As time passed, she knew she thought more of Healy than of the man whose bed she shared each night and wished it was Healy lying next to her. It was an impossible thought, of course, but one that gave her pleasure.

In the future she would talk of how she had ploughed what

money she earned, either through doing odd jobs, such as valeting or loaning out her home in Bellshill, into the Clova Street address or rather into ensuring that those who visited it, youngsters especially, were given a good time. At Christmas, she would buy a tree, decorate it and leave presents beneath the branches, imagining perhaps her own daughter being one of those ripping open carefully wrapped gifts and squealing with joy at discovering what lay inside. Apart from Isobel's birthday, this was the time she missed her daughter most and wondered where she was.

There was an inevitability that her affair with the salesman would drift to nothing. Two factors would set the seal on its eventual destruction. Mason, before meeting Hannah, had had a relationship with someone else whom we will call 'Daisy'. One night, as they lay in bed talking, Hannah asked him what had brought it to an end and was startled to hear his reply. 'I found the bitch in bed with another woman. To be honest, I'd always suspected she was bisexual because she had a way of looking at other females, as if she was asking them questions about their own sexuality with her eyes rather than her lips. Thinking of her in bed shagging another woman was just as bad as if it had been a man. But when I caught her at it, I told her I wanted nothing more to do with her.'

'Where is she now? Do you ever see her?' Hannah asked.

'No, I've had nothing to do with her since then and I haven't a clue what she's up to. She was the cause of my wife and I breaking up. My wife was and still is a lovely person, who has been very good and kind to me, even though we're not together.'

One night in the Thornlie Arms, while Mason was deep in conversation with Healy, Hannah mentioned the other woman to one of the regulars whom she'd come to know and like. 'Any idea where she went?' she asked.

The man gave her a puzzled look. 'Yes, she still lives around here and comes in now and again,' he told her. 'She and Graeme sometimes go drinking together.'

The words were a cruel blow. She had been cheated on many years ago, an act that had led to a night of madness, and now it seemed as though she was living through an action replay. From that day on, she would never again trust Mason. She wondered what other deceits were being played upon her, and would soon learn the answer.

One afternoon, sitting in the house on Clova Street, catching up on paperwork for Kays, the telephone rang and naturally she answered as Mason was out. She assumed he was working at the office, and so the likelihood was that the call was for her. When she picked up the receiver, she would discover it was for neither of them.

'Is Mr Balmer there?' asked a woman's voice.

'Mr Balmer? Sorry, I think you have the wrong number. Isn't it Mr Mason you want?'

The caller repeated the number written down on her notepad as that which Mr Balmer had given and, sure enough, it was that of the Clova Street address. There was no doubt she had dialled correctly.

'Well, can I take a message and when Mr Mason comes home he can sort it?'

'Right. Tell him Vardy Continental called. Can he ring us about the bus we are servicing for him?'

'Vardy Continental? His bus? You sure?'

'That's it.'

'Positive? And it's definitely Mr Balmer?'

'Yes, that's the name we have here.'

Later on in the day, when Mason came home, Hannah told him of the call and was astonished by his outburst. 'It's my phone! You should have let it ring!' he stormed.

'But I thought it might be for me.'

'And I thought you were going out, that's why I told them to call!' he shouted back.

The argument was short but bitter, with Hannah demanding to know what was going on. 'What's all this about a bus? Is this something to do with what you've organised? Is it connected to our trips with the money?' she asked.

Having already claimed to be the mastermind behind the scheme, he could hardly now pretend he did not know the details. At first, he fobbed her off by telling her to mind her own business, an order that only made her angrier. She knew she had taken risks for him and so was entitled to know what was going on. He, on the other hand, would have known how closely kept a secret was the drug-smuggling racket. Only a tight circle was supposed to be in the know, although as time had gone by more had learned many of the details. In time, the nagging rows sparked by her fury at being kept in the dark wore him down.

He would make a crucial, disastrous mistake. Mason spilled the beans. It may have been that he couldn't resist narrating the full story. Whatever his motive, he would have been in severe trouble with his fellow conspirators had they known then what he had done. By the time they found out, it was too late. By the tone and relentlessness of her demands to know what he was doing with a bus, he knew it would be hopeless to try to end her enquiries by simply relating that cash carried to Spain by couples like them, and families, was to buy hash. She was insistent that he tell her what part the bus played. And so he told her how he had bought for the gang first one bus and then a larger replacement. This second had had the seating on either side of the aisle raised in order to create two spaces running the length of the bus in which drugs were concealed. Side panels were lifted out to allow access and then screwed back into place for the journey back to Scotland. Youngsters were provided with free holidays in the sunshine, driven to their destinations and, after a week or ten days, brought home unaware that under their seats were secreted the drugs.

'But don't worry,' he told her, when he sensed she was about to make a protest at this evident use of children, 'it's only hash.'

To his credit, at no time did he mention anyone by name, simply referring to the others as 'them', and when she demanded to know who else was involved he told her only to forget it. 'Forget everything I've told you. I don't want to hear about the bus again,' he said.

'Who's Balmer?' she insisted. 'Is this the guy whose name you gave me for a catalogue?'

'Same one, he's just a friend and he has nothing to do with the buses.'

'Well, tell him it's about time he bought something,' she retorted.

Thinking, a while later, about what she had been told, she recalled hearing one of her catalogue customers talking of a benefactor who was paying for young footballers and kids from deprived families in Glasgow to have holidays overseas for free. 'Benji' Bennett was the coach driver, the woman had said, and that he was brilliant with the youngsters. When Hannah had asked about the millionaire who was footing the bill – she had been told it was a Mr Colin O'Sullivan, an Irishman with some sort of Glasgow connection but she did not know more than that – she had been told: 'He's a fine man and these are lovely people to give up so much time and money to help the children.' Hannah also remembered seeing a bus with a BMH logo parked in Clova Street. She wondered briefly if the initials stood for 'Balmer Mason Hannah', or maybe 'Bennett Mason Healy'. She would never know.

Hannah was not of a nature to be scared by what she had learned. Events that would cause fear in others simply made her curious. But she was hurt to think the man with whom she had been so intimate had kept so much from her. She saw this as a sign he could not trust her. She also realised he had overstated his part in the business: for something that was clearly so huge, his modest lifestyle suggested that far from being a leader he was but a bit player. The attempt by him to pull the wool over her eyes pained her as well. What other secrets, she wondered, was he keeping?

He had lied, humbled her and, she believed, been unfaithful: a recipe for separation. Throughout the summer, her anger simmered. The pair now rowed frequently, even over the most minor matters. In mid-September, he suggested another trip to Malaga. As soon as he mentioned he would book it through Square Deal Holidays, she knew this was no attempt at a romantic conciliation but only one more – the seventh – money-smuggling expedition. All the previous trips had been through Square Deal. She thought to herself how she had been used on previous trips and debated letting Mason down at the last minute by announcing at Glasgow Airport that she had changed her mind and leaving with the £70,000 cash in her bags. But she was certain John Healy was someone connected to the smugglers and while she cared not a jot about letting Mason down, she was too besotted to do likewise to Healy. And so she went.

At their Benalmádena hotel, she made no bones about what she intended doing during the break – and that was simply whatever she decided she wanted to do. So each morning Mason would be left behind while she sauntered off in the direction of the shops. As the end of the week neared, she could no longer prevent herself doing something she had determined not to do: look up James. And so she called in at the little bar where he had first introduced himself. He was not there and when she asked a pleasant young man if he might be popping in, he looked surprised.

'You know James?' he asked.

'Yes, we're old friends,' she said.

'You know him in Scotland?'

'No, I met him here a couple of years ago.'

'Ah, that is it. He is no longer here. He is back in Scotland.'

'On holiday?'

'Oh no, señora. He sold his bars to go back there.'

'He has made a lot of money and does not need to work?'

'No, no, his wife in Scotland made him do it.'

'His wife?'

'Yes, he has been married many years. When he was here, his wife was in Scotland. She used to come here sometimes with the children but told him he had to come home. So he sold up.'

She thanked him and left, knowing she had once more been taken for a ride, in more than one sense. 'You bastard,' she murmured to herself, as she headed towards the beach. 'Bastard, bastard, bastard.'

It was in the first hours of October that she and Mason returned to Clova Street, but the days of their affair were numbered. When she told him she was leaving, he neither asked why nor made any attempt to stop her. She packed her little car and headed back to Bellshill, all feeling for him gone.

She had learned the truth about his meetings with Daisy, the ultimate slap in the face. When she had challenged him about this duplicity, he had replied simply: 'Well, I like a drink; you don't and she does. That's all there is to it. We're just drinking buddies, nothing more.'

Depressed on the drive to Bellshill, her morale at rock bottom, she recalled his insults and complacency. 'I took on a lot when I set up home with him,' she would later tell her good friend, 'but I didn't expect it to end in such unpleasantness. Lots of couples lose their feelings for one another but hang on, thinking the good days might come back. They don't go out of their way to be offensive. Maybe towards the end he saw me as a negative influence, but he would come out with things like "You don't know what you're talking about" in front of others, or if I'd made an effort to look presentable "You look awful." In the end, I couldn't stand him.'

She settled down to life on her own once more. Christmas 1996 passed and then came the anniversary of Isobel's birth. The 'baby' would now be 27, she mused, maybe with a family of her own.

She was still knocking at doors, showing the latest catalogues, but was struggling to make ends meet. Then one day in mid-February, she answered a knock at her door to see a familiar face smiling down at her. 'Hello, Hannah,' said her caller. 'Can I come in? I have a little job I wonder if you might be interested in doing for me.'

Late on 29 March, Hannah and a woman friend set off in darkness from Glasgow in an unfamiliar vehicle, a Land Rover. They drove south, arriving at the Dover ferry terminal in time to take the quarter to six morning sailing to Calais. On board, they settled down to breakfast, studied a map and napped. At Calais, they drove carefully down the ramp leading to dry land and disappeared.

Their journey had not gone unnoticed. For months, the police – aware that hash was flooding into Scotland but baffled as to the source – had been studying the movements, telephone calls and meetings of a number of prime suspects, among them Tam McGraw, John Healy and the likeable Irishman Manny McDonnell.

Surveillance reports noted a meeting between Healy and Hannah, but the police were baffled by this unlikely combination. Their efforts were concentrated on him and it was as a result of this that they saw the Land Rover and subsequently spotted it motoring south with the women inside. It was watched off the ferry at Calais, though there was no need for it to be followed.

Telephone taps had indicated its destination to be Torremolinos, another resort just along the coast from Malaga. Had it been detained, a search would have yielded a fortune in cash, money to buy another consignment of hash. But it was not. It was allowed to proceed freely, and with the help of Spanish police the Land Rover was tracked on 1 April to the Scirocco Hotel, where the women were seen with two men, later discovered to be Glaswegians Robert Gillon and Donald Mathieson.

Two days later, the Land Rover driven by Hannah and her friend set off back to Scotland. When it reached Dover, it was stopped by Customs officers and police, who were convinced it was packed with drugs. The women were arrested, but a search produced nothing: no drugs at least, just some personal cash.

Suspicious that the authorities might be wise to what was going on in Spain, the smugglers had decided to use the Land Rover as a decoy, knowing that there was every chance it would be seized and searched, and confident that the forces of law and order would concentrate on it, thus allowing the drugs to be hidden away until they were to be carted back to the UK.

Working out what happened while the Land Rover was being dismantled in the search for contraband requires little imagination. The women were taken to interrogation cells and grilled, every technique, ruse and dirty trick available to the interrogators being used to scare them witless. And as the examiners knew it would, it paid off.

The friend genuinely knew nothing, a fact that quickly became apparent, but Hannah had been seen with Healy and that almost certainly meant she was a party to secrets. Just how much she told is open to speculation, but two days later Gillon, Mathieson and Liverpudlian Keith Barry were arrested. A helicopter dropped armed Spanish police into the grounds of a luxury villa used by the trio in Torreblanca and 470 kilos of hash, with a street value of nearly £1 million, was recovered. Chief Inspector Ignacio

Bulanyos – known as 'El Latigo' (The Scourge) because he was such a thorn in the side of drugs smugglers – admitted he had been told that Gillon and Mathieson would be using two hired cars to take hash to the villa in hessian sacks.

'They seemed surprised to see us,' he told reporters asking questions about the arrests. 'We acted on very specific information and were lying in wait.'

When, weeks later, the men – who would be given three-year jail sentences – were visited in their prison cells by detectives from Scotland, they said nothing. But there was a feeling among them that the police already knew too much. From the day Hannah was questioned, the surveillance in Glasgow and elsewhere of those suspected of being the smugglers' ringleaders was intensified.

Graeme Mason is in no doubt as to what happened. 'The friend probably knew nothing, but the feeling was that Hannah talked to save herself. From then on, things began to go wrong.'

TWENTY-TWO

SOWING SEEDS

Hannah drove back to Glasgow in the Land Rover and then to her home in Bellshill. The ordeal with Customs and police interrogators at Dover had left her frightened. She could not foresee it but never again would she breathe air not tainted with fear. The police in Glasgow would now step up their surveillance on prime targets believed to be linked to drugs smuggling to a remarkable degree. They bugged hotel rooms when the gang of which Mason had boasted to be the leader went for a weekend break and even put a tiny camera in a street light outside the McGraw home in Mount Vernon, the suburb where Hannah's elder sister Isobel had perished over 30 years earlier.

When he went out for a drink in the evening, Mason would be asked, 'Where's Hannah?' He replied that they had split up, unaware of the hate his treatment had planted within her. As she tried to gather together the threads that her been her life, desperate to weave them into something at least resembling normality, cracks were meanwhile appearing in the smuggling set-up.

Men who had been paid more money than they could have dreamed of wanted even more. The wise saved or let their womenfolk invest the proceeds. But not all were prudent. Many spent and wasted, often buying a brand new car only to change it a month later for a similar model in a different colour. One would later confess he had blown more than £200,000 on cocaine, his ability to afford the drug being, he reckoned, the worst thing that had ever happened to him. One or two decided to break away on their own, running their own little smuggling sidelines, none of which worked out but they all succeeded in bringing an even greater degree of police attention.

The bus runs continued, even though the gang suspected it was under surveillance. Strangers who were all too obviously policemen began appearing in the hotels frequented by the traffickers in Benalmádena, Fuengirola and then Torremolinos. Even petty Spanish criminals in Benidorm, the resort on the northern Costa Blanca, were making jokes about the policemen with strange accents who were in town. The outcome was inevitable.

One evening in September 1997, as she sat at home alone in Bellshill watching a television newscast, Hannah heard the presenter announce that a bus had been stopped near Uddingston on the southern outskirts of Glasgow and a fortune in hash found in it. Over the next few days, she read and heard of a growing number of arrests. Most of the names meant nothing, but others did, including those of Benji Bennett, who was driving the Mercedes when police surrounded it and forced it to a stop, and John Wood, whom she thought she remembered meeting once at the Thornlie Arms.

Mention of Benji made her heart race. She knew it would only be a matter of time before Graeme Mason was in the net. Then it would be her turn. She wondered if John Healy might escape, but he too was bagged, and then so was Tam McGraw. She had never met the Licensee but knew, from remarks made in the Thornlie Arms, that he placed huge dependence and trust in his wife Margaret, a shrewd woman and fiercely protective of her husband. What, she pondered, was the fate of Balmer?

No doubt his turn would come to be questioned. And what lay in store for her? She would not have long to wait.

There was an inevitability about the arrival one day of Strathclyde Police at her home because they already knew about the Land Rover trip. In a tone not of invitation but of threat, the officers told her they would like her to come to a police station to have a 'chat'. It would be helpful if she would come willingly, but if not, then they would haul her along anyway. It was up to her. Alone and scared, she realised there was no choice. Climbing into the Corsa, her heart beating, pale and feeling sick, she followed the two detectives to the police station at nearby Coatbridge.

Sitting in an interview room, a policewoman discreetly in the corner, she listened while the detectives told her how much they knew rather than, at that stage, asking her to talk. They were able to give dates when she and Mason had flown to Spain and the names of hotels in which they had stayed. What the men in shirtsleeves, seated opposite so composed and confident, wanted to know was what it was all about. When she hesitated, a voice rasped the reality of her position.

'Listen, Hannah. This isn't going to go away, nor are we. How you became mixed up in this we don't know, but mixed in it up to the neck we know you are. We have files a metre thick and your name features in them throughout. We are talking about millions and millions of pounds' worth of drugs being smuggled into Scotland. You don't have a family of your own, but you will still appreciate what those drugs can do, especially to kids. It is your decision whether or not you want to help us. If you do, and we find you are telling the truth, then you'll discover we can be very good friends to you. We're not going to make promises, but we'll discuss your situation with the Procurator Fiscal and it's very likely he will take the view that having your collaboration and help as a prosecution witness will be infinitely more useful than having you charged.

'On the other hand, if you decide you are going to bluff this out and hinder us, then we guarantee you here and now that firstly you won't be returning home but will be sleeping in Cornton Vale women's prison tonight, and second when this comes to court we'll make sure you get nothing less than three years' imprisonment. And that's a minimum. Given what we know already, you are more likely looking at five years.'

The police assured her that they had the entire gang in the bag. This was not true – others were yet to be arrested and the police case was far from complete or conclusive – but she was not to know that. Their words made her feel isolated. She thought of John Healy and wondered if he was alone in a prison cell. Hannah wanted desperately to be able to pick up a telephone, call him and ask what he wanted her to say and do. But, of course, she was on her own. The decisions that would come within the next few seconds were hers alone.

The interrogators were not to know it, but the tears that followed were not of fear but because they had forced her, by mentioning family, to think about her daughter. True, it had only been hash, but had Isobel followed the same path as so many youngsters into drug dependency, her arms and thighs a mess of bloody holes where the needles had gone in, her teeth rotting, her hair falling out, her speech incomprehensible? Could she have helped her on this road to destruction? No, she knew the answer to that. It was Graeme Mason who was responsible, Graeme Mason who had boasted of being the mastermind, Graeme Mason who had dragged her into this, Graeme Mason who had repaid her loyalty with humiliation and scorn. The sound of the two words that formed his name was enough to make up her mind. 'What is it you want to know?' she asked.

What followed was the ruthless extermination of her ex-lover. Mason's culpability extended page after page of a witness statement. And just as she painted venom over his canvas, so she lied and gambled with her own freedom by trying to draw a picture of Healy as a man in whom she had never seen wrongdoing. If he had been one of the plotters, then, she claimed, she had never been present when he schemed. True, she had met him when she and Mason visited one of his pubs, and once he had called to wish them well before they set off to Spain on holiday, but never had she heard him discussing drugs or buses. That was not what the detectives wanted to hear.

'You sure about this?' she was asked. 'You're not trying to protect him for any reason?'

'Definitely not,' said Hannah. 'The only person I want to protect is myself.'

In looking on Hannah as someone in whom he could confide, Healy had chosen well. Though the same could not be said of his choice of Mason as a partner. As Hannah's close friend recalls: 'Healy knew he could depend on her to do exactly what she was asked. But not Mason, who wanted to be a bigger player. According to Hannah, Healy would give tasks to Mason, such as "Go and find somebody who can buy a bus," but instead the salesman wanted to do it himself, and so have a finger in every pie, while at the same time keep what money there was in it for himself. It backfired because if he had passed on the job or the money he was given to someone else, then when the police finally got on to them they could never have traced the evidence back to him.

'By being such a busybody, Mason left his traces on the set-up everywhere. His friendship with Healy dragged him into it also. So in effect, Graeme Mason got John Healy caught. If Mason had kept his mouth shut, hadn't bragged so much, had delegated the jobs that he was meant to delegate out, things might have worked differently. But even when the hash arrived back in Glasgow, and he and others were supposed to leave it for others to deal with, he got involved in distributing it. The operation had been organised so everyone had a particular job that they were supposed to stick to, but not him.

'Hannah did what she could to save Healy, at least by playing down any connection he might have had in the whole thing, but the pressure exerted on her by the police was immense, terrifying. In a sense, she should have been grateful to Mason for being so unpleasant to her and causing their break-up because had she still been with him when the gang was caught it might have been impossible for her to wriggle out. She was informed in no uncertain terms that to save herself at least three years in jail she had to tell them what she could. She said afterwards that whatever she did it was because she wanted to protect Healy, but she felt no such duty to Mason. She liked Healy and admired him. Did she love him? Yes, it was obvious from the way she spoke of him that she did. But she never actually said she loved him, just that she was flattered by his attention.'

More than 30 men were eventually arrested as part of what the police had codenamed Operation Lightswitch, the name probably having derived from bugs that were planted in the lightswitches of hotel rooms, although others quote the source as a police officer who had advocated at a conference to discuss the smugglers, 'Right, let's switch off their lights.'

The investigation spanned more than two years and cost a fortune. It was so complex that prosecutors decided there would be three trials, with those accused split into three groups. Those they considered to be the ringleaders would form the first batch of accused and the prosecutors decided that they would throw the book at them, hit them with the strongest evidence they had. The thinking behind this strategy was that by blasting them with a full broadside any defence they hoped to put forward would be destroyed. All would be convicted and once the first group trooped out of the dock to face long jail sentences the remainder of those waiting to be tried would cave in and beg for deals, thus saving the taxpayer a considerable sum in legal costs.

The police were going for the jugular. They wanted Tam McGraw, the man they would accuse of being 'Mr Big', given a 24-year stretch. Hannah would be their star turn and as such she was given celebrity treatment. After her damning statement condemning Mason and blowing the lid on the real purpose of their trips to Spain, the secret under the floors of the coaches and the mysterious Mr Balmer, the police knew they had a jewel sparkling over their case.

In contrast to their initial threats, they were now polite, friendly and flattering, inveigling themselves into her life, addressing her as Hannah and pleading with her to call them by their forenames. They gave her their telephone numbers and insisted that if she thought of anything further or needed them for any reason whatsoever then she should call them day or night. They encouraged her loathing of Mason, egging her on when she spoke of how much she despised him. 'This is your opportunity to pay him back for the way he treated you and ripped you off,' they told her. 'And it's not as though you will be telling lies, just the truth. Stick to the truth, Hannah, and he'll get what he deserves along with the rest of them.' She was surprised at how easily the police had accepted her version and by the way in which, once having made her long statement, they did not press her to tell more or try browbeating her into being more forthcoming. Because hold back she did.

But it was not all sweetness and light. One day, two of the officers with whom she had become especially friendly came calling with news that was disturbing. 'They know you are going to be the star witness,' said one, 'and are aware how much damage you can cause. We think there may be an attempt to get to you to try persuading you to change your mind and not give evidence after all.'

'Am I in danger?' she asked.

'Not danger – we don't believe they'd dare try anything because that would be too obvious. But you ought to be scared of these people. Some are very rich and have everything to lose.'

'Is Mason behind this?' she asked, and decided the answer lay in their silence.

'We want to take some precautions for your benefit,' smiled the officers, rubbing salt into the wound. 'Nothing drastic, but better safe than sorry.'

The result of the visit was the installation in her home of an emergency telephone linking her directly to a nearby police station. A temporary alarm system was also fitted. Neither would ever be used. But the seeds had been sown.

TWENTY-THREE

THE MISSING BUNG

Isobel was discovering the fragility of happiness. Her marriage, like so many others past the early days in which love blows away failings and flaws, had now reached that level in which a couple establishes a routine that leads to either boredom or contentment. Invariably, the former is the beginning of the end.

She had been overjoyed at first, finding in her husband a friend, rock and lover, who made her feel needed. Now, the strands that had bound them were fraying and she feared the future no longer promised the security it once had. Picking up a newspaper one day while she worried of things to come, she read how 11 men were to appear before the High Court in Edinburgh facing charges that they had smuggled vast quantities of hash into Scotland. The report said the trial was likely to be one of the longest in Scottish legal history, with nearly 200 witnesses due to give evidence. She could, of course, not know one of them would be her mother.

Hannah, both anxious and fearful at the thought of the forthcoming court ordeal, had seethed after hearing the suggestion cleverly planted in her mind by the police that Mason was responsible for her need for extra security. After that first meeting when the question of a threat was posed, the detectives had visited her regularly, ostensibly to check the equipment they had left was working but actually to keep up the hints about who was behind the threat to her safety.

'You can never be sure that people such as him won't try something,' officers said. 'Did you know he's been given bail?'

'Bail? You mean he's out and about?' she asked, the shock and astonishment clear.

'Oh, yes. It's amazing what a good lawyer and a heart condition can do. He hasn't been in touch, has he?'

'No, if he had been, I'd tell him where to go.'

'Well, Hannah, how would you feel about getting in touch with him?'

'I never want to see or speak to him again.'

'We appreciate that after the way he treated you, but you want him to get his just deserts, don't you?'

'Of course, but I don't understand how my seeing him would achieve that.'

'Well, supposing you got in touch and said you were worried about him, were sorry for what had happened to him and wondered if he fancied meeting up for a chat.'

'He'd never believe that.'

'We think he might, because he wants to know how much you know and what you've told us. This crew are keeping their cards close to their chests and we'd like to know what's going on. Mason is the weak link, the one who can't stop himself talking. We'd like you to meet up for coffee or a bite of lunch and just listen to what he says.'

'And that's it? You'll tell me what to ask?'

'Sure . . . Just one other thing.'

'What's that?'

'We'd like you to carry a tape recorder.'

It would emerge that the police had already tried eavesdropping on some of the suspects, with bitter complaints later made

215

about attempts to bug the offices of some lawyers acting for the defendants. What was being proposed was an attempt to trap Mason into making a chance remark that could be used against him and his co-accused. Hannah did not know it, but the police and prosecution lawyers were beginning to wonder if their opponents knew something they did not because an air of confidence was exuding from across the battlefield. So it was time to introduce a dirty trick or two.

There was something else the police did not know: the intelligence of the alleged smugglers had been seriously underestimated. These were men who had dreamed up a scheme that had drawn admiration from criminals throughout Europe and even envy from some in Scotland who were smarting at having been left out of the chance to get rich. It had made millions and, had the foot soldiers stuck to their individual agendas, could have gone on considerably longer. In short, they were no mugs.

Nor was Graeme Mason. He was a clever, at times ingenious, salesman who had the seller's knack of being able to root out a customer's weaknesses. When someone wanted to give him something for nothing, he knew there was always a hidden motive. And Hannah wanted to give him something for nothing in the form of her company. When she telephoned, enquiring after his health and asking how he was, he was instantly cautious, sensing there was more to this than met the eye. He realised he had to be ultra-circumspect and reticent, but when she proposed a meeting he went along with it.

Hannah reported back to the police on her conversation with him. They had arranged to meet in Carntyne, in the east end of Glasgow. On the day of the rendezvous, a tiny tape recorder was placed in her handbag with a microphone stuck to the inside of the bag. As a ploy to gain information, it was not a success. Mason was certain she had been wired up and when she began going over old ground, recalling the arrangements for taking money abroad, who they met, what they did, how the buses had been bought and adapted, he realised she was simply trying to talk him into making incriminating remarks that were, he was sure, for the benefit of the police. So he let her do most of the talking, taking an active part in the conversation only when it turned to banalities.

It was friendly enough and they parted on good terms, she suggesting they meet again and he going along with the idea. When the police listened to the tape, they were disappointed but agreed it was worth another try. Hannah would set up two further meetings. The second, at a fast-food store in Baillieston, went the way of the first; at the third she was left sitting alone, waiting, before realising he was not showing up.

To friends in whom he had confided about these get-togethers, Mason said, 'She was clearly wired up and was asking me about the things we had done. It was obvious she was trying to get me to talk about what we had got up to, but I said nothing. She had been very well schooled by her police handlers, but it was pretty amateurish stuff. I knew right away when she got in touch what she was up to.'

Just as her mother and all the others had used her, now the police had done the same. The meetings had not been a good idea because the only consequence was to put Hannah in even greater danger by making it patently obvious she was working as a police spy. But just as she had tried to nobble Mason, now she was about to become a target.

Friends of Healy were deeply worried about his situation. Statements collected by teams of defence lawyers made his position appear precarious, although there was a feeling that if he, along with most of the others, opted not to go into the witness box – where the most likely outcome was that they would implicate themselves – then there was an outside chance of him getting a not guilty or at worst not proven verdict.

What evidence there was against him was largely circumstantial, but his friends felt that if Hannah would be willing to help out by denying she knew of any involvement by him, then it could prove the clincher in his favour. It was difficult making contact with her because her telephone was tapped in case such an approach was made. And she was encouraged to move around from time to time, staying with friends. But as one of those concerned with speaking to her has admitted, 'There are no secrets in Glasgow and in next to no time we knew where Hannah was and got in touch with her. She really was still besotted by John Healy. She was in love with the guy and everybody could tell. We were sure she would have done anything for him. Through one of her pals, a message was sent to her, asking if she would be prepared to help John, just he and nobody else. For a price. The deal was that she would be paid a £20,000 bung to change her story and say John was never implicated in the drug-smuggling racket. John had nothing to do with this. Hannah sent word she was up for it but stressed she would help only him because she felt very bitter towards many of the others, especially Graeme.

'The arrangement was that Hannah would be paid £10,000 up front to say she'd got it wrong about John Healy and once he was acquitted would receive another £10,000. The police version of events was that John Healy had arrived at the home she shared with Graeme Mason carrying a bag inside of which was the money they were to carry over to Spain to pay for the hash that would be brought back under the floor of the bus. Hannah had told the police it was Healy who turned up but as for the money she changed her story and said she'd been thinking things over and it hadn't been Healy but someone else she did not know.'

A bag containing £10,000 in cash was given to a woman to deliver to her. It came back with £9,000 still inside. What happened to the missing £1,000 nobody knows. Hannah would always swear she didn't receive money from anyone and her standard of living before and after the trial provided evidence that she spoke the truth. As for the second £10,000, it was conveniently forgotten.

She did receive between £200 and £500 in cash shortly before Christmas 1997. Hannah was told the money was a gift from Graeme Mason, but she could never be sure if that was the case. Within hours of it being handed over, it had been spent on presents for three children of whom she was especially fond. So at least some innocents were brought happiness by the events many hundreds of miles away.

In April 1998, the trial of the 11 men began. In the dock were Healy, McGraw, Mason, Wood, Bennett, Billy McPhee, Gordon Ross, John Burgon and Manny McDonnell, all from Glasgow; Paul Flynn from Rochdale, Lancashire, known to pals as 'Arthur Askey' because he looked so like the comic; and Trevor Lawson, who lived on a farm near Stirling.

As she waited at home to be told when to turn up and give her evidence, Hannah felt her fear spill over until she felt she was going mad. Her doctor had prescribed Valium to settle her nerves, which were at breaking point. She was anxious that her evidence would not prove disastrous for John Healy; she wanted only to destroy Mason. She had been selective about what she told the police, but now she wondered if, in doing so, she had sunk her friend as well. She felt the police had worn her down and could not even be sure as to what she had told them. On the morning she was instructed to arrive at the High Court in Edinburgh to give her evidence, she immediately asked for a meeting with the prosecution team and said she would be changing her statement and withdrawing any reference to John Healy.

'You haven't said anything incriminating about him. There's

no problem,' she was assured. 'If you try backing out now, you'll be charged with contempt or perjury and looking at a long spell in prison. Best to go ahead and get it over with, then you can go home and forget the whole thing.' That was impossible, of course, but there seemed no alternative.

There had been a variety of police witnesses, but it was on Hannah that everyone was waiting. Graeme Mason remembers as if it were yesterday the moment when she took the oath and began giving her evidence. 'When we were together, she used to ask me about what we were doing, but I told her nothing, nothing about anything and particularly nothing about the real reason why we were making these trips to Spain.

'But she must have listened to my telephone conversations, chats with others that I thought were in private, missed nothing, and it wasn't until after we were arrested that I discovered how much she knew. It was after she'd taken the oath and started speaking that I realised how Hannah had kept her ear to the ground from the word go. She knew everything, everything about what we had been doing, and she made sure she put that knowledge to full use. Furthermore she was going to make sure she stuck it on me big style. She nailed me to the cross like an executioner; the Roman soldiers who crucified Jesus had nothing on her.

'You could also see the hate steaming out of her when she was in court. If there is such a thing as looking daggers at somebody, she looked daggers at me and at Benji Bennett. We were her targets and at the same time she seemed determined she wouldn't do a thing to harm John Healy, or most of the others. She wanted me and if anybody else fell into her net, well, that would be a bonus. Her evidence lasted two days and she put on a performance that would have won her an Oscar had it been part of a Hollywood movie. She even wore a pair of dark glasses, so nobody would be able to see her real expressions. Hannah was a hell of an actress. She began giving evidence on a Friday and predictably, for effect, broke down. I'd been on bail for eight months, but when the case was resumed it was revoked, even though I'd never done a thing wrong in all that time.'

As he sat watching the proceedings from the public gallery, the Irishman chuckled when he heard the codename Operation Lightswitch. He remembered calling to collect money and Hannah wanting to switch on the bedroom lights. Now he realised how fortunate a decision that had been. 'The first time I saw Hannah's face was when she stepped into the dock to give her evidence,' he said. 'But more important for me was that if someone had asked how many times she had seen me, an honest answer would have been that this was the first. I wouldn't have recognised her as the woman I'd met a couple of years earlier in the darkened bedroom.

'She had been very well tutored by the police in how to give her evidence. For much of the time she laid on tears and, to hide her real feelings, wore sunglasses, even inside the courtroom. I was praying she would say she couldn't identify the man who had come to her room at the hotel. And she did.

'But she talked about how her life had been destroyed, how she was devastated by the way in which she had been used, and continually broke down. She set out to destroy Graeme, but because she had heard about Michael Bennett and had often heard Mason mention his name, she decided Benji must be one of his friends. That connection was enough for her to make allegations against him also, even saying Benji used to bring in prostitutes to work as couriers, a claim which was totally untrue.'

Another of the accused was staggered at the extent of her bitterness. 'After the arrests, we began getting an insight into the sort of evidence the police would be producing against us. Hannah was to be the prime witness and we learned she had made a very lengthy statement to the police. In it she nailed Del Boy Mason to the floor, hammered him. Hannah hated him because of the way she felt he had tricked her and in court she put the boot in big style, leaving him dead and buried. The trouble was Graeme brought it all on himself. When they'd met and started an affair he had told her a real story to end all stories. And Hannah had been through so much unhappiness in her life she was not the sort of person to forget when someone made an idiot of her.

'He had made the mistake of telling her, "I am the main man here. I set the whole thing up. I'm the brains behind it all, the organiser, the top dog, everyone else takes their orders from me and through me. I direct the whole thing." Unfortunately, she remembered his words. It was as though he had a gun and had shot himself in the foot, only his recovery from what she did would take much longer.'

The trial would last 58 days. After 45 days, Wood, McDonnell and Ross were released when it was ruled they had no case to answer. It was a blow for the police but from their point of view there was even worse to come. Benji Bennett, who had been driving the bus when it was stopped near Uddingston and who expressed disbelief when £263,000 worth of hash was discovered hidden under the floor, went home too, as the jury announced the charge that he had smuggled drugs not proven. There were similar verdicts for McPhee and Lawson, both of whom, said the Crown, had acted as couriers, taking money overseas. And as a not proven verdict was announced for Tam McGraw, friends in the packed public gallery hissed 'Yes'. John Burgon, too, walked free with a clear not guilty ringing in his ears.

Hannah, sitting at home, listened to the verdicts as they were announced on television. She wasn't particularly bothered what happened to the majority, it was the fate of two men that interested her. The outcome for one gave her a feeling that justice had won the day; for the other it brought bitter sobs. Of the three men who remained, all were found guilty. Paul Flynn was given six years, Mason eight and Healy ten.

For Healy, there was worse to come. Under legislation introduced to deprive criminals of their ill-gotten gains, the Crown financial experts had worked out that he had made £766,000 from trafficking in hash and they wanted £450,000 to be paid into state coffers. If it was not, then his sentence would be stretched even further.

For the Operation Lightswitch team, the outcome was devastatingly disappointing and, as is often the case, individuals looked about to see who could be blamed. Some who were high up pointed to the comments by the trial judge, Lord Bonomy, who criticised the way the case had been presented, making it clear he thought it was so complex the jury would almost certainly have had difficulty following what was going on.

Hannah would now be hung out to dry. She had served her purpose, helping to convict at least one of the three, possibly two, and had been rewarded for her efforts by not going to prison herself. She was being left to salvage what pieces of her life she could collect. A few days after the trial ended, a detective came to collect the equipment that had been fitted for her protection; evidently, it was felt she no longer deserved looking after.

'Can't you leave it?' she begged, trying to demonstrate how vulnerable she felt. 'Mason has a lot of friends and they know where I am.'

'Sorry,' she was told. 'You'll be OK. If you're really worried, why don't you pack up your house and move away? You don't even need to move out of the district.'

If it was meant to be helpful it failed abysmally. A few days later, she met an old friend, who asked about Mason. Hannah told her: 'I fell for his story. He knew he was stringing me along and I couldn't understand why because I wasn't impressed by his claims to be the leader of the whole thing. When I found out he'd been making a fool of me, I was so hurt and angry. But I simply sat back and waited for the chance of revenge. Del Boy used to get drunk and began boasting and rambling about what a big shot he was. I didn't drink, or hardly ever touched the stuff, so I'd sit and listen and take it all in. At the end of the day, he talked himself into jail but took a couple of others with him.'

TWENTY-FOUR

THE WRETCHED SOUL

Hannah, once part of a racket with a turnover approaching £50 million, had returned home penniless, empty and sad. Others had made fortunes, they drove flash cars and wore Rolex watches, while she had no jewellery, no clothes other than what she had bought from her catalogue earnings or made, and no savings.

Now, with the trial over, she felt abandoned by those she had helped on both sides of the law. The promise of a huge reward from the friends of John Healy had failed to materialise, although she never gave up hoping that one day it would arrive. There was no doubt that she had opened the door to the cell that was now home to Graeme Mason, but while he was locked inside the feeling remained with her that from now on she should move about constantly looking over her shoulder.

Hannah's problem was that as Mason had been garrulous, she was reserved, and now she needed to unwind, to uncork the bottle in which she had stored so many emotions for too long. A confession beckoned. She knew one of her closest friends would sit on the other side of the curtain and would understand and not punish. It had been in the days before Mason that the two had last shared a heart to heart and her confidante could never forget what she had been told then.

'Hannah was an amazing storyteller but persuading her that opening up was sometimes the best remedy for sadness could be difficult. After her dad died, she had been at a very low ebb and it was only then that she told me about having Isobel. I had probably been as close to her as anyone, yet I hadn't had a clue about the baby. That was how closely guarded a family secret it was. We'd sat in a café for two hours and throughout that time it was Hannah who did the talking.

'Then one particular night, some time after that, she had walked down the road with me as though she was heading for home. But it seemed as if she had nowhere to go and so she came to my house and began going over old times, old memories. When midnight came, I wondered how I was going to get up for work the next morning, but to Hannah it was as though time did not exist. She talked on and on through the night, soul searching and crying, and I could tell she wanted to get something into the open.

'When eventually Hannah decided to talk about her baby, she was distressed and distraught. It was the story of Isobel from the night in the back of the car up to her birth. It simply poured from her, as if a dam holding back the words had burst. It was, I suppose, like a relief to her, but she went over who she had spoken to about the baby, who hadn't to know and who was told, who helped, who was in favour of her keeping the child and who against it. She cried her way through from half an hour after midnight to half past five in the morning and came back the next night and did the same.

'Now, a few years on, I had the sense she needed more of these long sessions, and it was only after she and Mason split up that she really, really opened up. Maybe she had thought that in Mason there was an escape from the past and perhaps finding he was not the answer made the experiences she had with him appear all the worse. "He's a wee weasel," she said. She rarely referred to him by name, usually as "that wee weasel".

226

'For a long time after they parted, she kept herself to herself because she could not face going out. She went to her job, selling catalogues, and then came straight home and went to her bed. That's how she lived for months. Part of living like a hermit was down to her always having that fear after giving evidence of somebody putting a contract out on her, even though she had no alternative. In reality, it was probably Mason who had more to be scared of than her because but for him she would have known nothing and the others would not have been in jail.

'I thought the drugs thing was an ingenious plan and I told Hannah, "Maybe more of a punishment for the weasel is the thought he might get done in for opening his mouth too often rather than simply being locked up in prison."

'During another meeting, I asked what she was doing with herself, but she simply sighed and said, "Absolutely nothing, I haven't been anywhere lately. We'll have to have a night out."

'One night, I again asked her into my house. She came in and that was the resumption of the long unburdening sessions we'd had before she lived with Mason. Hannah started coming to my house on a regular basis, before she started work, after she finished work, often right into the early hours unless I was going somewhere else and even then she would wait until I returned and ring up, although it might be midnight, and ask if she could come to see me.

'Some nights she told stories about her mother, crying from one end of the night to the other, about the things her mother had done. Then she'd look up as if she was a wee girl and ask, "How could she do that?" I'd felt part of Hannah's family but, in my naivety, because her mother was nice to me and in many ways kind to me, had I really overlooked the fact that she just wasn't the same with Hannah?

'There had been times when she was living in Clova Street when we'd met one another as she came over to check her own house and we'd chat. Then she had talked about Mason and Healy, especially Healy. She didn't mention any of the others or the involvement she had with them at that time, but after it was over and the trial was finished and she had laid low for months, she really opened up.

'She'd had all her pain, living through the unhappiness of her childhood and then suffering the tragedies of her sister dying, her mother dying, her father, granny and granddad too. And there had been the disappointment and heartbreak of everybody else who was supposed to care about her at some point or another slapping her in the bloody face and turning their backs on her when she needed help. She got everything out. That's why I knew of all her bitterness, all her hatred, all her love even.

'Was she a sad, hurt person? People say "You bring it all on yourself" and I did say that to her about her fears over the Mason situation. But there's always a lot more to it than that. You actually don't just "bring it on yourself" because it's like there is fate, as if it's bloody meant to happen to you, the karma experience again. I said to Hannah, "I'm shocked by what was going on, all the drugs and the kids in buses, and yet I'm not shocked at your involvement. Maybe you were destined to be there and to do something about it, as you did in the end."

'She believed she had been part of something very, very big and yet she hated drugs and drug users. "I know it's hypocritical," she would say, "because I took part in bringing them in, but it was only ever cannabis."

'Hannah had felt this was one way, maybe the only way, in which she might make some money in life. Yet despite all the bad things that happened to her, she could remain a dreamer. Sometimes when we'd sit talking at night, she would say, "See, when I get that money from John's friends, because John will make sure I get that money, I'm going to buy my house and then I'll not have rent to pay. I'll struggle on for the next couple of years until I can claim the pension I built up when I worked at Hoover. Then things will be so much better."

'She so looked forward to getting the tax-free lump sum that would come with her Hoover pension and had even thought about how receipt of the pension itself would adversely affect her right to housing and other benefits. Owning her own house would be the best way around the problem and that's why the money she expected for helping out John Healy was so important to her. She was sure that if he knew it had not been paid he would send word from prison to his friends who had made the arrangement to honour it.

'Hannah was such a changed person after the split from Mason and the long build up to the trial. The whole experience had a devastating effect and for a year or two afterwards she laid low, not having relationships and not seeking them. He had slowly demoralised her, and if she had been in love with him the thought that someone to whom she had given her heart could put her down in the cruel way he did would have been so much worse. But she had never loved him, although maybe at the beginning she wondered if love might come with time. Now she had to begin all over again.

'When she'd been happy and everything was going along fine, she would shine. But there were two faces to Hannah; she had a split personality after the years with Mason. That affair destroyed her mentally and materially.

'Once she sat in the dark at her home for a week because she had no money with which to buy a card for her electricity meter. Each day bills and final demands dropped through her letterbox. Anyone else might have sought help from their friends, but not Hannah. She was suffering from depression but could not see it and like many depressives was too proud to seek help.

'I wondered why, when she was staying with Mason, she had continued to slog around the streets, looking for catalogue customers. Why, I asked her, had she not packed it in and looked for something more profitable? She would shrug as though she didn't know the answer, but it was clear she was hiding the truth, which was that she felt insecure when she was with him, unsure as to how it would all end. For all his bragging about money, she still paid bills and bought food. When they broke up, she returned to Bellshill with so much baggage she was never fully able to sort her head out. She tried doing that by dressing up to become a different person, applying make-up in a way that actually made her feel differently about herself. "I'm putting on my personality," she would say, dressing in very stylish outfits by the likes of Frank Usher, even though they might be second-hand, telling us when she was ready to go out, "Now the act begins."

'She was probably more comfortable playing these smart, bright characters that she pretended to be than her actual self. Getting dolled up gave her such confidence. Others might need a couple of drinks to get enough courage to take to the dance floor but not Hannah. If she liked the music, she would walk straight on and begin, even if she had no partner. She loved making an entrance, being noticed, and yet while others thought she was too full of herself she was the first to put herself down.

'And the reason was that the hidden Hannah was a wretched, depressed soul who must have shocked even herself when she opened up into the other jovial, laughing woman she could become. It was like watching a chameleon. She used to say, "I know I'm not pretty and men don't find me attractive, but when I put my face on and go out I can become a different person." And people who knew her would say, "Hannah gives you her heart and soul."

'She always gave the impression she couldn't do enough for you. If she had it, she would give you it, but all the brightness went out of her after Mason. What was especially sad was that in the later years she didn't have anything to give; she had to be a taker.

'She was paranoid knowing that someone blaming her for the demise of the gang would come after her bent on revenge, and friends tried persuading her to shake off the distress this caused her by going out socially. We'd take her to different clubs but, although she appeared to be having a good time, it was never enough for her. If we suggested somewhere different, she would say, "I've never been in there in my life, why should I go now?"

'Despite the trauma caused by the affair with Mason, she still hoped to find someone with whom she could settle down. On nights out, Hannah would say, "If I get into a relationship that works, I won't dump my friends but I'll stop going out with them. Instead I'll be going out with whoever I meet. He'll come first."

'One night, when we were with her at a club, she met a guy – big, bloody dumb and you could tell from the little conversation he had how dull he was. But he bragged about having money, and when you have none that's an attraction. That was the bait that caught Hannah. He asked her for a date and when she agreed he took her for a meal and even gave her a red rose. They arranged to meet again and he telephoned to say he was taking her out, but didn't. Instead he turned up and suggested he stayed the night. The reason was that her home was along the route he would be taking to get to work and he thought he could have his fun with her, use her, then clear off. Hannah saw through that right away, blasted him and told him to bugger off. She told me, "It took me an hour and a half to tell him everything that was wrong with him."

'She met a local man who had been living in England and had returned to Scotland. They went out for meals and he'd turn up at her door with fish suppers and ice cream so they could stay in and have a cosy night. At weekends, though, he would disappear and then telephone her to make excuses, such as "My dad is ill" and "I'm in casualty, come and get me." We told her he had a drink problem, that he was phoning from a pub, but at first she didn't want to believe this because she felt comfortable in his company. Then she realised he drank and told him it was over. He called her a bitch and lots of other unpleasant names. She was deeply upset because she'd had high hopes of things working out.

'Another man whom she'd known for years saw her at a dance one night and put a note on her car windscreen then told her it was there. She rushed out and found his telephone number written on it. She became totally besotted with the guy, but he wasn't looking for a relationship, just a woman for the night. It was the old story of him promising to meet her then not turning up.

'None of us knew it at the time but she was ill, constantly moody, depressed, crabby as could be, and it was all made worse by her having no money. I found myself paying bills and settling other debts for her. What hope Hannah had was dying. It was as though her eyes could see only sadness; they had lost the ability to pick out joy. And she was pining for Healy. Someone told her he was being held at Shotts prison in Lanarkshire, just ten miles from her home. Day after day, Hannah would drive there, park in the big prison car park and just stare at the barbed wire and walls, knowing that he was somewhere behind them. They were the strangest vigils you could imagine but doing it made her feel closer to him.

'Sometimes she would take me for a drive past the jail, stopping and pointing and telling me, "I think that's where John is." I'd ask, "Where is Mason?" and she would just say, "I don't know and I don't give a damn. Maybe he's dead because I don't believe he has the bottle to serve out his time and with a bit of luck one of the others will arrange for someone to get him." She read in a newspaper that one of the hash smugglers had died of a heart attack in prison and she thought it must be Mason, but instead it turned out to be Paul Flynn, who had collapsed in the shower.

'One day she said, "I wish we could get away for a wee while," and so we arranged to stay in a caravan near Luss. We had no intention of going for nights out or drinking, it was just a trip away. It was around this time that it really became evident she was becoming ill. At night, she would talk and talk, as though she had so much to tell and wanted it all told before it was too late. It was a trip down memory lane for her because Luss had been one of the places where the family used to go in the car for Tea in the Grass. We'd go walking or out for a drive and everywhere seemed to have some significance, some story attached to it.

'She relived those days, when she was too young to know real unhappiness, talking of days out, places she had been with boyfriends. It was like her memories were being awakened, but physically she was losing her appetite, hardly eating, poking at her food.

'Since telling me about the baby, she had never mentioned it again, but now she wanted to talk about her daughter, starting off by going back to being attacked by the man she thought was Bible John, then how Isobel came to be born – how it happened, the one night stand, being sick all over him, wondering later if that might have been Bible John, sex meaning nothing to her, being asked "Are you pregnant?" – and at that she broke down and cried. She said she had kept it from everyone because she was so scared of the shame that would have been piled on her if news of the birth had leaked out. She'd say, "I look at you with your family about you and think that could be me. Maybe Isobel's got kids of her own."

'I suggested "Why don't we go around the adoption agencies and try to find out? They don't tell you, but they can pass on messages." She said no: "I have got nothing to offer. If she ever comes looking for me, I'll welcome her with open arms, but I won't go looking for her because I could upset her whole life and I don't want that. We don't know what she's been told or anything. Better leave things as they are."

'Maybe her parents should have been sterner, knowing she was going to the Barrowland during the Bible John era. But there was always a kind of morbid curiosity about her. There was a lot of fear about at the time: many parents wouldn't let their daughters go, but Hannah almost enjoyed wondering if there would be another victim. She was fascinated, drawn by the sensationalism of it. Don't get me wrong, she wouldn't have wanted to be murdered, but it was almost a dare to continue going. She knew she was dicing with danger, but that attitude summed up so much of her life. I used to call her "Hard-hearted Hannah" and yet one of the tragedies was that she was so brilliant with kids. She had an ability to mesmerise them, thrill them with her stories. She would have been such a wonderful mother to Isobel.'

In June 2001, while Hannah was unburdening her memory, the past was being recalled in the High Court in Glasgow. Since the night in 1978 when little Mary Gallagher had been attacked and brutally murdered, her family had never given up hope that one day they would see justice for her. At the time of her death, a police scientist had cut a sample of the dead girl's body hair and it had lain in a box locked away in a police-station storeroom with the rest of the evidence. More than 20 years later, following a decision to have another look at unsolved cases from the past, a fragment of DNA was found in semen on the hair.

The sample matched that of an inmate in Peterhead prison who was nearing the end of a life sentence for other offences against girls. He had denied being Mary's murderer, but a jury found him guilty and he was jailed for life. Mary's mother Catherine watched, along with other family members and friends of the dead girl, many of them in tears, as the man was led away back to his cell in the grim Aberdeenshire jail that had in centuries past housed French prisoners of war, knowing he would never ever be freed.

The sensational case was widely reported that night on television and in the following day's newspapers. It demonstrated that, even many decades after an offence was committed, thanks to the advances in DNA testing, no criminal was now safe.

Mary had died in the east end of Glasgow and, as with the violent death of any woman in that part of the world, reference to it brought back thoughts of Bible John. Those same thoughts flashed through the mind of Hannah, as she took her meagre breakfast the next day. She mused, too, about DNA and wondered, 'Could it have told me who Isobel's father was?'

TWENTY-FIVE

BLOOD ON THE WALLS

Just as her mother had realised the time had come to leave Graeme Mason, so Isobel knew her marriage was doomed and the only thing left to do was to walk out in the hope of starting afresh. She felt she had given the relationship her best shot, but living with a man she once loved had become a nightmare. Marital break-up is nothing unusual: more than 40 per cent of all unions end in the divorce courts.

It was a sad ending, but then while she and her husband had been together, there had been plenty of gloom and disaster in the world around them. The fairy-tale life of Diana, Princess of Wales had come to a tragic conclusion in August 1997 when the car in which she was a back-seat passenger crashed in the Pont de l'Alma road tunnel in Paris. Her 15-year marriage to the heir to the throne had ended the previous year and now her life was over too. One-time American football star O.J. Simpson, having been found not guilty of murdering his wife, Nicole Brown, and a friend, was instead ordered that same year by a civil court in America to pay £20 million in damages to their families. The marriage of US President Bill Clinton, however, survived after his affair with Monica Lewinsky was made public.

And murder and mass killing would always dominate the

media. Dr Harold Shipman would opt to take his own life after being found guilty of poisoning 15 elderly patients, although the real figure probably ran into hundreds. Television pictures showing the horror of 11 September as it happened, taking nearly 3,000 lives, were almost too incredible to be believed. In a Scottish court sitting in the Netherlands, Libyan Abdelbaset Al-Megrahi was sentenced to life after being convicted of blowing up a Pan Am jet over Lockerbie.

These were mass killers indeed, yet Bible John, with a mere three murders to his credit, would always fascinate, such was the allure of mysterious death to the Scots public. The hunt for him continued to make occasional headlines, although most were for spurious reasons, not least the fact that one of the detectives involved in the inquiry was related to John McInnes, whose body had been exhumed.

'That is common knowledge and no big deal,' said Joe Beattie, the detective, and most agreed. He was convinced there had been more than one killer involved in the deaths of the three women attributed to the madman. Joe went to his grave in 2000 perhaps wondering if he might meet in the afterlife at least one of the men he had spent so much of his life hunting. The old cop never doubted that if he came face to face with whoever had squeezed the life from Helen Puttock, he would instantly recognise him. 'I know more about this man than I do some members of my own family,' he used to say.

The public never lost interest in the case of Bible John. From time to time, the police would investigate tip-offs that named someone as a killer. Rarely, if ever, did newspapers get wind of these, but invariably the old files would be dragged out by detectives, only for them to discover the name had already been checked out and cleared three decades before. There were approaching 50,000 names in those files, most of them witnesses, dancers who had been to one or other of the halls at the time of the killings. Was the name of the man who attacked Hannah from behind among them? Was Isobel's father? Was Bible John? Perhaps all three were the same person. It was assumed only one man knew the answer, but did someone else?

And so the mother and daughter whose paths seemed in so many ways to run parallel began anew the course of the rest of their lives. But while Hannah shunned a new partnership, Isobel would quickly meet someone else. It was hardly surprising: young, single, attractive women are rarely without offers of company. She was hesitant at first about allowing this new friendship to develop, but after a handful of dates realised she had become fond, very fond she would admit to close friends, of her new man.

As the weeks rolled into months and the bond between them strengthened, she realised she was in love and could only hope that this time it would last. The closure of her marriage had been a traumatic experience, although throughout her adoptive family had as ever been there with support and kindness. They knew, having gone through their own separation and divorce, how she was suffering, feeling alternately guilt and anger, warmth and hate, reliving the good days and bitter that they had not lasted.

She had planned for a life once more as a single girl, even to the extent of buying her own house – a fortunate move, as it turned out, because her boyfriend was married with children and although separated from his wife needed a place of his own. Eventually, Isobel and her lover settled down in a home he bought for them. But the ghosts of the past were about to enter her life: the murdered women and Bible John, a lost mother and outings drinking tea by the roadside, nights in dance halls and a wedding guitar. These and a hundred other interwoven pieces would begin to slip into place.

Having committed herself to the new man, Isobel decided to start afresh and so she sold off the majority of the possessions she had built up during her marriage, believing a clean sweep would remove any lingering traces of a relationship she now wished only to forget. The couple warmed to their new home and became as many of the married couples that surrounded them: going out at weekends, enjoying chats with neighbours and calling on their respective families.

It seemed idyllic and the future looked bright. They had mutual friends and friends of their own, whose companionship they enjoyed. Then a maggot found its way into this rich harvest of love and trust. Isobel suspected her partner had a special woman friend, one he could not and would not discuss with her. 'I thought everything was all right between us until he started having his mobile phone turned to silent so it would not make a sound when someone called it. At first this did not seem peculiar because he worked much of the time away or late in the evenings and, as I worked unsocial hours too, I just wasn't used to hearing the sound of his phone. And then he began cooling towards me. When I asked him if he still loved me, instead of pressing my hand and answering "Yes", he'd look away and mumble something to the effect that there was no need for me to ask.

'To me, it was obvious what was going on and I began to get very suspicious that he was seeing somebody else. Friends who had gone through this sort of experience told me their partners would become very subtle and devious, but he either did not care that I'd find out or he simply didn't think I'd work out he was being unfaithful. One day, he told me he and some friends from work were going off to Glasgow the following evening to play ten-pin bowling. I asked if the others were taking their wives and girlfriends and he said they were not, that this was just a bunch of guys getting together.

'I asked if a few of us could come and watch, then they could all go off and we would have a girls' night, but he told me that would spoil the evening. The next night, when he came downstairs to go bowling, he was dressed in his best suit with a collar and tie. I had been ten-pin bowling and I knew that was not how you dressed for it. That night, I went to bed on my own and cried myself to sleep, knowing he was with another woman.

'Two days later, he made another excuse to go out, claiming it was work-related. His expression said it all: he was meeting his new girlfriend again. That night, he came in late and I pretended to be sleeping. I waited until he drifted off, then quietly slipped out of the bed and went to look for his mobile. Normally, he left it in one of his pockets, but it was nowhere to be seen. So I found his car keys, opened up the glove compartment and there was the phone. I was reading through text messages that were so obviously from a woman arranging to meet up with him, giving him intimate promises of wild sex, when I heard a noise behind me and there he stood. He had woken up and followed.

'There was a huge row. We shouted and screamed at one another, making such a din in the middle of the night that the neighbours were woken up and lights went on in the houses around us.

'Eventually, it calmed down and we went to bed. The next morning, he telephoned but when I answered, hoping to receive an apology, he demanded: "What was all that about last night?" I told him to stop treating me like an idiot, to just be upfront and honest with me. Then I heard him tell me he was seeing somebody else. He reminded me I was living in his house and ordered me to quickly find somewhere else to stay. I was devastated.

'A day later, I was off work and, because it had been a really rotten week emotionally, decided to sit down with a couple of bottles of wine. It was the night of one of the *Big Brother* finals on television. By the time my partner arrived home, I was steaming. By eight, I was pissed. A friend was texting me on my mobile telephone and I was sending messages back to her. Eventually, I was too drunk to type a reply and went into the hall to contact her using the landline phone but, as I did so, he turned the sound down on the television in order to listen to what I was saying. He heard me calling him a few names during the conversation and sprang up, barged in the hall and grabbed the telephone from me.

'It developed into a fight, and as my shoes were lying on the floor I picked one up and battered him with it. It had a wedge-type heel and he must have felt it when I whacked him. There was a lot of pushing and shoving while we struggled and eventually he rang his parents, pleading with them to come to the house. When they arrived, they obviously sided with him because blood is thicker than water.

'But there was lots of blood: his. It was all over the walls and, being a man, he was really milking this situation for all he could. The four of us stood there arguing and shouting. It was getting to the point of no return, so I phoned the police. I phoned the bloody police.

'Two policewomen arrived and spoke to each of us in turn, asking what had happened. An ambulance was called to take my cheating boyfriend to hospital while I was arrested and carted off to a local police station, where, after being made to empty the contents of my handbag, I was locked in a cell while they went off to the hospital to interview him. A couple of hours later, they returned, cautioned me, asked why it had started and what had happened. So I went through the story from day one.

'When I finished I was asked to stand up and they said I was being charged with assault. They then told me that they were entitled to take my fingerprints and DNA. I knew what having fingerprints taken meant, the ends of your fingers were rolled in a pad of ink and then onto a sheet of paper. Giving the DNA sample was very simple; a small swab was put into my mouth and removed and that was it. I was puzzled why it was necessary but thought nothing more about it. Why should I? I had whacked my boyfriend, but that was all. In any case, it meant my being released and all I wanted was out of there.

'They said he had made it clear he didn't want me anywhere near the house or anywhere near his work, so that night I stayed with friends.

'My car and all my belongings were at his house, so the next day I tried continuously to get in touch with him to find out when it would be convenient for me to collect them. He would not answer my calls but eventually telephoned the friends I was staying with to say I could get in at a certain time, as long as one of them was with me and I did not touch anything. When we arrived and he opened the door, I saw that the blood splashes were still on the wall. That was for effect, of course; he could have washed them off because he was still there looking sorry for himself but had instead left them for all to see. No doubt he'd had the neighbours in for a look as well.

'My friend went inside, spoke to him and came out with my clothes. That night I went back to see the police because I really did not understand any of what was happening, but all the two policewomen could tell me was that his injury had not been serious.

'The following week my boyfriend promised to write a letter, asking for the charge to be dropped, explaining that it was a domestic dispute that had got well and truly out of hand. He and I decided to meet up, but when we did he played the sympathy vote, patting his head and saying how painful it was and telling me how long it would take to heal up. It was pretty pathetic really. He was being so patronising it made me feel sick. He was telling me, as he pointed to his head, "At least these scars will heal but getting over you will take a hell of a lot longer, particularly because of everything that has happened." I thought to myself "Yuk".

'As for his promised letter, he left it too late and, by the time it arrived, the formal report had been typed up and sent to the

Procurator Fiscal. A fortnight later, I was summonsed to appear before a sheriff. I was frightened, as I expect anyone else would be who has not been in trouble with the law before. My solicitor asked me to write a letter to him that he could present to the sheriff, describing what had happened and how it was so out of character for me and that I was now left with nothing: no belongings, furniture or home.

'At court, sitting among people who were so obviously career criminals because of the way they clearly knew how to play the legal system to their own benefit, waiting on tenterhooks for my name to be called, I was terrified as to what was going to happen. Finally, after what seemed like hours, I was told to go home and forget about it. The matter had been dropped.

'Those were the worst weeks of my life and I told myself I would never again go near a sheriff or a court. I was not to know how wrong I would be.'

TWENTY-SIX

GO HOME

At the time Isobel was at her happiest, content and in love with a partner who in a few months would betray her trust and lead her to face a court, Graeme Mason and Hannah had good reason to be worried. Del Boy in particular was wondering if an avenging angel, the spirit perhaps of some victim of the drugs he had helped smuggle, had contrived the demise of the gang of which he had been a member.

Without warning, Paul Flynn had succumbed to a heart attack in an English jail. Then, in April 2002, Trevor Lawson, fleeing home to escape a fight at a local bar, was knocked down and killed as he ran across the M80 motorway. In September that same year, Gordon Ross, fit and handsome, legendary for attracting beautiful women, was lured outside a bar in Shettleston, Glasgow, and murdered by four men. Many of the remaining smugglers wondered who would be next. They would not have long to wait.

In March 2003, Billy McPhee was stabbed in the middle of a crowded restaurant as he watched teatime television, but before him the Grim Reaper would collect one more participant of the plot. Hannah would live to see neither Christmas 2002 nor enjoy her 53rd birthday.

As the death toll piled up of men she had not met but of

whom she had known, their names having regularly cropped up in conversations at Thornliebank and occasionally in Spain, Hannah questioned why Mason had been released early. 'He's responsible for John being in prison and for everybody being caught,' she would angrily tell her close friend. 'Why have the others let him live? Why haven't they arranged for somebody they know in prison to take care of him? Surely something will be done.'

But nothing would be. The drug-smuggling plot had been good while it lasted, but it was over and the chapter had been closed the day he, Healy and Flynn were jailed. There was nothing to be gained by seeking retribution now.

Her long confessions to her friends continued. It was as though she had heard a whisper that her time was running out and had to explain everything that had happened before it was too late. 'She needed to explain herself, almost to justify herself,' said her old friend. 'She wanted to talk about the things that had hurt her most – being treated as the gopher during her youth, Bible John, Isobel's birth, Mason – hoping perhaps that in talking she would find answers.'

Hannah's confidante remembers her friend helping so many along the way but receiving little or nothing back in return. 'Hannah was especially kind to one individual who had suffered his own share of personal tragedies; in fact, she had been more of a help to him than his own family. If he needed his grass cut, or shopping done, he would phone her. She didn't resent doing his chores, only that others whose duty it was to care for the man did not help him.'

Perhaps it was down to her hard upbringing among families who, before the advent of the welfare state, objected to having to pay for a doctor, but when she was ill Hannah would shy away from surgeries, preferring to let nature work out a remedy. 'She wouldn't go to the doctor for help because apart from a dose of flu when she worked at the Hoover factory she had never known illness,' said her friend. But there came a time when she had to.

'We'd been shopping in a supermarket and Hannah had bought a pack of porridge and a pint of milk. As she laid them on the conveyor belt, she spotted a special offer – three little teddy bears for £3. She grabbed them and put them beside the other items. The checkout girl burst out laughing, and so did I. "All you need is Goldilocks," I said to Hannah, and she broke into a giggle, but she had to hold her side. I had noticed she had been doing that quite a lot and knew it was a classic symptom of gallstones. When I said so, she asked, "What are they?" I had to try describing how things were growing on the side of her gall bladder and that simple keyhole surgery would remove them. Finally, she did go into hospital to have them sorted.'

In November 2002, her friend had arranged to holiday abroad with friends and promised to bring Hannah duty-free cigarettes. Before setting off, she had felt ill herself and Hannah had pleaded with her to stay at home, probably because she simply did not want someone on whom she relied so much to disappear, even for a short while. Nevertheless, the holiday went ahead. When she returned, she was horrified at her friend's condition. At first, she thought the sickness had been caused by tablets prescribed for Hannah's high cholesterol, but when Hannah called to collect the cigarettes it was obvious she was a sick woman. She stayed only 20 minutes; it would be the last time she visited her friend's home.

Soon afterwards, she began complaining of leg pains and persuaded a friend to drive her to Monklands Hospital. After a brief examination, doctors ordered her to be admitted and she was put into a bed she would never leave. The following day her old friend visited her and was shocked by her gaunt look. Hannah toyed with the bedding, running her fingers along the blanket wrapped about her body. It was clear she had something to say but did not know how to form the words. After a silence, she decided that someone who had been such a close friend since childhood would understand and forgive the indelicacy in which the words were framed.

'It's cancer, you know,' said Hannah, embarrassed at being the bringer of bad news.

'Yes,' replied her friend, struggling to retain the tears that wanted to cascade from her misting eyes.

'It's secondary. You know what that means?'

'Yes. What are they going to do for you?'

'They're going to give me steroids, fucking things. They say they're going to build me up and give me chemotherapy. I would like you to do something for me.'

'Anything.'

'Before I came in here I was ill in my house. I wouldn't want anybody else to see it like that.'

'Don't worry about it.'

Her confidante of many years took the key to her old friend's home and did as she had asked. But she knew the clean-up was not for Hannah's benefit; it was because the next time the front door would be opened it would be to admit mourners. Hannah wanted them to be entering a clean, neat house.

'When I got back to the hospital, she was really bad, kicking her legs about. I could see one was black, dead, and she was very agitated. The doctors had put her on morphine to try easing her distress. I didn't think she had long to live, but she did not want anyone knowing or worrying about her and when I suggested telling a particular relative, she insisted, "Just tell him I've got a sore leg."

'The following morning, at a quarter to nine, the hospital telephoned and asked if I would like to sit with her. I called to inform the relative and then we sat in a vigil by her bed. We could tell Hannah's death rattle because at first she was breathing from her stomach, but every hour the source of her breathing rose higher into her chest and then further up still. There was a lot of dark blood escaping from her nose, then her mouth, and then I noticed it coming from her ears.

'It was absolutely horrifying at the end, yet I never saw her look so peaceful; her features had sharpened until she was her mother's double. You could have sworn blind the person lying in the bed was her mother. At one time, she said, "I can't stand this pain, I give up. I can't take pain like this, I give up."

'And then she told me, "Go home, lass. I'm away to my bed." She was, of course, already in bed in hospital. Those were the last words she spoke, then she went off to sleep. "That's her going now," I said and I told her once more, as I had so many times already that day, "Let yourself go, Hannah. You're OK, hen." And then came her last breath; it was like a sigh of relief and then, oh Jesus, the blood started pouring out of every orifice.

'We were asked to leave the room where her body lay and it took the nurses an hour to clean up before we could come back in. It was horrible. But she was gone. It was over.'

Hannah died at teatime on 10 December, four days before her birthday. She had been suffering from cancer, the origin of which could not be found because by the time she entered hospital it had spread over too much of her body. Officially, the cause of death was liver disease brought on by cancer.

Hannah's childhood friend arranged for her to be dressed in an expensive suit made by Frank Usher and bought specially for her last journey to join the others in her family. 'We were determined she would go out in style and put her birthday card in the coffin with her. But when we came to see her for the last time, the peaceful look I remembered from the hospital had gone. Her face was distorted, swollen. I'd rather that was not my very last memory of Hannah, but it is.'

Hannah had made the journey to Daldowie crematorium three times already, with Isobel and her parents. Now it was her turn. There was no longer any need for the hearse to make a detour to avoid the spot where Isobel had died. During her final five years, she had lived a never-ending nightmare of financial shortage and terror that someone might seek her out for having spoken in court. Throughout that time, she had lived for the day when she would reach her 55th birthday and receive the Hoover pension.

Then there was the other windfall she was certain she would receive, one that meant more than the £10,000 at which it was valued. Every day, Hannah would rush to her front door after the postman called, looking for a brown envelope in which she was convinced John Healy's friends would have sent the promised cash. That it did not arrive each morning did not mean it would not turn up the next. Her eternal optimism was based on her love for the man she tried to protect. Like so many aspects of her life, in this too she would be disappointed and she died poor, lonely and sad, with not even a picture to remind her of her daughter.

There were few to mourn Hannah, and Graeme Mason was not among them. As she could find no forgiveness for him, so he could not pardon what he saw as the malice she had shown him and Benji. Del Boy still makes no secret of the detestation he feels towards her.

'After I was released, someone rang me one day and told me Hannah was dead. "You certain about that?" I asked. "Don't crack jokes. Her dead? I'm not that lucky." But it was true and I regret to say I'm glad she died because if she hadn't died in the way she did, someone, sometime would surely have murdered her because of the damage she caused to so many families.'

TWENTY-SEVEN

SERIAL SEARCHING

Hannah Martin died never thinking she could possibly have been the trigger that shot down the shield protecting Bible John. A clue had perhaps been left, a fragment of evidence dropped, when she was attacked near Landressy Street. However, her violator had certainly left a pointer as to his identity: Isobel would forever carry traces of his DNA. Was her father the serial killer who quoted from the Good Book?

Scotland has had its fair share of serial killers and it has usually been a solitary slip that has opened the door to revealing a catalogue of death. For example, to boost their miserable wages as labourers helping dig the Union Canal, William Burke and William Hare were said to have dug up dead bodies in Edinburgh and sold them to medical schools in the city. Then they worked out it was easier just to strangle anyone who happened to be handy. However, the disappearance of their 16th victim, Mary Docherty, aroused too much suspicion and Hare was arrested. He was given immunity from prosecution and guaranteed freedom in exchange for spilling the beans on his old business partner and, as a result, Burke was hanged in Edinburgh in 1829.

In the case of civil servant Dennis Nilsen, originally from Fraserburgh in the north-east of the country but who moved to London, his homosexuality and loneliness led him to invite homeless men to his flat, where they were strangled and their bodies cut up and burned in his garden. When he shifted to an upstairs flat, he tried flushing their remains away, blocking drains. Workmen who were called to investigate discovered his gruesome secret. He was convicted of six murders in 1983 but is suspected of killing at least twelve others.

Robert Black from Grangemouth was known to school pals as 'Smelly Bob'. He went to London where, working as a delivery driver, he travelled all over the UK and the European mainland. Between 1982 and 1986, police were horrified and baffled by the murders of three children, Susan Maxwell, Caroline Hogg and Susan Harper. In 1990, Black was arrested trying to abduct a child in the Borders. He was convicted of murdering the three children and has been questioned by police about the disappearance of many more.

Archibald Hall put behind him a Glasgow birth and his upbringing as a petty criminal to become a butler to the aristocracy, using his contacts with both to steal from them. When David Wright, one of Hall's previous cell mates, tried blackmailing Hall about his past, he was murdered and buried on an estate in Dumfriesshire. Hall went on to kill his London employer, former MP and Labour government minister Walter Scott-Elliot, and his wife, Dorothy, before dispatching his lover Mary Coggle and his half-brother Donald, a child molester. Hall was arrested in 1978 because a North Berwick hotel owner thought he was going to leave without paying his bill. He died in prison in 2002.

It was largely luck that had brought about the downfall of these evil men. But good fortune appeared to have deserted the police hunting Bible John. If he had made a slip during the killings in 1968 and 1969, it had not been sufficiently obvious to lead to his capture. Any clues that might have been left from his earlier

251

attack on Hannah near Landressy Street had been lost long ago due to the incident going unreported. And while his DNA might always remain within Isobel, it was many years before Hannah would tell of the circumstances of her conception and DNA sampling would become routine.

As far as the 1977 slayings of Anna Kenny, Hilda McAulay, Christine Eadie, Helen Scott and Agnes Cooney were concerned, other reasons would be cited for the failure to arrest whoever was responsible, including inter-force jealousy and an apparent refusal to see what, to a number of officers, appeared to be an obvious connection between their deaths. There would be another spate of killings of women in Glasgow between 1991 and 1998 and police again were adamant that there was no connection between the victims: Diane McInally, Karen McGregor, Leona McGovern, Marjorie Roberts, Jacqueline Gallagher, Tracey Wilde and Margo Lafferty. They would be proved correct. In a number of the cases, men would be charged and appear in court, although the prosecutions did not always end in convictions.

However, the feeling persisted that the 1977 slayings were linked, even though two of the deaths had obviously taken place far away from the others, while in the case of poor Anna the suspicion was that she had been killed where her body was discovered. It nagged at the men who had worked on the cases but were now retired, and continued with others who came along to take their places.

There was another factor that may well have contributed to the lack of arrests. Scottish police are traditionally jealous of their territory and it is only in recent years that this attitude has softened. They do not like the thought of outsiders – especially from a neighbouring force, but even from another division – not only being brought in to give a fresh opinion on an unsolved case but also offering advice. Could it be, then, that this hard-line attitude had hindered solutions?

The National Crime and Operations Faculty functions within the National Police College are based on a campus housed around a superb Jacobean mansion in Bramshill, Hampshire. One of the many tasks the faculty performs is to study various crimes and look for similarities that suggest the same individual or gang may be involved. Because of its intense workload, the faculty tends to concentrate on major incidents – attacks on children, rapes and other sex offences, bank raids, art thefts and, of course, murder. At the time Hannah Martin was losing her hope and her health, officers at the faculty were examining a series of files sent by detectives in Scotland that they found increasingly interesting.

Police forces all over the UK, and sometimes from overseas, send details of major incidents to the faculty in case it discovers that a bank raid carried out in Yorkshire has a likeness to one in Devon and another in Warwickshire. Detectives of these three forces then meet up to see how they can help one another and alert yet more police forces to be on the lookout for a travelling gang of robbers whose methods can be described.

The faculty looked at the 1977 murders along with two further homicides for which the culprits had not been found. In March 1979, the body of Carol Lannen, aged 18, was found in Templeton Woods on the outskirts of Dundee; days later, her clothing turned up on the banks of the River Don in Aberdeenshire. She had last been seen alive on Exchange Street in Dundee. Almost a year later, Templeton Woods yielded the body of 20-year-old nursery nurse Elizabeth McCabe, the last sighting of whom had been a fortnight earlier, when she left a city discotheque and told friends she was about to get a taxi home.

The fact that experts at the faculty were examining these cases was sensationalised in the *News of the World* in September 2003. Police had been desperate to keep the faculty's role a secret and officers who might have had access to this information were surprised and in some cases not a little amused to receive visits from colleagues asking questions about any links they might have had with the newspaper. There were a number of reasons why, in this case, it was advantageous that the role of the faculty was kept under wraps, not least because if it was determined that the killings could be the work of one man, or the same men, then evidence taken at the time would have to be brought out for re-examination – if any of that evidence had been mislaid or lost, it could prove highly embarrassing for those responsible.

It was clear to police that the *News of the World* knew that the faculty experts believed there were connections between the murders. Eventually, the newspaper would give some of the reasons why this view had been arrived at and in a further report it would state that there were at least ten points that gave rise to it.

Meanwhile, the hand of the police had been forced. A series of high-level meetings was arranged, at which the September article was high on the agenda. The result was that in early 2004 three forces – Lothian and Borders, Tayside and Strathclyde – announced the setting up of Operation Trinity to re-examine the killings dating back to the late 1960s. It was a long-awaited development that would mean both heartache and hope for the families of the victims. They faced the agonising ordeal of having to recount the lives and last hours of those they had loved; but there was hope that whoever had taken these lives would finally be held accountable.

Therefore, teams of specially chosen detectives began going over ground that had been covered years earlier, realising that memories were sure to have faded in that time and many witnesses might have died. To reassure themselves that the faculty was on the right tracks, the police decided to seek a second opinion by looking across the Atlantic. Not so many moons earlier, to have sought assistance from a force 30 miles away would have been unthinkable; now officers 3,000 miles off would be called in to help.

The Federal Bureau of Investigation (FBI) is tasked 'to protect and defend the United States against terrorist and foreign intelligence threats and to enforce the criminal laws of the United States'. It is also a tool that frequently helps turn cogs in the law-enforcement agencies of many other nations, priding itself on good relations with the UK in particular. Security-conscious America does not stint on supporting organisations such as the bureau and, as a consequence, it can boast the finest crime study and investigation facilities to be found anywhere on the planet.

The FBI's National Academy is housed on the United States Marine Corps base in Quantico, 40 miles south-west of Washington. Here the Investigative Computer Training Unit offers highly specialised training in how to use computers for criminal investigations, research and in the analysis of evidence. It runs a Violent Criminal Apprehension Programme – VICAP for short – which among other things collects, collates and analyses crimes of violence, specifically murder. It studies, for example, unsolved homicides that involve an abduction and are apparently random, motiveless or sexually oriented, or are suspected to be part of a series; or missing persons, where the circumstances indicate a strong possibility of foul play.

Only police forces existing in the Dark Ages are unaware of the existence of VICAP. What it offered was manna from heaven to the officers engaged in Operation Trinity. When the FBI was approached for help, it immediately made the latest and most powerful computer equipment available to the officers from Scotland.

The Scots force suggested that details of the crimes the Operation Trinity team had been asked to look into were fed into the FBI computers. It sounded sensible and practical, but the

Americans had other ideas. Why not put details of every murder committed in the last three or four decades into the system, they suggested? It was a staggering proposal. The computer was being asked to analyse literally thousands of murders and decide which had been committed by individuals and which were the work of serial killers. Some, such as those that had been the work of the likes of Black and Archibald Hall, would be obvious and in any case they were already solved. The Lockerbie bomber, too, would be classified as a serial murderer.

Early on in the work of Operation Trinity, it was decided that the Dundee deaths were not connected to the others and could be discounted. Now, the FBI computer was being asked to find series of other murders that appeared to have clear similarities. The search offered a remarkable conclusion.

Had the computer been human, it would have been accused of stating the obvious by putting forward that the 1977 atrocities were the work of the same person or team. But in doing so, it confirmed what was now suspected. Tens of thousands of words had already been written pointing the finger at two men, accusing them of being the killers, naming one but not the second. But what staggered Scots police was that the computer added another name to the list of their victims, that of Frances Barker. Thomas Ross Young had been jailed in October 1977 for her murder in the July of that year. Young, despite his deteriorating health due to a heart condition, was then being held at Peterhead prison.

If the computer was correct and all the killings were down to the same culprit or culprits, it of course meant that Young must not be that man. It was a complication the police could have done without but one that could not deflect from the fact that, as far as the other deaths were concerned, they were on the right track. The FBI involvement proved how computers had become the new detectives.

Cyber science would now take a further hand and seek out

from the life of Hannah Martin a night in April 1969 near a Glasgow dance hall.

The Operation Trinity team asked scientists to examine every exhibit still held from the 1977 murders to ascertain whether any would give up DNA. Whose DNA that was could vary. It might have been from the victim, the killer or someone not involved. The findings were then matched against all the DNA samples held by police in Scotland on the computer.

It is correct that no two people, with the exception of identical twins, have exactly the same DNA. But in seeking to compare samples, scientists carry out a number of tests, with the result that some may match in every one, while others in most but not all. This means that the odds of a match being correct can be worked out, although there are categories of similarity; some are completely identical, others nearly the same, yet more pretty similar, and so on. The experts told bosses of Operation Trinity that around 200 samples held by police in Scotland from men and women taken at some stage into custody matched closely enough those taken from the murder scenes to warrant a more detailed investigation. The time had come to begin knocking on doors.

TWENTY-EIGHT

WORLD'S END

As detectives were tracking down men whose DNA may have, though not necessarily, put them at one of the murder scenes, Isobel was trying to get her life back in order after the traumas that followed the violent end to her relationship.

There were times when it was hard for her to fight her tears, but she was a practical woman and knew putting her head in the sand and pretending it had never happened was not the answer. She still had her job, her family and her friends; however, she felt she needed to fill her empty house with belongings and memories that would make it a home.

Her good looks ensured she had no shortage of candidates to entertain her, but with the hurt left by the previous experience still fresh she was wary of offers. Finally, she struck up a friendship with another young man but, for the time being anyway, decided against making it a live-in arrangement, so each day she went off to work, returning in the evenings to solitary meals and thoughts of what might be. Through the letterbox would have come the usual handful of cheap money offers, vouchers guaranteeing cheaper boxes of soap powder, applications for credit cards . . . junk mail that she binned. As she arrived home one evening in 2004, though, as the lightening skies signified the coming of another spring, she found a neighbour waiting for her.

'Two men were at your door, Isobel,' she said. 'They were asking where you were and what time you'd be back from work, but I thought it best not to tell them. They did not say who they were but put a card through your letterbox. I thought you should know. They didn't look like Mormons or Jehovah's Witnesses, or like they were selling something, but they didn't knock at any other doors.'

Isobel thanked her and went inside. On her doormat lay what looked like a yellow postcard. But immediately she picked it up she saw the heading 'Lothian and Borders Police'. Mystified, and already beginning to worry, she carried it into her living room, sat down and examined it. The card asked her to contact the police station in Dalkeith, the town to the south-east of Edinburgh, and gave a telephone number.

On a printed line beginning, 'If possible on . . .' had been written the single word 'Anytime'. Another starting with the word 'Regarding . . .' had written after it 'An ongoing inquiry'. It requested her to ask for two detectives, whose names were given. Baffled, she turned the card over. It appeared to be a standard message asking for information about stolen property.

'A police officer called to speak to you to find out if you saw or heard anything suspicious, but there was no reply,' it read. 'If you have any information that you think may be of help in solving this crime, please contact . . .'

She stared in bewilderment, with not a little anxiety, as she read the word 'crime'. Had someone living close by been burgled and the police thought she might have seen or heard something? One of the neighbours would have been sure to mention it, she figured. Had she been involved in a car accident, perhaps nudging another vehicle without knowing it and driven off? She frantically began running through places she had been, people she'd met and things she'd done in the past few weeks. It could not be, she was sure, anything that had arisen from the incident involving her boyfriend. That had been almost a year earlier and, as far as she knew, it was over, if not forgotten.

She switched on her television and began watching the evening news, still uncertain as to what to do. She was reluctant to call the police without knowing why they wanted to speak to her. Should she first speak to a lawyer, she wondered?

The lead item on the news programme concerned the arrest that same morning of 15-year-old Luke Mitchell, who had been seized at his home in a dawn raid by police and charged with murdering schoolgirl Jodi Jones, aged 14. Immediately, she was convinced she knew why the detectives had called. The key lay in the reference on the police message card to Dalkeith, a town she knew well, frequently travelling through it on her way to England. In June 2003, Jodi had left her home in the Easthouses part of the town, telling her family she was visiting Mitchell and would be home later. When she failed to return, a huge search was mounted with Mitchell joining in. He was among those who found her body on a woodland path. It was clear she had been the victim of an appalling attack. Her hands were tied behind her back, her body had been mutilated and her throat cut. The police immediately appealed for witnesses.

Mitchell was accused of killing her and in February 2005 was convicted of murdering Jodi. He was sentenced to life imprisonment by the judge, Lord Nimmo Smith, who described it as 'one of the worst cases of a single victim to have come before the court in many years' and ordered Mitchell to spend at least 20 years behind bars.

Isobel speculated that CCTV footage had shown her van as having been in Dalkeith at around the time of the murder and, she mused, the police wanted to jog her memory in case anything significant lay hidden in her subconscious. She desperately tried recalling where she might have been at that time, but when nothing came to mind she decided to take the bull by the horns and dial the number on the yellow card. It rang several times, then her call was automatically switched to an answering machine. To her surprise, the message revealed she had been diverted to the World's End murders' inquiry unit.

Almost in a panic, she hung up, thinking she had dialled the wrong number, then desperately worried if her own number would show as having called. She thought she had heard of the World's End murders but was uncertain, and in any case could not recall what had happened. What she was sure of was that this could have nothing to do with her. Carefully, she rang the number again and listened to the same announcement before hanging up a second time. She reckoned it unlikely the detectives would have left a wrong number and decided, before trying to phone once more, to find out about the World's End murders.

Switching on her computer, she connected to the Internet, where she found scores of references to the tragedy. Reading the words on the screen before her telling the awful story brought back recollections of hearing it discussed by her adoptive parents when she was a schoolgirl. But Isobel was still baffled as to why the investigators wanted to talk to her. Deciding there was only one way to find out, she dialled the number in Dalkeith a third time, leaving a message to say who she was and where she lived, quoting the names of the two officers on the card and giving her home telephone number.

Promptly, at eight the next morning, her telephone rang and one of the two officers whose names she had given identified himself. 'Thank you for calling us back, can we come and see you?' he asked.

'Sure, but what's it all about?'

'Well, we'd rather not say anything on the telephone, but when we see you everything will be explained in full.'

261

'OK, but should I get a solicitor?'

'Oh no, there's absolutely nothing for you to worry about. We simply believe you can help us.'

'It's all a bit mysterious. When do you want to come?'

'How about right away?'

A little over two hours later, a car pulled up at her house and two men stepped out. Considering the distance involved, she guessed they must have ignored speed regulations. She opened her door as they introduced themselves and showed her their warrant cards; she invited them inside. One of the men was tall with dark hair; the other smaller, stockier. She could not remember which name to attach to which, but it was the stockier of the two who seemed to be doing most of the talking. The men exchanged pleasantries with her, she made them coffee and then the talking started in earnest.

'We're with a unit which is part of an investigation taking a look at a series of unsolved murders going back to the 1970s: 1977 in particular. Very shortly, there will be an official announcement that three forces, ours, Tayside and Strathclyde, have set up a joint inquiry called Operation Trinity. We are told about 100 detectives will be working on it, so that's an indication of how seriously this is being taken. Do you buy the *News of the World*?'

'No, why?'

'Well, in September last year the newspaper carried an article suggesting that there was evidence to suggest an individual it named might be responsible for a number of these deaths. The article was extremely accurate and some of the top brass have actually been trying to find out where the reporter got his information.'

'I didn't see it.'

'Well, you might want to go to your local library sometime and look it up.'

'But what has this to do with me?'

'Officers from Lothian and Borders police are looking into

two of the murders, those of Christine Eadie and Helen Scott. You might have heard of them, they're usually known as the World's End murders.'

'Yes, I looked them up on the Internet.'

'And naturally you want to know what could be your connection. These girls were brutally attacked and raped. Their families have a right to find out who was responsible and so do we.'

'I still don't see . . .'

'Don't worry, we're coming to that, but as this is a murder inquiry our hands are pretty much tied when it comes to giving out information. We can assure you this is important, however.'

'But you can surely tell me something.'

'We'll tell you as much as we are allowed to and try to fill you in on the background to all of this. You remember going to a police station last year and having your fingerprints taken and giving a DNA sample?'

'I can hardly forget it.'

'Well, your DNA closely matches a sample found at the scene of one of the World's End murders. That sample did not belong to the victim, so it had to come from someone who was there.'

'Such as who?'

'Well, perhaps a suspect or even the killer.'

'You're saying I know the killer?'

'No, nothing like that, this is just a routine check of everyone whose DNA is similar to that found at one of the scenes. It's a process of elimination.'

'But you think I could be involved?' Isobel instantly felt cold and frightened, and the detectives realised the impact of what she had just been told.

'Please don't get upset or worried. We know you can't possibly have had anything to do with what took place.'

'So why are you here? How could my DNA be there? I was only about seven when the girls died.'

'You got your DNA from your parents. It's your mother and father we'd be looking to speak with.'

'So you think it was one of them?'

'No, not at all, we'd just like to speak with them.'

'But I was adopted.'

'Yes, we know that. You had to give details about yourself when you were arrested last year. Do you know the name of your natural mother?'

'Yes, when I was younger I decided to get my birth certificate. It said she was called Hannah Martin and that I was born at Rottenrow.'

'Did it give the name of your father?'

'No, that space was left blank.'

'You understand it's crucial we find out who your father was. It is hardly likely your mother would have been involved, but she may tell us who your father was, even though for reasons of her own she left his name off your birth certificate. Have you ever tried tracking down Hannah Martin?'

'No, I was very happy with my adoptive parents and there didn't seem any point.'

'So you've never made contact with her or spoken to her?'

'No.'

'Have you any idea where she is?'

'No.'

'Any idea who might know her whereabouts?'

'Sorry, no.'

They discussed adoption and Isobel's thoughts on having been given away when she was born. Suddenly, one of the men asked, 'Isobel, would you be willing to get your adoption papers?'

'Why?'

'Because they might give us a clue as to where Hannah is or was living at the time you were born.'

'Can't you find that out?'

'No, we would never get permission. It would need to be you who requested them.'

'But how would those details help?'

'As you were adopted, there would certainly have been a social work report and it would have gone into who your father was. It would also give the reason why you didn't remain with your natural mother.'

'I'd want to think about this. It would be a very big step into the past for me.'

'It's really important. Please try to see how helpful this would be. Think about it.'

'What would I have to do?'

'Write off asking for permission.'

'And where would I write to?'

'Don't worry. We would sort all that out for you. We would draft a letter for you to sign. All you would need to do would be to sign it. We'd even post it for you.'

Isobel insisted she would need a few days to think this over and then asked near which of the dead girls the DNA that closely matched hers had been discovered. She found the men evasive and the longer the chat lasted the more reticent they became about telling her anything. Their refusal to be more forthcoming caused tension and they realised that, having scored one minor success in persuading Isobel to consider going along with the idea of applying for her adoption details, it would be a good time to end the interview. Just under an hour after arriving, they departed, and asked for her mobile telephone number, promising to be back in touch.

As she watched them drive off, she found herself shaking. Since discovering her mother was called Hannah Martin, she had never felt the need to try tracing her to ask why she had been given away – and a hundred other questions that were now racing through her brain, especially why her father's name was not on her birth certificate.

It was a strange sensation being told that the mother who bore her might have been mixed up with a savage sex killer. Until the police visit, having answers had never seemed important; now, she felt something of a drama queen, at the centre of something involving many families other than her own, and suddenly she desperately wanted answers.

She climbed into her car and went to see the family that had cared for her since her birth. They were equally surprised by the police visit but just as ignorant of the whereabouts of Hannah Martin. Their advice was not to become involved. 'What point is there in raking up the past?' they told her. 'It's not fair on anyone.' In any case, they could see no reason why the police should need to pursue their inquiries with her because she could tell them nothing.

Two days later, with the weekend looming, she returned home one evening and had barely stepped into her home when the telephone rang. The caller identified himself as one of the detectives who had visited. 'Isobel, I'm sorry, but I have to give you bad news,' he said. Without stopping, he carried on, 'We did some checks and traced Hannah Martin. Sadly, she died in December 2002. I am really sorry, but this makes it all the more important that you look at your adoption papers to see if there's anything in them about your father. We'll need to come back and see you.' It was arranged they would call the following week.

In the meantime Isobel, though unable to feel desolation over the death of a woman she had never known, nevertheless felt a sadness, not just for herself but also for Hannah. As curiosity had from time to time gripped her about her mother, she knew Hannah must often have wondered about her. Now it had taken an investigation into murders almost three decades old to reveal her mother was dead. She had known that the police would somehow track Hannah down and that once that was done Isobel would be unable to resist the urge to meet up with her. Now questions she had been mentally preparing for that rendezvous with the past would never be asked or answered.

The fact that Hannah was dead changed Isobel's thinking towards resurrecting what had gone before. Now, by taking further the quest to uncover the truth about her parentage, she would no longer be disrupting Hannah's life, only her own and that of her adoptive family, and so it was to them she sped with the news. It caused them also to rethink.

'It's clear the police are going to give you no peace until you have your adoption papers,' they told her. 'Maybe you should just go ahead and get it out of the way. Then perhaps they'll leave you alone.'

Over the weekend, Isobel thought long and hard about what she was being asked to do. She returned to her computer and once more scanned through details of the World's End girls' deaths. How would she feel, she asked herself, if one of them had been her friend or older sister? It would be wrong, she knew, to hinder any chance those parents had of seeing justice done. 'What if I was in their situation and knew somebody who could help was refusing to do so?' she asked herself. In the same breath, she realised, 'I can't prolong their ordeal.'

TWENTY-NINE

FINDING OUT

By the time the police returned the following week, Isobel had all but made up her mind to cooperate. 'I'm about to go on holiday and will be away for three weeks,' she told them. 'I'll start off the procedure now, so long as I can have the option of changing my mind when I return. While I am away, I'll make a definite decision. I'm very sure I know I am doing the right thing, though.'

She had in fact arranged to holiday with her new boyfriend. She wished the trip could have been put on hold: holidays could be taken at any time, decisions affecting so many futures were a one-off. Whatever she did had to be the right thing; there would be no second chance. When the past came out, it could not be hidden.

The detectives produced a letter to the Scottish Court Service in which she asked permission for access to her adoption details. After reading it over, she signed it. They promised to mail it off that same day, assuring her that when she returned from holiday a reply would be waiting.

In between their visits to see her, the men had not been idle. Not only had they discovered Hannah was dead, a bitter blow because it deprived them of the one party who might know for certain the identity of the man who could have crucial information about two murders, but they had traced a close relative of the dead woman. This relation had never known Hannah had had a child, so closely guarded was the secret, but remembered Malcolm Martin as a control freak who dominated his remaining daughter until his death. The relative was happy for Isobel to be put in contact and gave the police her telephone number, together with a plea for it to be passed to her.

Both met up shortly afterwards, an emotional reunion of two people who had not known the other existed. They decided to seek out other friends of Hannah and placed an advertisement in a local newspaper asking for anyone with information to call a telephone number.

Sadly, mistakes can easily be made. The number that appeared was the wrong one, turning out to be that of the local council's social work department, who said at least five callers had responded. Not knowing what it was all about, the social work staff had been unable to help but after a visit from Isobel agreed that if anyone else made contact as a result of the advertisement they would pass on her number. The newspaper admitted its mistake and happily ran the advert once more, this time for free and with the correct telephone number.

The outcome was that Hannah's close childhood friend made contact, told them about another close friend of Hannah's and suggested the two should get together with Isobel and the relative. Ironically, the meeting was at Strathclyde Country Park, a convenient spot on Isobel's route into Glasgow. As the four sipped tea and coffee, beneath the waters of the nearby lake lay the remains of Bothwellhaugh, which had been such a part of the dead woman's life. It was at this point that Isobel learned how Hannah had become pregnant and had been forced to give up her baby, then had become embroiled with a gang of drug traffickers and had fallen in love with a major underworld figure.

She remembers listening to the stories. 'I fluctuated between awe and astonishment, shock and embarrassment, and found it difficult at times not to get up and walk away so I could be on my own and have a little cry in private. I had never known her and still could not look on her as my mother, but it was impossible not to feel involved with her. I learned that one of the very few friends who knew Hannah was pregnant and was being made to give up her baby had offered to take me as her own. But her husband had thought it would not be a good idea to be so close to Hannah, who would see me often but know I could not be hers.

'As it was, I'd had a relatively quiet upbringing, but this woman, so naive in her understanding of her own body, had become drawn into the Bible John horror, had calmly walked through Customs checks with hundreds of thousands of pounds hidden in her underwear, had driven to Spain to help a drug baron, had been subjected to horrific pressure from police, had helped wash away clues from cars used in killings and robberies, had carried on while cancer ate away at her and had died without a farthing. And only I knew, now that she was dead, how she had become drawn into mass murders.'

She set off on a break she by then did not want to go on and within a few days realised her new relationship was going nowhere. She was in New Zealand, spending ten days each on the North and South Islands, but her mind was not on the sights or the sun, rather on what faced her when she returned to Scotland. The trip became an ordeal that could not end soon enough. On the final day, while shopping for presents in Wellington, she spotted a two-day-old English newspaper and, for a reason she would never know, bought it. Sitting in a café with a coffee, she scanned through the pages, then almost dropped her drink. 'World's End Killings Linked to Five Other Murders' read the headline over a brief two-paragraph item that went on to explain: 'Seven unsolved murders of young women – including the notorious World's End murders – are being linked by new scientific evidence, police said. Three Scottish forces are investigating the links between the series of deaths in the 1970s and early 1980s.'

As soon as she read it, she knew Operation Trinity had officially been announced and she, strangely, felt part of it. When she returned to Scotland, it was still major news and would continue to be the source of considerable speculation.

She went home alone. Opening her front door, Isobel stared at the pile of mail awaiting her and quickly rifled through it for an envelope with an official stamp. It was there, from the Scottish Court Service, and after ripping it open she read:

> I refer to your recent request to view your Adoption papers and write to advise you that I will require the names and address at the time of your Adopted parents. This information is required to ensure the correct Adoption papers are located in Edinburgh and sent to this court for you to view.
>
> The procedure is for you to come to the Court one morning at 9.30 a.m. along with proof of your identity, a passport or a driving licence is sufficient for this purpose. You will be required to meet with one of our sheriffs, who will grant you permission to view your records.

It was cold and formal, but she knew no outsider could be expected to understand the many emotions the application had aroused. Court officials would, in fact, contact the General Register Office in the Scottish capital. This is the government department responsible for keeping records sent by more than 300 local registrars of every birth, death and marriage, along with civil partnerships, divorces and adoptions. Much of the information it holds is available to any member of the public – by giving basic details, for example the date of a birth and the name of the child, it is possible to have a copy of anyone's birth certificate; adoptions, which need to be approved by courts, are the exception. Information on anyone involved is only issued to those who can prove they have a close, normally a family, interest. It is looked on as highly confidential. The numbers of adoptions are slowly dropping each year, the trend being blamed on a combination of factors. In the years that followed the end of the Second World War, Scotland saw an average of nearly 2,000 adoptions each year. Now that figure is just above 400.

She responded immediately, also enclosing her telephone number. A few days later, she was called. A voice told her the name of a Sheriff Court at which an appointment had been made for the papers to be shown to her. It was in three weeks' time. She let the two detectives know and they arranged to meet her there.

'You've made up your mind to go ahead?' they asked.

'I don't think I ever had any doubts,' said Isobel. 'It's the right thing to do.'

Then she sat back to wait. She recalls becoming increasingly nervous as the day neared. 'I was both excited and worried. Excited at the probability that details of my life I'd previously only be able to wonder about were being made known to me, nervous because it kept nagging at me that I could be opening a can of worms. If there was something in the papers I'd prefer not to have known, then it would be too late to turn back. I would always have to live with whatever I found in there.

'My own curiosity was not strong enough to be the reason for doing this; my motivation was the help this would give the girls' families. But as time went on, I became more and more hyper, filled with strange emotions, a sense of daring mixed with uncertainty as to how I would handle all the things I had never before encountered. It was then I knew I didn't want to be alone when the papers were opened and told my family I needed them to be there beside me.'

The night before the appointment, Isobel was unable to sleep. She sat late in front of her television screen, drank endless cups of coffee, read books and magazines, and began doing chores about the house. In bed, she was still restless, through her curtains seeing the first light of dawn slowly rising.

Eventually, she rose early, knowing she had a two-hour drive ahead, but was too filled with trepidation to eat breakfast. Isobel dressed in a demure navy-coloured skirt with matching shoes and a white top. It was not an occasion to be daring or gaudy.

She met up with her family and headed to court, arriving early and able to have her choice of spaces in the giant car park she spotted nearby. Waiting while time moved on depressingly slowly, she watched others arrive for work or shopping and began to envy them, assuming they knew everything they needed to know about their own pasts.

'I had discovered I was part of the life of a woman who had done the most daring and outrageous things. Yet we also had so much in common. Both of us had suffered hurt through relationships that had not worked out and in which we had been badly let down by men in whom we'd put faith and trust; we had each of us become outgoing, probably as a result of having been forced to stand up for ourselves against manipulative partners; we had jobs that entailed us getting out and about to meet strangers. Hannah had died in the same hospital in which I'd come within a whisker of suffering a similar fate.'

At a quarter past nine, she and her family saw the two detectives drive up and park close to them. They strode across and introduced themselves, one asking Isobel if she was nervous.

'I'm dreading this,' she admitted.

Walking through the doors of the court building, she got a

feeling for how the guilty must feel before turning up to hear their sentences. The policemen introduced her to a clerk who examined her passport and, satisfied she was who she claimed to be, took her to meet a sheriff. She remembers him as being kind and sympathetic and that he was anxious to be reassured she wanted to continue.

'It's not too late to change your mind,' he told her.

When she said she had thought her action over carefully and still believed she was doing the right thing, he told her she could not take away any of the documents she would be shown or photocopy them, although she could make notes. They were together only a few minutes and then he called the clerk back.

'The sheriff wished me all the best,' said Isobel, 'and I thought that was exceptionally kind of him because he seemed to understand I wasn't finding any of this easy.'

With the others from her family and the police officers, she followed the clerk through the court building. 'I felt as though I was in a maze and wondered if I could remember how to retrace my steps when I came to leave. I was absolutely terrified and quite worked up as well because I thought I was going to find out an awful lot of information that until now I had not known. The fact that Hannah was dead and now I was about to find out her greatest secret gave me a strange feeling. I didn't know her, and you can't really grieve for somebody who is a stranger, but all the same I felt sad.

'Eventually, we stopped outside a door. It was opened and we found ourselves in a small room, almost like a storage cupboard, with a couple of chairs. The clerk handed me a small A4-sized envelope and told me to go inside with my family and open it up.

'"Take as much time as you want," she said. "But if it's any help, read it over very slowly so you take everything in."'

She closed the door, leaving the tiny group alone looking at the envelope. The detectives had sympathetically announced they would wait outside in case what was about to take place proved too upsetting for Isobel and she needed her family to comfort her.

Finally, she opened up the letter and a handful of papers fell out. Only two mattered, but after all she had tensed herself to meet with what she discovered felt a huge letdown. There was her original birth certificate with, as she knew it would be, the space for the name of her father left blank. It was as if she had read a murder mystery at the end of which the author had omitted the name of the killer.

What she really wanted to see was the report from the social workers who organised the adoption and, after scanning it, she realised why Hannah had not filled in the father's name. It was because, as she had confided, she did not know it. The report simply said he was thought to have been a 20-year-old Glasgow shipyard worker. Isobel knew how creative Hannah had been in telling them that. Too drunk to learn or remember anything about her companion in the car, in order to avoid embarrassment and the realisation she might be thought of as having loose morals, she had invented an age and occupation. It stood to reason, Isobel was convinced, that had the man gone that far in telling her about himself, he would certainly have added a name, any name if necessary. That the report included the fact that Malcolm would not let Hannah keep the baby came as no surprise. She had already gleaned that during the chat with the dead woman's friends. The social workers had concluded it was in Isobel's 'best interests' to grow up with another family.

When she had finished reading, she passed the documents over to her family, waited until they had read enough, then went outside and asked the two waiting CID officers to enter. She handed them the papers and, after asking permission to read them, they scrutinised them closely before looking up, clearly trying to hide their disappointment at the absence of a father's name.

'They kept apologising for putting me through what they had to put me through and said they were pleased for my sake that the name they were looking for hadn't appeared on it. Whose name was it? We had never discussed any particular person, although the name of a man being linked to the World's End and other murders had been splashed over a lot of newspapers for some considerable time.

'I had been afraid that his name might turn out to be in the social work report as being that of the man who had sex that night with Hannah and therefore be my father. Of course, it was not.

'I had assumed the detectives were referring to this same man in the context of him being one of the killers they were looking for. They never spoke his name but when I mentioned it they said my DNA was not linked to him but to another person who had probably been with him at the time.

'Again, they never gave the name of this second man and it came as a surprise to me to hear someone else could also have been involved. I told the police I had been fascinated as much by the intrigue of their investigation, by the part my role, as it unfolded, played in the overall picture, as by discovering a name that would probably mean nothing to me. Probably they could not understand my feelings and I cannot blame them for that.

'They were still apologising when we parted and promised to keep me in touch with developments, but I knew they would not or, more likely, could not. At least now I could get on with living, knowing – or maybe hoping – there were no more skeletons to fall out of the cupboard.'

THIRTY

THE WEST WING

Many women have a fascination with the future. It is illegal to take money by claiming to tell what course a life will take, but there is nothing to prevent legions of crystal-ball gazers, decoders of tealeaf formations and tarot card readers telling their armies of devotees what the stars would seem to have in store for them and making a very prosperous living from it. How their customers then choose to interpret these omens is up to them. Hannah Martin was no exception.

On most of the schemes that are home to the working classes, there will reside someone, often a female, who is regarded sometimes with awe, sometimes with caution, because she is known to have a gift to look into the unknown and see what awaits. At times of great family stress, she will be invited in to lay her tarot cards on the table and explain the meaning of each of the figures they show. She will perform this task at the drop of a hat and customarily for free, although the handing over of a small gift is the norm.

Hannah was an avid student of anyone willing to sit down with her and prophesy. As years slipped past and the unknown beckoned, the need to continually update what lay in store became an obsession, like that of the 60-a-day smoker waiting for a church service to end, trying meanwhile to recreate the taste of that first draw. There were occasions when Hannah would hear her portents twice or even three times in a single day, desperately hoping to be told good fortune awaited, that a tall man with dark hair would change everything.

It was not as though she needed reassurance that John Healy's £10,000 would materialise. She remained certain of that and even bought herself a tarot pack, perhaps with the intention of teaching herself to somehow hurry along the prediction for which she yearned. As we know, it would never arrive, but was her longing so strong that it held her to an earthly solitude? Did she chain herself to the life that had treated her so badly in the hope of somehow receiving the rewards she was convinced would someday arrive? This is not as fanciful as it might seem because of two incidents that left those who witnessed them believing, wondering, if Hannah had wanted to make known her presence long after she was dead and her body turned to ashes.

While she was alive, she would often take out the black velvet cushion cover that had been handed down to family members, bearing her forename, an ancient Hebrew word meaning 'Grace of God'. It was a beautiful piece of work that carried with it decades of love. She guarded it jealously and took seriously her commitment to ensure the line of its ownership was continued. But her death, sudden at that, meant she had been unable to fulfil that duty, something Hannah's old friend in particular knew would have upset and distressed her. Someone else, with whom she had been distantly involved, announced they knew of the existence of the cloth and insisted it should be given to them. It was not a matter in which the old friend could intervene, but she knew where in Hannah's home the relic had been stored and indicated a particular cupboard in which it would be found.

The friend gave an assurance there was no lock to the door,

that it opened freely and easily, but when an outsider pulled at the little handle it refused to budge. It seemed an unseen hand inside was holding it closed. Hard as the door was pulled, it could not be moved. In the end, a joiner had to be sent for and, with chisel and hammer, he eventually succeeded in gaining access.

'It was,' said the friend, 'as if Hannah was watching what was going on, was holding the material and saying to herself, "I don't want this person to have this."'

Most of us take for granted the fact that we have friends. We use and occasionally abuse them, not realising that to the lonely a single friend may be all he or she has, and need the constant assurance that friendship exists. In her childhood friend, Hannah had found someone on whom she could lean. When she emerged from the isolation she'd imposed upon herself in order to recuperate from the bitterness of the Mason experience, Hannah needed this friend's constant presence and it was one she could not relinquish even after the curtains had closed on her life.

One of Hannah's favourite television programmes had been *The West Wing*, an American drama starring Martin Sheen as the fictional Democratic president. It is set in the west wing of the White House, the president's command base. Hannah was an avid watcher from the start, although her death would deprive her of many episodes. Or would it?

Soon after Hannah had died, her friend's television set for no apparent reason ceased to work. There was no outward sign of a problem and tests could not discover any internal malady. Its failure was put down to simply being a problem associated with modern technology in which a microscopic part for some reason known only to itself decides to play up.

In her home one night, the friend heard a noise and, upon investigating, was startled to discover her television had returned to life. It was switched off and had not functioned for some time, but there was a picture with sound and the programme was just beginning. It was another episode of *The West Wing*. The friend decided not to tempt fate by running through the other channels, so instead sat down and watched the show, a tear trickling from the corner of her eye as she thought had Hannah still been alive this was precisely what she would have been doing at this hour. She sought out a newspaper to see what other programmes there would be later, but as *The West Wing* ended the set turned itself off. She twiddled with the controls, but it didn't come back to life. It was a bizarre and unnerving experience.

'Maybe Hannah wanted to let me know she was still around,' she said. 'I'd like to believe it was she who switched on the television, and my set at that.'

CONCLUSION

According to friends, Hannah Martin died still convinced the man who attacked her near Landressy Street was the man, or at least one of the characters, known as Bible John. They do not doubt she manufactured the scant information given about her attacker in April 1969. After all, the natural reaction to being offered a lift home by a stranger would be to ask his name and where he lived rather than his age and occupation. The circumstances of this incident point to the man who fathered Isobel being Bible John. He alone knows the truth, but where is he? Theories abound, most of them fantastic. Again, only he knows, but what is certain is the astonishing physical similarity between his daughter and the portrait painted by Lennox Paterson.

It is remarkable that an American-inspired investigation into a series of murders in Scotland should have led to Isobel discovering the likely identity of her father. Two years ago, she left Scotland and now lives on the south coast of England, where she is a highly respected and regarded executive. Most days she takes from her purse a photograph of Hannah and wonders about answers to the secrets her mother took with her. She is proud of her natural mother and devoted to the family who adopted her.

* * *

Hannah was not to know it but, during the last weeks of her life, John Healy was moved to Castle Huntly open prison in Angus and would be allowed an occasional weekend at home in Thornliebank. After he was released from jail, he had a brief flirtation with Dundee Football Club but now lives quietly in Glasgow.

At the time of writing, Angus Sinclair has been charged with raping and murdering Christine Eadie and Helen Scott and is awaiting trial.

By yet another of the odd quirks that punctuate the Hannah Martin story, Sinclair and Thomas Ross Young were both held in the jail's 'C' Hall until the latter was moved in the autumn of 2006 for health reasons to Saughton in Edinburgh – the same prison that Hannah would visit to smuggle cigarettes to a relative. Two years earlier, Young, now 72, was arrested on suspicion of murdering Pat McAdam in 1967, though it was later decided that he was too unwell to be tried.

Graeme 'Del Boy' Mason still lives at the home he once shared with Hannah on Clova Street. In 2003, he set up Magnetspruce Limited, describing himself as a domestic-appliance engineer, but formal records indicate the business was later dissolved.

The Barrowland lives on, hosting packed concerts, the gaudy lights of its glittering sign still a much-loved landmark. The streets that surround it have changed, but there are some who believe that on dark nights they can hear the voices of the dancers, many now dead, ghosts sailing a sea of sorrow, among them a teenager called Hannah, seeking affection but finding only disappointment.

Mummy, Take Me Home
A Mother's Tug-of-Love Torment

by David Leslie

Publication date: October 2007
ISBN: 9781845962296
£9.99 (paperback)
www.mainstreampublishing.com

'Mummy, take me home,' sobbed little Jasmine Dodds as she was ripped from the arms of her mother. But there was nothing that Morag could do, as a court in Scotland had given custody of the child to her Texan father.

When her parents' relationship had ended, the couple had fought bitterly about their daughter's future. Fearing that she would lose her child, Morag fled with Jasmine, only to be hauled back in shackles and incarcerated in a grim American prison. When she was eventually freed, and both mother and daughter were sent back to Scotland, Morag thought her nightmare was over. In reality, it was only beginning.

Back in the UK, every move she made was watched and every mistake recorded. When a new legal challenge was mounted and Jasmine was returned to her father in the US, Morag sank into deep depression and became lost in a haze of booze and drugs. Police cells and hospital beds became her home and the once beautiful and desirable young woman's life spiralled out of control.

Mummy, Take Me Home is the gripping, disturbing true-life story of a tug of love that no mother should ever face and no child should be forced to endure.

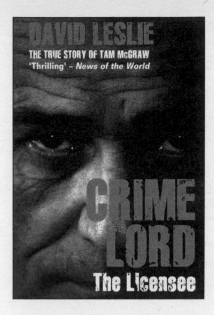

CRIMELORD
The Licensee

by David Leslie

Available now
ISBN: 9871845961664
£7.99 (paperback)
www.mainstreampublishing.com

'Thrilling' – *News of the World*

Crimelord is the gripping life story of elusive multimillionaire gangster Tam McGraw. A notorious criminal kingpin, McGraw has risen from extreme poverty in the East End of Glasgow to become one of Scotland's wealthiest men.

When hash started to flood into Scotland from the late 1980s onwards, suspicion centred on McGraw, leader of the infamous Barlanark Team. After a two-year surveillance operation, police discovered the drug had been hidden in buses carrying young footballers and deprived Glasgow families on free holidays abroad. It was a scam reminiscent of the movie The Italian Job, only this time Scots kids had been sitting on hash worth over £40 million. Police claimed McGraw was the financier and mastermind but in 1998 a jury declared him innocent while other suspects were jailed.

As McGraw refuses to discuss his life publicly, his remarkable tale is told through friends, fellow crooks and the occasional rival. It is an outrageous, often hilarious, true gangster story.

The Happy Dust Gang
How Sex, Scandal and Deceit Founded a Drugs Empire

by David Leslie

Available now
ISBN: 9781845962616
£7.99 (paperback)
www.mainstreampublishing.com

Charlie, snow, toot, white: cocaine goes by many different names. But in Glasgow in the early 1980s, they called it Happy Dust.

At no-holds-barred parties of the glamorous and wealthy, cocaine was the new aphrodisiac. A few lines of Charlie and a humdrum party could become an orgy.

Hot from the forests of Colombia, Charlie flooded onto the streets of Glasgow and was passed along the line to the cocktail set, highly paid sports stars and yuppies desperate for kicks and thrills. Behind it all was a man they called the Parachutist.

But all too soon, the party was over. People became too greedy and the Parachutist was double-crossed. Some of the gang did shady deals with detectives in hotel rooms; others flew to seek shelter in the sun, their reputations destroyed but not their fortunes.

The good times might have been over for the Happy Dust Gang, but their legacy lives on to this day.